"Lone Wolf" Gonzaullas, Texas Ranger

(Courtesy Texas Ranger Hall of Fame and Museum.)

"Lone Wolf" Gonzaullas,
Texas Ranger

BY BROWNSON MALSCH

FOREWORD BY MARY NELL GARRISON
INTRODUCTION BY HAROLD J. WEISS, JR.

UNIVERSITY OF OKLAHOMA PRESS
NORMAN

To Albert Charles Egg, Jackson County sheriff after the turn of the century, who, like "Lone Wolf" Gonzaullas, was a faithful, fearless officer and an implacable foe of wrongdoers—and to his wife, Louise Traylor Egg, who, like Laura Scherer Gonzaullas, heroically endured constant anxiety for the safety of her man—this book is affectionately dedicated.

Library of Congress Cataloging-in-Publication Data

Malsch, Brownson, 1910–1999
    "Lone Wolf Gonzaullas, Texas Ranger / by Brownson Malsch; foreword by Mary Nell Garrison ; introduction by Harold J. Weiss.
    p. cm.
    Rev. ed. of: Captain M. T. Lone Wolf GonzauUas. 1st ed. c1980.
    Includes bibliographical references and index.
    ISBN: 978-0-8061-3016-3
    1. Gonzaullas, Manuel Trazazas, 1891-1977. 2. Texas Rangers—Biography. 3. Peace officers—Texas—Biography. 4. Crime Texas—History—20th century. I. Malsch, Brownson, 1910– Captain M. T. Lone Wolf Gonzaullas. II. Title
F391.G65M35 1998
363.2'092—dc21
[B]   98-6495
                                                                                                    CIP

The paper in this book meets the guidelines tor permanence and durability of the Committee on Production Guidelines for Book Longevity of the Council on Library Resources, Inc. ∞

Puhshed by the University of Oklahoma Press, Norman, Publishing Division of the University. Copyright © 1980 by Shoal Creek Publishers, Inc., returned to author and transferred in 1997 to the University of Oklahoma Press. Introduction by Harold J. Weiss, Jr., copyright © 1998 by the University of Oklahoma Press. All rights reserved. Manufactured in the U.S.A. First printing of the University of Oklahoma Press edition, 1998.

CONTENTS

Illustrations vii
Foreword by Mary Nell Garrison ix
Introduction by Harold J. Weiss, Jr. xi
Preface xv
    I. Baptism of Fire 1
   II. North Texas Cleanup 17
  III. Even the Cows Were Drunk 31
  IV. Indicted for Murder 41
   V. On Again, Off Again 57
  VI. Santa Claus Is a Thief 67
 VII. Purification at Borger 75
VIII. Thwarting a Panhandle Mob 81
  IX. Sherman: The Prisoner Was Roasted Alive 93
   X. Boom in East Texas 103
  XI. First of the New-Type Rangers 119
 XII. Science Against the Criminal 129
XIII. Sixth Sense at Work 141
XIV. Martial Law at Beaumont 151
 XV. The Phantom Killer 159
XVI. Manhunt in East Texas 169
XVII. A Fitting Climax 177
XVIII. The Last Years 189
Bibliographical Note 210
Index 213

ILLUSTRATIONS

M. T. Gonzaullas	frontispiece
Captain John R. Hughes	3
Texas Rangers, 1890	4
Gonzaullas' cartridge belt, chaps, spurs and scabbard	11
Gonzaullas on border duty, 1920	33
Personal guns of "Lone Wolf"	47
Field shotgun	48
Gonzaullas' bulletproof vest	56
Decorated Colt revolvers	66
Altered revolver	74
Colt .38 Detective Special revolvers	87
Gonzaullas' revolver recovered from car of Clyde Barrow	102
Kilgore, Texas	104
30-06 Mannlicher-Schoenauer rifle	109
Chrysler coupe scout car	115
Gonzaullas as head of Bureau of Intelligence, 1937	118
Gonzaullas in DPS gun room, 1938	123
Crime section laboratory	124
M. T. Gonzaullas, C. G. McGraw and J. Edgar Hoover	128
Gonzaullas on his horse Charcoal	144
Ornamented Colt .45 revolvers	150
Rangers at Camp Mabry, Austin, 1943	155
Company "B" bloodhounds	162
Bust of "Lone Wolf" Gonzaullas	167

Gonzaullas' license plate 168
Company "B" headquarters in Dallas 176
Rangers at Gonzaullas' retirement party, 1951 191
Captain Gonzaullas and Colonel Homer
    Garrison, Jr. 193
Certificate of Appreciation and
    Honorable Discharge. 194
Ranger and Mrs. Ernest Daniel and Captain
    and Mrs. M. T. Gonzaullas 197
Captain Gonzaullas and Jarvis P. Garrett 203
Certificate of election to Texas
    Ranger Hall of Fame 205
Captain Gonzaullas and Captain
    Robert K. Mitchell. 207
Gonzaullas' gold badge of captain 209

FOREWORD

We often find our lives touched by that of another, and then it is never the same. So it is for me. Friendships I have known because of my late husband, Homer Garrison, have molded my own life and given it a dimension I never suspected would be mine when I married in 1939.

Captain M. T. Gonzaullas and his vivacious wife, Laura, became a part of me through the interwoven fabric of the Texas Department of Public Safety. My husband was a longtime director of that department. In the early days of the DPS, we knew quite intimately the men in the field as well as those in the Headquarters Division in Austin; the staff was markedly smaller then. Informal gatherings offered opportunities for the men to reminisce about the "good old days," and I never lost my fascination for the tales that unfolded on those occasions.

We called him "Cap," and he was always the star performer—because his had been such a startlingly dramatic career, and partly because even then there was something of the legendary associated with him. He and Laura were always the most fashionably dressed, the most articulate, the most polished and I might add, the most engaging. They would talk at the same time—she had almost as many stories as he to tell—and you could take your choice of whom you wanted to hear. But "Cap" was modest in his recollections, and Laura would often add the necessary reminder of his valor, his professionalism, his determination and his uncanny ability to solve the most involved case.

Brownson Malsch's book dramatically recreates many events that I can remember hearing Captain Gonzaullas tell. As fascinating as a novel, this factual account of his exploits is more exciting than fiction ever could be. The author documents Gonzaullas' experiences as a young Texas Ranger in the 1920s, his flexible transition from the "one riot, one Ranger" era to the increasingly scientific techniques of law enforcement during the forties and fifties, and his post-retirement career as a Hollywood technical adviser. For those who remember law enforcement before the introduction of crime laboratories and high-powered cars, and for those who are intrigued with the modern processing of crime data, *Lone Wolf* will be a source of valuable information and reflection.

I find that the book clearly describes the basic philosophy of this remarkable man, who was never boastful, never swaggering, never bullying. The intrinsic fairness and total integrity of "Cap" are evident throughout the book. He made no distinction between "big men" and small-time criminals; he brought all to justice with impartiality. Captain Gonzaullas was a man whose life excites the imagination and whose dignity, perseverance and wisdom made him a living legend.

Mary Nell Garrison

MARY NELL GARRISON

INTRODUCTION

The life and times of the Texas Rangers can be approached from three different vantage points: the charging horse soldiers with six-shooters, blazing away in bloody battles with Comanches and Mexican troops during the frontier days; the old-time lawmen who chased desperadoes in a changing Texas by the early 1900s; and the modern Rangers who now use high-powered weapons, cars, and crime labs to maintain law and order in today's urban-industrial state. Correspondingly, the images of these Rangers in popular culture also changed across two centuries. The stories about the Texas Rangers as intrepid fighters and brutal foes on battlefields had been replaced in the late nineteenth century by tales of white-hatted peace officers who gunned down bandit gangs bent on robbery and murder. By the time Manuel Trazazas "Lone Wolf" Gonzaullas (1891–1977) had entered the field of law enforcement, the Rangers in Texas had gained a national reputation in fact and fiction:

As tall as he his story from the borderland uncouth—
Some of it is legend but most of it is truth. . .
For fact stands out of hard fought fight, or years of stand-up
  strife—
The Ranger rode the border and the outlaw rode for life.[1]

The Rangers kept their place in Texan affairs because they adapted to the changing times. Their operations in the field were carried out in three distinct, yet interrelated time periods.

First, from 1823 to 1874, came the birth and sporadic deployment of those engaged in the ranging service as citizen soldiers—mounted gunmen, spies, and volunteers. In this era Anglos, Amerindians, and Hispanics competed with each other, often in deadly warfare, for control of the land in frontier Texas.

In the second period, during the coming of the railroads, the discovery of oil, and the settlement of West Texas, the Rangers moved from conducting military operations to carrying badges as law officers in struggles with feudists, cattle and horse thieves, and killers on the run. This transition began with the creation of the Frontier Battalion under Major John B. Jones in 1874 and lasted, with the formation of the Ranger Force in 1901 after a legal dispute about arrest powers, until the Great Depression in the 1930s.

In 1935 a new state agency appeared to house the Texas Rangers and the Highway Patrol: the Department of Public Safety (DPS). Still in existence in present-day Texas, the DPS allowed the Ranger service to lessen political patronage, improve communications and training, and become more involved in the developing field of criminal investigation—from fingerprinting to the use of crime labs. With this move, the new-style Rangers had taken center stage. They had become full-fledged members of the movement to make state police agencies a more permanent part of American law enforcement.[2]

The career of Texas Ranger Gonzaullas spanned both the second and third periods of Texas Ranger history. In one sense he epitomized the old-time horseback Rangers who, like Gonzaullas, became adept at using revolvers and rifles, searched for clues at the scene of a crime, stood against feudists and mobs bent on extralegal justice, and received their orders in a command system stretching from companies in the field to the adjutant general's office in the state capital. These Rangers combined two traditions: the martial spirit of the early nineteenth-century soldier-Rangers under John Coffee "Jack" Hays, and the law-and-order attitude of the peace-officer Rangers in the early twentieth century.

Yet Gonzaullas also took on the characteristics of the modern Texas Rangers during the Great Depression, World War II, and the years after. He became head of the intelligence bureau in the newly created Department of Public Safety, accepted an appointment as captain of a Ranger company in the field, and increased his knowledge of criminal science methods being used by police agencies in today's technological world. As a laboratory detective Gonzaullas knew that without a crime lab, law enforcement in Texas would be "back in the horse and buggy days."[3] By the time the famed captain retired from Ranger service, he and other local, state, and national law officers had brought an end to the outlaw tradition in America, as typified in 1930s Texas by the crimes of Bonnie Parker and Clyde Barrow.[4]

Gonzaullas, known as "El Lobo Solo" or "Lone Wolf" for his ability to get in and out of scrapes by himself, was not the first Texas

Ranger of Hispanic origins. Before and after the American Civil War, Mexican Texans or Tejanos served in the ranging service of the Lone Star State, sometimes in separate companies and sometimes in mixed units with Anglos and American Indians. Yet Lone Wolf, with his roots in Spain and with his celebrated status among the common people, can be seen as a unique Hispanic Ranger. Few if any Latino Rangers in any generation can match his service record.

Like other well-known Texas Ranger captains, Manuel Gonzaullas was a law-and-order person who could operate alone or join others in a crusade against crime and disorder. By the early 1900s the careers of the "Four Great Captains"—John A. Brooks, John R. Hughes (whom Lone Wolf admired), William J. "Bill" McDonald, and John H. Rogers—were winding down. McDonald's motto had set the tone for the old-time Ranger organization: "No man in the wrong can stand up against a fellow that's in the right and keeps on a-comin'."[5] In time, these Ranger officers were replaced by the "Big Four."—Gonzaullas, Francis A. "Frank" Hamer, Thomas R. "Tom" Hickman, and William L. "Will" Wright. Although Gonzaullas and the other seven captains had no death wish, all of them had one thing in common: a desire to take on those who committed crimes.

The Texas Rangers were always a mixed bag. Some served with distinction and others were drummed out of the service. Some stayed single and others married and raised families. Some could hardly write a sentence when others wrote poetry and newspaper stories. Some killed without mercy while others carried their Bibles with their guns. These "Christian Rangers," as one writer called them, saw crime and their law-enforcement duties through the eyes of their religious faith, and their ranks included Captains Gonzaullas, Rogers, and P. B. Hill.[6] As a member of the Presbyterian Church and the Masons, Gonzaullas tempered Old Testament sayings—an eye for an eye—with repentance and forgiveness found in the teachings of Jesus Christ. These men not only carried Bibles, but also followed the Good Book.[7]

The life and times of Manuel Gonzaullas will continue to intrigue future historians of the Texas Rangers. Yet one thing is certain about the flamboyant personality and storied career of Gonzaullas—he was instrumental in guiding the Ranger service into the modern era of law enforcement. A newspaper headline about Gonzaullas and the use of forensic science says it all: "State Takes Sherlock Holmes Role."[8]

HAROLD J. WEISS, JR.

NOTES

1. William B. Ruggles, *Trails of Texas* (San Antonio: Naylor Co., 1972), 17.
2. For a more complete study of the changing nature of Ranger operations in two hundred years, see Harold J. Weiss, Jr., "The Texas Rangers Revisited: Old Themes and New Viewpoints," *Southwestern Historical Quarterly* 97 (April 1994): 621–40. For a look at Manuel Gonzaullas and twentieth-century Rangers, see Ben Procter, *Just One Riot: Episodes of Texas Rangers in the 20th Century* (Austin: Eakin Press, 1991) and Mitchel Roth, "Courtesy, Service, Protection," in *Courtesy, Service, Protection: The Texas Department of Public Safety's Sixtieth Aniversary*, ed. Mike Cox et al. (Dallas: Taylor Publishing Co., 1995), 8–86.
3. M. T. Gonzaullas Scrapbooks, vol. 2, 197 (five volumes at the Texas Ranger Hall of Fame and Museum, Fort Fisher, Waco, Texas).
4. Mitchel Roth, "Bonnie and Clyde in Texas: The End of the Texas Outlaw Tradition," *East Texas Historical Journal* 35, no. 2 (1997): 30–38.
5. Harold J. Weiss, Jr., "Organized Constabularies: The Texas Rangers and the Early State Police Movement in the American Southwest," *Journal of the West* 34 (Jan. 1995): 29–30.
6. William W. Sterling, *Trails and Trials of a Texas Ranger* (Norman: University of Oklahoma Press, 1968), 376.
7. For further enlightenment on this subject, see Green Peyton, *For God and Texas: The Life of P. B. Hill* (New York: Whittlesey House, 1947).
8. M. T. Gonzaullas Scrapbooks, vol. 2, 197.

PREFACE

J. P. Bryan, Jr., of Houston recently told of his chance meeting with Captain M. T. "Lone Wolf" Gonzaullas. It occurred in the early 1950s at the Broadmoor Hotel in Colorado Springs, where Bryan was vacationing with his family. He was then a budding teenager.

The young Bryan had watched a trim-figured, silver-haired man sunbathing beside the pool and rowing on the lake. Swim trunks revealed the upper part of his body, on which there were several small scars, the obvious result of bullet wounds. Fretting to know more, he asked his father who the man was. No doubt the senior Bryan knew, but he suggested to his son that he approach and introduce himself. When he did that, the man amiably said, "I'm Captain M. T. Gonzaullas, Texas Ranger. Some people call me 'Lone Wolf.'" Bryan related, "Had he said, 'I am GOD,' I couldn't have been any more awe-struck."

The spell that Captain Gonzaullas cast during his lifetime has not abated since his death in 1977. His story clamored to be told. He was, after all, one of the most colorful of all the men who have worn the badge of Texas Ranger in the long history of that world-renowned law enforcement agency. Thanks go to Mr. and Mrs. Henry Rosser of Willingboro, New Jersey (formerly of Fort Worth, Texas), for making this book possible. As executor of the estate of Laura Isabel Gonzaullas, Mr. Rosser kindly made available to me Captain Gonzaullas' immense file of newspaper and magazine articles on his career. Their keen sense of history led Captain and Mrs. Gonzaullas to maintain a complete record of all phases of his work, beginning in 1920.

Mr. Rosser also loaned pertinent portions of the captain's personal library, his collection of more than five hundred Ranger photographs and other items, without which this book could not have been completed. Invaluable were Captain Gonzaullas' handwritten notations (always in red ink) elaborating on printed material in his possession. He was a meticulous man who penned detailed comments to ensure that the record was kept precisely correct in all news stories.

The captain's lively taped reminiscences provided the icing on the cake! Yet, there were some things he would not talk about. He steadfastly declined to state how many men he had been obliged to kill in the line of duty. He would never discuss those incidents, nor would he speak about encounters during which he himself received a wound. Momentous as those events were, they remained a closed book insofar as elaboration by the "Lone Wolf" was concerned.

In a career that spanned more than three decades in Ranger service, Captain Gonzaullas was involved in hundreds of cases. Only a representative number could be described in this book. From those selected, the reader can visualize the role and the scope of activity of a twentieth-century Texas Ranger caught up in all kinds of situations involving enforcement of the law and protection of life and property . . . some humorous, some tragic, but none dull.

I
Baptism of Fire

To that Texas Ranger patrolling the wild, rugged border region of the Rio Grande from Comstock to Del Rio in 1920, one question on the Daily Scout Report clearly had a double meaning. At the end of the day of May 10, he wrote, among other things, that he had traveled thirty-five miles on horseback scouting and cutting trails on the river for smugglers, as well as checking brands for stolen cattle. He had apprehended a law violator on the charge of cattle theft, but the arrest was resisted. Working by lamplight as he filled out the report, he progressed to the question "Disposition of prisoner." After chewing on his pencil stub and staring out into the blackness of the night, he tersely inserted, "Damn bad. Had to kill him in a gun fight."

Just twenty weeks later on October 1, 1920, a promising new recruit at El Paso joined the Ranger force intending to serve first along that same great river separating Texas from Mexico. Manuel Trazazas Gonzaullas was twenty-nine years old. Born in Cadiz, Spain, on July 4, 1891, to a father of Spanish and mother of German ancestry, American citizens visiting there at the time, Gonzaullas was destined to be the only man of Spanish descent to become a captain in the Texas Rangers. He was to earn the nickname "Lone Wolf" because, as he explained it, "I went into lots of fights by myself, and I came out by myself, too!" Border outlaws later came to know him as "El Lobo Solo."

All boys need a hero, a man of honor, of good character, who can serve as an example of true manhood for them to emulate.

Young Manuel found such a hero in the person of Texas Ranger Captain John R. Hughes, the "Border Boss," whom he frequently saw astride his horse riding down the streets of El Paso. Tall and ramrod straight in the saddle, the brown-haired Captain Hughes was clean shaven at that time, except for a pencil line mustache. Plain, knee-high black boots were pulled on over trim black pant legs. On his head, there was a fine quality, wide-brim white hat. His long-sleeve white shirt with black string tie was set off by a smooth leather black vest. Hughes always wore a tie. Contrasting with the somber black and white of his clothing was the sunlight glinting off the row of cartridges in his hand-tooled belt, and off the pistols at his hips.

It was no wonder that the boy Gonzaullas was impressed by this man, whose reputation for honesty and fair play was acknowledged on both sides of the river throughout the border country. Hughes had joined the Ranger force at Georgetown on August 10, 1887, and had become head of Company "D" when Captain Frank Jones was killed by a band of smugglers not far from El Paso in 1893.

Manuel Gonzaullas' desire to become affiliated with the Rangers stemmed from his intense hatred for outlaws. It was a natural feeling for one who had helplessly witnessed the murder of his only two brothers and the wounding of his parents in a bandit raid on their border home. The vivid memory of that tragic and senseless attack when he was fifteen remained with Gonzaullas until his death at eighty-five on February 13, 1977.

One of the most colorful of all Rangers in the 150-plus years of the service, Gonzaullas became poison to criminals. His life was a crusade to eliminate or place behind bars smugglers, bootleggers, thieves and murderers wherever he was assigned in the state of Texas. His coolness under fire, his utter fearlessness and his deadly accuracy with pistols and rifles are generally credited as the basic reasons he survived innumerable gunfights, in a great many of which the odds were clearly against him. Gonzaullas himself went further. "It was more than that," he said, "much more. Sure, some luck was involved, but you can't make it just on luck at all times. The good Lord has to have His arm around you and has to help you in a situation like that. You can't count on judgment or luck alone. I know that He had His arm around me many, many times."

Gonzaullas' nature was a pronounced blend of sternness on the one side, and gentleness on the opposite. He was an intensely religious man. A staunch Presbyterian and active in his church

This portrait by Keith Martin of Captain John R. Hughes in his older age hangs in the Texas Ranger Museum in Waco. Hughes was a boyhood idol of Gonzaullas. (Courtesy Texas Ranger Hall of Fame and Museum.)

Texas Rangers at Shafter Mines, Presidio County, El Paso district, in 1890. *Left to right, standing:* Bob Speaker and Jim Putnam. *Left to right, seated:* Lon Odem and John R. Hughes, who held the rank of sergeant at the time. (Courtesy Texas Department of Public Safety.)

throughout his long life, he had a deep-seated belief in the justice of "eye for eye, tooth for tooth . . ." as laid down in Exodus 21:24-25. It was a belief that had its root in the indelible mark left on his young mind by that border outlaw raid. Yet, he was a man completely without prejudice against others because of race or national origin.

As a law enforcement officer, he was like a thundering prophet of old who brought down the wrath of God on wrongdoers. On the other hand, there were times when he interceded with a plea for mercy on behalf of individuals when, in his opinion, a severe sentence meted out by a court far exceeded the gravity of the crime committed. He was a keen student of the Bible, which he read regularly. The several Bibles which he possessed were copiously marked with underlining of passages that pertained to sinning and the seeking of forgiveness and peace in the eyes of the Lord.

Later in life, he made it a practice always to have in his pocket and in his car copies of the New Testament with markings that pointed to the powerful message of repentance and forgiveness. Those New Testaments would be given to errant men whom he believed might be remolded into useful members of society. He had no sympathy for incorrigible criminals, men who rebuffed efforts at rehabilitation, but there was compassion in his heart for those who had fallen into the error of their ways and were genuinely sorry. On the first page, he would have a handwritten note in red ink directing attention to the first of the readings, Romans 3:23. On that page, there would be the next notation which moved the reader to Romans 6:23, and so on through Ephesians 2:8-9, Luke 18:13, Romans 8:38-39, 10:9-10, II Corinthians 6:2 and Acts 8:35-39. In the margin of the page containing the last passage, he wrote in red ink, "Amen. Believe what you have read and you are saved forever." In his old age, he cherished memories of men whose lives had been changed by a gift testament.

Not the traditional towering Texas lawman, "Lone Wolf" Gonzaullas was an average 5 feet 10½ inches in height. There was never an ounce of fat on his broad-shouldered, lithe 170-pound body. His full head of dark hair turned to a silvery gray in later years. Gonzaullas' gray-green eyes disconcerted men who had something to hide. Their stab of swift appraisal made the subjects of their scrutiny flinch as the "Lone Wolf" appeared to be reading their innermost thoughts. In his long service as a law enforcement officer, there were times when it appeared that he actually did read the mind of another. Some of his associates firmly believed that he was endowed with extrasensory perception. He might well have been, though he never admitted it.

One who took pride in personal appearance, Gonzaullas wore well-fitting clothes, the broad-brim western type hat that is typical of the Rangers, and fine, custom-made boots that were polished to mirror brightness. A man of obvious quality and good breeding, Gonzaullas was noted for his unfailing courtesy and gentlemanly deportment toward men and women alike, except when confronting outlaws. In those encounters, his steely courage and determination to have and keep the upper hand were notable characteristics.

Handsome and an undeniably flashy dresser, in later years "Lone Wolf" Gonzaullas was able to satisfy a liking for diamonds that was sometimes compared with Mae West's appreciation of the gems. He wore them in rings, on handsomely crafted silver and gold buckles fastening gun belts of hand-tooled leather. He even had them on some of his pistols. Those gold and silver embellished guns, which were gifts from admirers, sported a glittering array of diamonds. In addition, the more elaborate were decorated with such emblems as those of the Shrine, Masonic Blue Lodge, Scottish Rite, etc., as well as a miniature Ranger Captain badge, his initials "MTG" and his brand. They were spectacular enough to dazzle the beholder, whether friend or foe. After he acquired those works of art, an untold number of outlaws had the distinction of having their epidermis punctured by bullets fired from Gonzaullas' fancy pistols. He had a code that was engraved on some of them. It was "Never Draw Me Without Cause or Sheathe Me With Dishonor." A Colt .45 was inscribed, "God Created All Men Equal. Col. Colt Made Them All the Same Size."

His regular working pistols had the trigger guard cut away and were made with safety catches on each side of the hammer. The spring holsters were cut deep so the trigger itself was exposed and readily accessible. On numerous occasions, those refinements enabled him to get in the first shot, undoubtedly saving his life. Although he has been credited with killing as many as seventy-five men in his career, Gonzaullas said, "That is a gross exaggeration," but would not state just how many had fallen before his guns. He knew, but kept his counsel. Despite the fact that he enjoyed publicity, he avoided it like a plague when it would have dealt with fatal gunfights.

By the time of his retirement from Ranger service in 1951, Gonzaullas had acquired a collection of 580 guns of various types, plus knives, daggers, clubs and other weapons he had removed from the persons of criminals he had captured. Whenever asked about their origin, he always declined to tell. "Some have real stories behind them," he would say, "but it's nobody's business where they came from!"

When he enlisted in the Ranger force on October 1, 1920, Gonzaullas had been married for only five and one-half months. He had transplanted his bride, a native New Yorker, to the desert Southwest. Manuel Trazazas Gonzaullas and Laura Isabel Scherer were married in Riverside, California, on April 12, 1920. His father was Manuel Gonzaullas, a native of Spain, and his mother was Helen von Droff Gonzaullas, a native of Canada. Both were naturalized citizens of the United States.

Laura's parents, Abraham Scherer and Caroline Greenbaum Scherer, were born in New York. Laura was less than three years old when her mother died. The child, who was reared in Brooklyn by a grandmother, grew up with the ambition to become a dancer in Broadway shows, but she met Manuel T. Gonzaullas and ended up in California where she married him. A petite, graceful woman with delicately beautiful features, she had innate good taste in clothes. Laura and Manuel Gonzaullas complemented one another. He was an extrovert. She was an introvert, content to remain in the background.

She was destined to face long absences by her husband while he was on assignment in distant places. His was a strange career choice for a man who held home life in high regard. Separated from his beloved Laura, he would be obliged to lay his head on pillows in hotel rooms, or in private homes when hotel space was not available. During his service in wilderness areas along the Texas-Mexican border, his saddle served as a pillow while he lay on his bedroll, looking up at the stars shining brilliantly in the clear night air, and longing for his young wife. Occasionally, the opportunity would be presented for her to go to him when he would be stationed at one place for days or weeks.

Although he fully expected to be permanently assigned to service along the Rio Grande, Gonzaullas quickly received his Ranger baptism of fire elsewhere. He was ordered by the adjutant general's office to the command of Captain R. W. Aldrich in Wichita County. Presence of the Rangers had been requested to help bring a semblance of order to the chaotic oil fields of Northern Texas in the vicinity of Burkburnett. Robbery, murder, bootlegging, gambling and prostitution had become so prevalent that local authorities were powerless to enforce the law.

Immediately, he became involved in steps to put the finger on criminals responsible for the reign of terror in the area. A substantial number of people were ready and willing to tell all they knew, but not surprisingly, others were reluctant to do so. Among the latter were some business and professional men who had been clamoring in private for state help. Typical of their craven attitude was the remark of one. "For God's sake, don't talk to me, sir. The hijacking bunch will kill me if they see me speaking to 'the law.' "

In the 1920s, mob action was still a final resort of citizens aggrieved by lawlessness and the failure of local officers to maintain order in a community. Frustrations in Wichita County surfaced over a relatively minor incident in which a highly respected man was the intended victim. That event was the culmination of a lengthy series of unspeakable acts by the criminal element against the long-suffering public. An attempt was made by two men to rob R. C. Vandiver of Wichita Falls and to make off with his seven-passenger Packard touring car. The attack occurred at about 10:00 P.M. on the outskirts of Bridgetown while Vandiver was traveling from Iowa Park. As he topped the ridge from which the road descended into the valley, he was stopped by two highwaymen and jerked out of his car. That was in the days when the state speed limit was twenty-five miles per hour but conditions on the rough, rutted roads seldom allowed movement faster than fifteen.

Although Vandiver had a pistol which he carried for protection, it was, unhandily, in his pocket and he did not have time to pull it out before he was rushed. Not a man to submit timidly to such indignity, Vandiver's first defense was with his fists. He gave a good account of himself by pommeling the offenders, although he was smacked upside his head by a blow from a gun used in the manner of a blackjack. The result was a bloody scalp wound. During the fracas, he eventually managed to get to his pistol. At that, one of the would-be thieves turned tail and ran, considering flight more sensible than standing his ground. Vandiver and the remaining hijacker commenced firing at one another. A bullet went through Vandiver's coat but missed his body. The attacker was not so lucky. A trail of blood from the scene demonstrated that he had been struck by a bullet fired from the victim's pistol. Two women who resided near the spot, their attention attracted by the sound of shots, saw a couple of men load a third into a Model T Ford, after which they drove away as fast as the four cylinders would take them.

When word of the attempted hijacking spread and evidence was noted that one of the heisters had been shot, an alarm was sent out in Wichita and surrounding counties in Texas, also in Oklahoma. Hospitals were alerted in case medical aid was sought. A mob of over two hundred men quickly formed, breathing threats to summarily hang the offenders if they could be caught. Lines of automobiles moved out, filling the roads in all directions. Local officers set up roadblocks, not to interfere with the movement of the mob but to nab the suspects. After combing the countryside the balance of Saturday night and all day Sunday, the mob dispersed, having met with failure to track down the quarry.

It was into that tense atmosphere that newly appointed Ranger Gonzaullas went, in the company of several other members of the force who had been in service and exposed to similar troubles during tenures of varying lengths. Gonzaullas was not new to law enforcement. He had been intimately involved in investigative work with the United States government for five years as a special agent of the Treasury Department and was well trained. That training was to serve him in good stead during the next thirty-one years. Prior to that federal service, he had been a major in the Mexican Army at age twenty.

Independent in thought and action by nature, Gonzaullas' "style" as a Texas Ranger soon became apparent. He entered into crime control with zest. In a short time, his name was striking fear into the hearts of even the most arrogant, swaggering outlaw bullies. To him, the law was to be impartially enforced. Its violators merited his utter contempt.

Arrival of the Rangers in Wichita County had a pronounced, if temporary, quieting effect on crime. Their reputation for vigorous pursuit brought about a short-term holding action on the part of the criminal element as the new situation, which was not at all to their liking, was sized up.

Wichita Falls, as the major city of the region, was headquarters for companies which engaged in various lines of business connected with the booming oil fields at such places as Burkburnett, Bridgetown, Newtown and Bradley's Corner. Bridgetown received its name from the fact that a ramshackle bridge over the Red River was nearby at that time. Because of confusion with the name of Newton in Newton County, Texas, the post office at Newtown in Wichita County was given the name of Thrift.

Gonzaullas found living conditions in the oil fields to be primitive in the extreme. Therefore he, too, made Wichita Falls his headquarters. Habitations and businesses in Bridgetown, Newtown and Bradley's Corner were primarily tents or tar paper covered shacks. Many were placed among and between oil derricks. There were a few unpainted frame buildings. Some people were living in dugouts, over which tents were stretched. The dugouts were less than satisfactory living quarters when rain fell. In the "towns" themselves, rainy spells turned the dirt streets into quagmires. Vehicular traffic, whether wagons, trucks or cars, came to a complete standstill at such times. Enterprising individuals would lay a long, wide board across particularly deep mud holes at street intersections. Pedestrians could cross on such a board after the payment of ten cents.

There were no public toilets, so other persons who were equally industrious erected crude privies at street corners. Early day versions of modern pay toilets, those privies could be entered only upon payment of ten cents to the custodian. They were of the roughest construction imaginable, consisting of one-by-twelve-inch planks raised to chair height. The planks, which would have holes cut in them for seats, were erected over open pits. There was no roof to such privies, the walls themselves being of canvas or tar paper.

Lawlessness was rampant throughout the Wichita County oil fields. Gambling of all kinds was carried on in tents, outside which lookouts were stationed to guard against law enforcement officers slipping up on them. However, except for the fines involved, raids hardly mattered because the operators had little investment. If the places were shut down and equipment destroyed, all they had to do was get another table or two, some more dice, cards and chips, then they were ready to go again.

As the "Lone Wolf" explained it, the gamblers were as difficult to control as were the prostitutes. "You could put a woman in jail for prostitution," he said, "but, what good would it do? As soon as she got out, she was ready to go back in business. She didn't have to buy any merchandise, and she didn't pay any taxes on her stock in trade. We soon learned that the best way to handle prostitutes in the oil fields was just to make them move on." In those days, a quart of whiskey was said to have commanded a price three times that charged by a prostitute. The ratio of the fees clearly demonstrates the relationship of supply to demand.

Robbery of workers, either on the drilling rigs or while they were in transit to and from their jobs, had become so routine that men carried a lunch pail in their hand and a pistol in their belt.

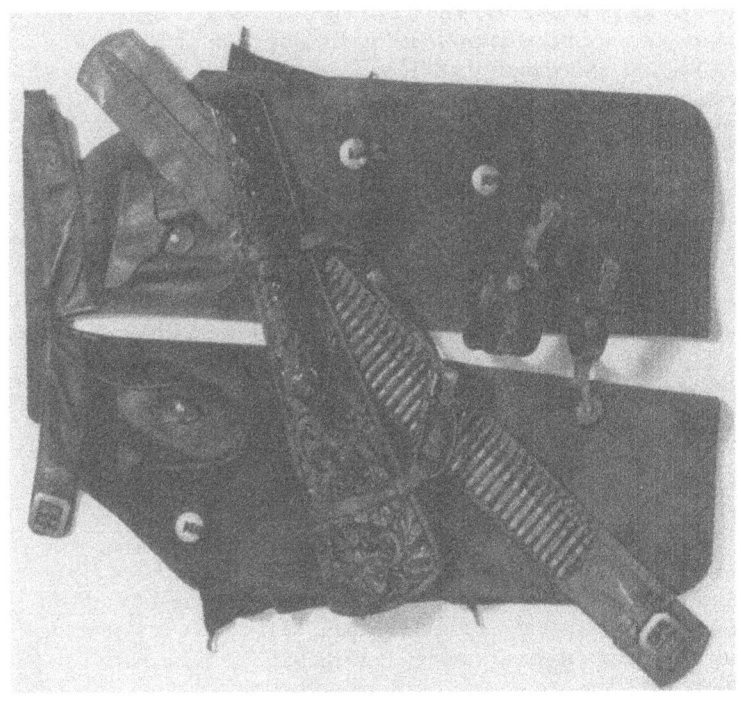

Cartridge belt, chaps, spurs and scabbard used by the "Lone Wolf" are now displayed at the Texas Ranger Museum in Waco. (Courtesy Texas Ranger Hall of Fame and Museum.)

They were prime targets for hijacking, as it was the custom at that time for each rig worker to be paid in cash for each day's work at the end of his shift. The thieves who would stick up the crews were so brazen about it, and they felt so secure in being beyond the reach of the local law enforcement officers, that few even bothered to conceal their identity by wearing a mask. They lost their security when the "Lone Wolf" arrived.

A great percentage of county holdups and murders had occurred in gambling dens. The lewd women were targets of the Rangers not only because of their "profession" but also because it was common knowledge that they were, in numerous instances, accessories to crime by providing places of refuge and safety to thieves and murderers after commission of their illegal acts.

The drastically changed atmosphere in Wichita County had two clear results. One was expressed by a newspaper: "Church and Sunday School are being held now in oil towns of Wichita County which before their [the Rangers'] coming had never heard the name of God except in blasphemy." The second result was that hordes of gamblers, bootleggers and others left after it became too "hot" for them to operate with impunity, as had previously been the case. It was standard practice for that element to move to other territories where they could ply their trade for a while until public outcry brought a contingent of Rangers in, thus obliging the outlaws to move on again. Sometimes they would go back to a county that had been cleaned up and, after the Rangers had left, renew their operations.

Automobiles or saddle horses were used by Rangers for personal transportation. During rainy spells, patrol duty could only be conducted properly on horseback. Mounted Rangers brought in arrested law violators by subjecting them to the indignity of being handcuffed to a stirrup or obliged to walk in front of the horses, depending upon the severity of the crime with which they were being charged. The speed of forward movement would be dictated by the Ranger on the horse, which meant that the criminals afoot would have to maintain a lively pace to avoid being stepped on by the animal or being dragged by the handcuff fastened to the stirrup. Slogging through the mud under those conditions had a sobering effect on many lawbreakers.

Following the subduing of the crime wave in Wichita County, the Rangers began to put in surprise appearances at other towns in the North Texas oil fields, notably Ranger, Desdemona and Breckenridge. Here today and gone tomorrow, their strategy kept the law violators on nervous edge, never knowing where the force might next make a pop call. It was being noted that many criminals had simply shifted operations from Wichita County to the Eastland and Stephens County oil fields. The Rangers headed there in hot pursuit. They were welcomed in Desdemona by the Law and Order League, which had been involved in numerous direct encounters with the criminal element whose purpose was to separate the oil field workers from their money. The responsible citizens of Desdemona had been sufficiently courageous to stand up for their convictions. They and their property became targets for retribution by their enemies. One such incident occurred on Saturday night, November 27, 1920. An attempt was made to destroy the Baptist Church by dousing a part of it with oil and then setting it afire. The act was clearly aimed at members of that congregation and especially the pastor, J. A. Kidd, who was a prominent leader in the Law and Order League. The beginning of the blaze was spotted by near neighbors and the alarm turned in. The fire was extinguished before great damage was done to the sanctuary. The deed backfired on the perpetrators by arousing the indignation of the populace, which threw its weight behind the Ranger force in cleaning up the oil field there. Earlier that same night of November 27, the Rangers made flying raids on gambling joints in Desdemona and arrested 125 men. Prostitutes picked up in the raids were not booked but were given orders to leave town at once, which they did.

Ranger, Texas, residents did not unanimously welcome the Texas Ranger force making raids in their city during the first week of December 1920. The people protested that the sending of state officers gave the town a bad name. Included among those complaining was the Chamber of Commerce. Local officers had not called on the state for help in crime control. The relationship of citizens toward the Rangers was described as "unfriendly." The hard feeling became crystallized in the aftermath of a raid on a bootlegger, in which Rangers M. T. Gonzaullas, H. P. Brady and Martin N. Koonsman were aiding Deputy Sheriff J. B. Ames. The prisoner was said to have made a threatening move while being conveyed to headquarters. During the ensuing affray, he was wounded by gunfire, a not uncommon occurrence. However, in this instance there was fierce reaction. The Eastland County sheriff arrested and jailed Gonzaullas and Koonsman, charging them with assault with intent to kill. His action was an unheard-of procedure. As might be expected, the response from Austin was strong. The adjutant general's office ordered an entire company of Texas Rangers to the city of Ranger, and the presence of an assistant attorney general was requested.

News that the company was on the way fell like a bombshell in the city. It was totally unexpected. The immediate result was that Gonzaullas and Koonsman were released from jail on fifteen hundred dollars bond each, a face-saving gesture by county authorities. Captain C. J. Blackwell and nine Texas Rangers arrived at 7:40 P.M. on December 7. State Assistant Attorney General C. L. Stone, who set up his office at Breckenridge in adjacent Stephens County, stated that the sending of the additional men to the city of Ranger was "due to the failure on the part of local authorities to cooperate with the Rangers." By the middle of December the Eastland County grand jury met but returned no indictment of Gonzaullas and Koonsman, then issued a statement in which it was said, "They [the Rangers] are needed in this county and ought to receive the cooperation of the citizens of every section . . . ." The Chamber of Commerce prudently withdrew its complaint and the whole matter was permitted to cool off. Raids by the Rangers continued unabated.

Before going to the Eastland County oil fields to stay, Gonzaullas by chance had taken part in a Wichita Falls police action soon after midnight on the early morning of Monday, November 29. That was during the transition period when he would be in Eastland or Stephens County for a day, then back to Wichita County for a day or two. Coming in to town from late duty alone in the Burkburnett area, he stopped at the police station before going to his hotel and to bed. While he was at the station, a call came in from a residence on Brook Street reporting a robbery in which money and jewelry valued at ten thousand dollars had been removed from the unwilling victims.

A poker game had been in progress in the house. Involved was a group of prominent Wichita Falls business and professional men and their wives, all close friends who made it a practice to play poker together at frequent intervals. The men were playing at a table in the living room, and the women, also playing poker, were gathered around the dining table. Thanks to the oil boom, Wichita Falls was prosperous. It had almost tripled in population to forty thousand in two years. Money was plentiful and the high stakes in the game reflected the financial affluence of the city.

To the astonishment of the players, a masked man wielding a sawed-off shotgun entered the front door. At the same instant, another man, who also had a white handkerchief tied over the lower part of his face, stepped into the house through the back door. He was carrying a .45. They scooped up the cash on the two tables, relieved the players of additional money in their wallets and purses, then demanded rings, watches and other jewelry items, all the while filling the air with obscenities and threats. They reeked of whiskey and appeared to be sufficiently under its influence to make a slow, sauntering exit from the house.

After a second of stunned silence that followed the thieves' departure, the alarm was telephoned to the police station. Only Patrolman Homer Palmer was available for the night chief to send out, so Gonzaullas volunteered to go with him. They got in the patrol car and sped to the nearby residential section. Approaching the place from the rear, they noted a parked automobile a couple of blocks from Brook Street, standing at the end of an alley. With their uncanny instinct for smelling out clues, the officers stopped to examine the vehicle. In it were a half-empty bottle of whiskey, a partial box of shotgun shells and several articles of clothing. The key was in the ignition switch. On the hunch that this was an intended getaway car, they removed the key, pulled spark plug wires and then began to stealthily reconnoiter the adjacent area. If this were, indeed, a getaway car they knew that the two men would be making their way toward it and, by that time, must be near.

The officers separated, Palmer walking in front of the houses in that block, whereas Gonzaullas cautiously moved up the dark alley, pistol in hand, stalking the unknown. His sharp ears picked up a slight sound of movement only a short distance in front of him. He stopped, motionless, straining to hear any telltale noise that could indicate to him what was ahead, and where. A street light at the next intersection was too far distant to cast any illumination into the alley, its rays being blocked by residences and garages. There was only starlight, and that was not enough.

Then there was a burst of fire from a pistol down the alley and the bullet struck a garage wall near him. Gonzaullas dropped to a crouching position, at which time his eyes spotted a barely perceptible white blur which he assumed was a shirt. A second streak of fire gave away the hijacker's position. It *was* a white shirt. Gonzaullas fired twice in rapid succession. There was a screamed oath, so he knew he had hit his mark.

He heard a body fall, but held his ground suspecting that the fall could have been a ruse. Almost simultaneously there were mumbled words followed by the sound of two pair of feet running through a gate into a yard and on around a house. In the yard, a bloody handkerchief was found, but not until morning light was discovery made of the bag of jewelry which the thief had dropped in his flight. Residents in two houses along the escape route, awakened by the firing of the pistols, reported hearing the groans of the wounded man as he ran, supported by his accomplice. The automobile had been stolen from the Arcadia Oil Company and was returned by the police. Not until Gonzaullas was temporarily stationed in the Eastland County oil fields did Wichita Falls officers take the two criminals into custody.

II

North Texas Cleanup

Whiskey making was big business in the fields, and very profitable for the still operator until he was caught. Ingenious methods of camouflage were used to conceal each enterprise from the unwelcome eyes of the law. There was a never-ceasing, around-the-clock, cat-and-mouse game between officers and offenders as the former worked diligently to track down the bootleggers and the latter used every artifice at their command to escape detection and seizure.

Just outside Ranger on the road to Graham, Rangers Gonzaullas, Brady and Koonsman, again working with Deputy Sheriff Ames, found the best camouflage yet when they seized an elaborate still setup which utilized a coal-fired, steam-powered ten-ton farm tractor. Attached to the tractor was a regular trailer, whose high sides concealed a five-hundred-barrel wooden tank and still, for which the heat came from the boiler of the tractor by means of tubing. It was no problem to adapt the tractor-trailer unit to still operation when needed.

The tractor was moved around the farm property frequently to allay any possible suspicion. Sometimes it was in plain sight and at other times it was not visible. It was the fact that the tractor was to be seen here and there on the farm, though soil was not being turned, that first attracted the notice of the sharp-eyed Gonzaullas. He knew something about farming and was aware that farmers would not shift massively heavy mechanical equipment to different

17

places without good reason. He became suspicious, so a watch was set to determine the reason for the wanderings of the gargantuan tractor and trailer. Christmas was approaching and the demand for whiskey was rising, so the still operators became just careless enough to lead to their undoing. The tank was about one-third full of mash when it was seized by the officers and converted to kindling by the free use of axes. The still was confiscated, as was the supply of liquor found on the premises.

Also in December, a mobile unit was drawn up to the Stephens County courthouse in Breckenridge by an old gray mule and an old bay horse, whose gaunt appearance showed they would have benefited by a diet of the corn before it was converted into the mash they were pulling. Then a second covered wagon creaked to a stop behind it. The equipment had been captured by Rangers Gonzaullas and W.L. LeSeur. Gonzaullas' keen nose had scented the wildcat still southeast of town, and the search was on. In a secluded area of dense brush half a mile from the nearest public road, they spotted a tent and then quietly watched the unsuspecting distiller hard at work. Two wagons were nearby, both hitched up and ready to go.

As the wagons rolled away, moving out of sight and sound, the Rangers entered the tent and arrested an astonished bootlegger, handcuffing him and taking his complete still into custody. Their next step was to follow the drivers. As the vehicles were separated by sufficient distance, slowly wending their way along the tortuous trail in the brush, Gonzaullas and LeSeur were able to seize the second wagon and arrest the driver without the lead wagon occupants being aware that anything amiss was going on right behind them.

In that first seized wagon, they found two barrels of corn mash, a quantity of corn liquor, bottles and miscellaneous items. Next, they grabbed the other, a large covered wagon, and arrested the driver and his wife. It contained living quarters and a complete still, as well as a valuable stock of corn whiskey. The Rangers deposited at the sheriff's office the two stills and two five-gallon jugs of whiskey as evidence, also two pistols and two rifles. The balance of the booze-making equipment which they took over at the tent was smashed with heavy axes. Mash, hops and syrup were scattered on the ground and made unusable. Following the filing of charges, Gonzaullas and LeSeur assumed a new role in their official duties as they went about watering and feeding the half-starved beasts.

Gonzaullas and his fellow Rangers continued to hammer away at law violators in the Breckenridge area to the delight of most townspeople, who, along with the local press, praised their work. The newspaper commented, in part, ". . . The cleanup is on and it will be but a short time, Captain Aldrich assures us, that the undesirables in the district will be weeded out and the scourge . . . suppressed. Breckenridge has attracted many undesirables in the past several months who have found a fertile field here for their work. Hi-jackers, invading the isolated drilling rigs, have held up the drillers and . . . this type of piracy of the oil fields has not been at all uncommon. With the coming of the Rangers and the thorough cooperation of the sheriff's office, it will not be long before the district will breathe easier. Let the good work go on!"

As was their policy in high crime areas, the Rangers, acting in conjunction with Breckenridge city and Stephens County authorities, spread the dragnet for men who were without visible means of support. The system used was to examine the palms of their hands. If the hands were rough and calloused, the men were judged to be workers and released with the admonition, "Go about your business and behave yourself." Where the hands were soft and showed no evidence of manual labor, those men were checked out to determine their means of livelihood. In most instances, the latter proved to be gamblers and fellow parasites who preyed on the oil field workers.

"If they [the authorities] didn't have anything on them, we would just lock them up for 30 days or give them two hours to get out of the state," Gonzaullas commented in later years. "You could do it in those days! And, in Wichita County they generally gave us about an hour and a half back, as they could be over the line into Oklahoma in 30 minutes. Later on, in the East Texas field, that warning would put them across the Louisiana line in just about the same length of time."

In the first pickup of that kind in Stephens County, twenty-five men were held for questioning. Other drives followed, as Captain Blackwell proposed ". . . to make the district a poor winter resort for silk-shirted lounge lizards and their ilk," pointing out that ". . . under the law, they can be arrested on a vagrancy charge every 24 hours." The constant pressure soon had its effect and there was a general exodus of unwanted persons. Before long, Wichita County was complaining that some of those who had exited from Stephens County were turning up back in the county from which they had been chased in the first place.

19

In another drive of two days, in which the Rangers, federal prohibition agents and Stephens County officers worked closely together, thirty-nine more men were rounded up and jailed, and a hundred barrels of whiskey were seized along with a massive quantity of narcotics. At one place that was raided, no liquor was evident, but officers noted an elaborate wall panel in the corner of one room. Its presence in that setting seemed so unusual that a check was made. The panel was removable. To the dismay of the operator of the house, there was discovered behind the panel a very narrow room ten feet long and ten feet high, which was used as a storage place for whiskey.

Just after Christmas, the adjutant general's office in Austin ordered Ranger Gonzaullas back to Wichita County to conduct an additional purge of the oil fields. It was to be a hard-nosed roundup of the criminals who had drifted in from Eastland and Stephens Counties when the pressure there became too great for them to take. As Gonzaullas expressed it in Wichita Falls, "The idea is to keep them on the jump so they'll have no time to settle down and make plans. Although we made a large number of arrests in the other oil fields, a majority of the criminals took to their heels and are right back here where we originally chased them out."

He was already becoming known as the "Lone Wolf," the first newspaper reference to that nickname being in the *Wichita Falls Daily Times* on December 29, 1920, when it was stated, "Ranger Gonzaullas, who is known throughout the oil fields where he has been on duty as 'Lone Wolf,' was recognized by at least a dozen characters in the field [here], who approached him and said they were leaving for other places immediately. Proper warning was issued to all of them. Mr. Gonzaullas stated Wednesday morning that the cleanup raids would be conducted periodically, and with a few words was away for another trip." He liked publicity. It flattered his ego and it conveyed to the world a desired image of toughness. That made his job easier.

The periodic cleanup raids met with active resistance by some lawbreakers, and there were several scrapes pitting the Rangers and local officers against offenders. One such affair occurred at Bradley's Corner, a short distance out of Wichita Falls on the night of January 5, 1921. It almost assumed comic opera proportions. It was led by Gonzaullas, assisted by Ranger J. W. McCormick, a deputy sheriff and the county attorney. A tip had been given on an alleged retailer of corn whiskey in Bradley's Corner.

The party arrived in the community at about 10:00 P.M. and headed for the business establishment in question. It was located in the old post office building. They did not know until after the dust settled that there had been a leak and their arrival was not a surprise. The suspect's wife told the officers later that a couple of hours before they appeared on the scene, a tip had come to her husband that a search party was on the way. That gave him sufficient time to remove liquor from the premises. However, in his haste, he overlooked one cache. That was his undoing.

McCormick and the deputy went to the rear and side of the two-story structure, County Attorney John Davenport guarded the front door and Gonzaullas went inside. The suspect was completely cooperative. Nearing the end of a thorough check, during which he had found nothing, Gonzaullas remarked he believed he had received a tip on a "dry hole." But, there was one door he had not opened. The man told him there was nothing beyond but a balcony at the top of an outside staircase. On the balcony was a tank which held water for the shower. Nevertheless, Gonzaullas decided to have a look. Perhaps he recalled the tank attached to the farm tractor.

There was no outside light, so the suspect obligingly procured a long electric extension cord, on the end of which there was a socket with a bare light bulb. He had completely forgotten what was in that tank. Proceeding with the search, the "Lone Wolf" spotted two quart jars of corn liquor on the bottom of the tank. Upon discovering them, he turned to the man and told him he was under arrest, whereupon the fellow lost his head. Gonzaullas leaned over to pull out the jars. While he was in that position, the suspect reached up on a shelf, grabbed an empty bottle and struck the Ranger on the head with such force that it momentarily knocked him out. He dropped the end of the extension cord he was holding, whereupon the bulb hit the balcony floor and exploded.

From below, Ranger McCormick and Deputy Sheriff Weaver had watched the proceedings as best they could. When the bulb blew up and Gonzaullas collapsed, their first thought was that he had been shot. The suspect dashed back into the building, raced down the inside stair and exited through the side door. Weaver called to him to stop, but he would not, so the deputy fired two warning shots. McCormick also fired and commanded him to halt, but the man was so intent on getting away he speeded up. A fourth shot was aimed at his legs. He hit the ground rolling and howling. The sound of the pistol shots attracted a crowd from the street. The men endeavored to rush into the building but were stopped in their tracks. County Attorney Davenport, his back to the front wall, vowed to use his gun on the first man who stepped onto the gallery. None did.

While the light bulb episode and the suspect's flight were in progress, with the shots being fired, a resident of the house next door thought the place was being robbed. He ran to his window with a rifle and started to draw a bead on McCormick and Weaver. He was spotted by those men, whose natural reaction was to fire at him in self-defense. At that split second of the action, before any triggers were pulled, the man's wife, who had been remonstrating with him without success, put herself in front of his gun and called a halt. Her courageous act saved his life.

Continuing sweeps of the oil fields in Wichita County netted dozens of stills and large quantities of whiskey and mash, as well as the persons of individual bootleggers, retailers of the illegal liquid refreshment, and gamblers of all types. It was a never-ceasing enterprise for the officers. Again and again they went out, at all hours of the day and night. In a typical raid which Gonzaullas, acting alone, made at Bradley's Corner, he came across a fifty-gallon still complete with coils and burners, plus a bottling machine and mash. There was also gambling equipment, consisting of dice and poker tables, and chuck-a-luck games. All of the bootlegging and gambling paraphernalia was in a single large tent, characteristic of the temporary nature of most of the setups there.

On another run-of-the-mill action, Gonzaullas went alone and raided a cafe, also at Bradley's Corner. There he found a thirty-gallon still which was hidden under counters in the rear of the place. Wrapped in flour sacks and concealed under the range in the cafe kitchen were the coils of the still. The tubing connecting still and coils had been run through a wooden partition and covered.

Although the operators endeavored to disguise its characteristic scent by utilizing formaldehyde as a deodorizing agent on the surrounding ground, Sergeant McCormick and Ranger Gonzaullas ferreted out a still in the countryside between Newtown and Burkburnett. On the downwind side, they sniffed its existence, despite the formaldehyde and, like bloodhounds, were on the trail. They found one twenty-five-gallon and one four-gallon still in an isolated farmhouse, the smaller unit being used for second run. Two men were arrested and the Rangers confiscated sixteen gallons of first-run whiskey, eight barrels of mash, together with a quantity of hops, corn and sugar. The still operators had surreptitiously tapped a natural gas pipeline to secure free fuel and had run a water line into the house for use in cooling and condensing the vapor. At another location in the vicinity, they took possession of a large quantity of apple wine and raisin wine.

The "Lone Wolf" was joined by two associates in an expedition near Bradley's Corner, during which a man and a woman were arrested at another farmhouse. Though unmarried, they were living in the place together. In the house, the officers turned up copper coils for two stills and a batch of bottled corn liquor, which the woman attempted to destroy. The presence of the coils was sufficient grounds for belief that stills were not far distant. A determined search of the premises disclosed an underground room, or "dugout," in which there was a complete thirty-gallon still, a thirty-gallon tank and three barrels of corn mash. Not convinced that they had found everything, the officers continued looking and probing, watched intently by the baleful eyes of the handcuffed man and woman. Eventually, they pinpointed another underground room, that one containing a fifty-gallon still. In an outbuilding, there was a barrel of molasses which was being used as a sugar substitute. When the two were brought in to Wichita Falls, they were not only charged with the manufacture and sale of liquor but also with adultery, then a punishable offense in the eyes of the law.

A heavily armed group of officers left the city hall in Wichita Falls in the middle of January headed for the fields in the northwestern part of the county, their plans being to capture the ringleaders of a band of bootleggers. Unfortunately for the lawmen, the main quarry got wind of their approach and eluded capture by fleeing in automobiles the short distance across the Red River to safety in Oklahoma. That was a bit of frustration that frequently plagued officers in Wichita and other counties lying along the border river. Although the main prize escaped them, the raiding party members did come back into the city with three stills, three men and an eleven-year-old boy. The youngster, acting under orders, made a futile hundred-yard dash from the back door of a soft drink parlor, trying to get away with a gunnysack containing the evidence, a quantity of bottled "Choc" beer, as the Choctaw Indian recipe beer was commonly called.

Residents of the area saw only the surface indications of law enforcement as M. T. Gonzaullas and the other Rangers went about their routine work in cooperation with the local officers.

One activity unseen by the public was an undercover investigation that had been pursued since the middle of December. The focus was on a "hot" oil theft from one company and sale to another unsuspecting firm by middlemen. Those engaged in working up the evidence were Gonzaullas, McCormick and oil company special agents W. R. Johnston and T. W. Shannon, together with two confidential operatives of the Pinkerton and Shelton detective agencies.

Back on December 15, 1920, Empire Oil Company gauger G. B. Avant had observed that a thousand barrels of oil were missing from a large storage tank belonging to that company. The same thing was true on the succeeding day. At almost the same time, an employee of Interocean Oil and Refining Company discovered a three-inch tap line running from Empire's pipeline to that of another company, whose gathering line was used in common with Interocean. That other company was Uniform Oil and Gas, which had started receiving the oil in good faith under a contract that had just been made with a group of Wichita County men. The connection, which was underground, was located by seepage where the tie-in was made with Empire's line. It was a distance of about one-half mile from the storage tank.

Empire's office in Bartlesville, Oklahoma, received notice of the tap almost simultaneously from Uniform and from gauger Avant. The quiet investigation got under way to determine who had made the connection, and when. In all, some twenty-five thousand barrels of oil were moved through the illegal line up to the time the detective work was completed and charges filed. The connection had not been shut off so the surveillance could go forward without alerting the malefactors. Ten men were involved and were indicted by the Wichita County grand jury.

Most of the raids by Gonzaullas and his associates were run of the mill, with smashing of stills and gambling equipment, confiscation of whiskey, and a steady procession of arrested men and women being brought in and charged. Occasionally, there were interesting variations in that routine. One occurred in Wichita Falls itself when Gonzaullas and McCormick watched as a five-gallon glass container of whiskey was delivered beneath a residence at night and then hoisted inside through a trapdoor in the floor of the kitchen. The house sat on brick piers, as was the construction style in that era, and was a few feet above ground level. When the messenger returned to his car, he was arrested along with a woman companion. On the approach of the officers, the suspects, realizing they could not make a run for it, threw out two half-gallon glass jars of corn liquor, one of them breaking on impact. Why they tried to dispose of only those two was a mystery. Perhaps they panicked. More bottles and jars containing whiskey packed in straw and carpet material were on the floor and rear seat of the Dodge car.

When the Rangers then went to the back door of the residence, the woman in the kitchen saw them through the glass pane, whereupon she promptly broke the five-gallon container of whiskey, allowing its contents to run all over the floor. If she thought that by destroying it she would be beyond the reach of the law, she was mistaken. She was arrested, as was her surprised husband on his return to the house later in the evening. The arrests climaxed an investigation over a period of several days. At a safe distance to allay suspicion, Gonzaullas and McCormick had followed the Dodge to the house that night. Not only was its cargo of liquor confiscated, the car was also placed in the custody of federal authorities in Wichita Falls.

Another variation occurred in the existence of a gambling house being revealed in McCleskey to the alert eyes of Ranger Captain Tom Hickman, Gonzaullas and Deputy Sheriff Weaver. They were driving through the town on a night inspection of the oil fields. The giveaway was the sight of a man clearly walking post as a sentinel on duty. That was an extraordinary sight on a street, so the automobile was stopped. Upon being questioned, the guard admitted that he was, indeed, supposed to be protecting a gambling den from interference by the law. After taking him into custody, the officers entered the building and caught nine men engaged in games of chance. They, the operator of the house and the inefficient sentry were turned over to the Young County sheriff at Graham, whereupon the three continued their night tour of Eliasville, Ivan, South Bend, Lake City, Harding and Newcastle.

In a switch from carrying out their work on foot, on horseback or in a motor vehicle, on one occasion, at least, they made their way on their stomachs. Rangers Gonzaullas, McCormick and Roy W. Hardesty were on the trail of a whiskey-making operation in Archer County. The still they sought was located northeast of Scotland. The distillers had displayed better than average ingenuity in choosing the site for their illicit business. The still operation was concealed in a camouflaged spot amid trees, brush and tall grass. It was about three hundred yards east of a farmhouse, which was situated on the top of a high hill. In the house, there was stationed a twenty-four-hour lookout to guard against a surprise raid. The location of the farmhouse on the hill was such that an approaching automobile could be seen for two miles in any direction. Because of that, it was impossible for the Rangers to drive up to the place and capture the equipment intact and arrest the men. Nor could they approach across the fields and pastures without being readily spotted.

A careful and detailed reconnaissance disclosed that the only possible means of undetected approach would be up the bed of a shallow, low-bank creek that flowed near the house and emptied into the Little Wichita River. When they were ready to implement their plan, the Rangers were driven past the site in a touring car that traveled on the bumpy dirt road. They lay on the floor of the car that chugged along at a distance of several hundred yards from the house in the late afternoon when visibility was reduced. A couple of miles further, the road entered a small grove of trees in the creek bottom where the view from the lookout was completely obstructed. The officers quickly slipped out of the car, which continued on the road, again coming in view from the farmhouse as it passed out of the grove. The automobile went down the road until lost in the distance.

The next phase of the plan was a slow, dirty and laborious process, but foot by foot the Rangers progressed up the creek bed, crouching, crawling, even inching forward on their stomachs as they neared the target. By the time they reached their destination, they were covered with mud from head to foot, but success was theirs. Gonzaullas reported that nine hundred gallons of corn mash in eighteen barrels, a sixty-gallon still and other operating accessories were seized in three large dugouts. The whiskey-making equipment was chopped to pieces with axes and the mash strewn about and made unusable, then the ope.ators were placed in the custody of the Archer County sheriff.

It was always disturbing, and understandably so, to "Lone Wolf" Gonzaullas to find young boys involved in bootlegging operations, no matter how indirectly. He was an ardent supporter of the then-new Boy Scout movement. Throughout the remainder of his life, he worked hard encouraging youths to be a part of the Scout program and live up to its principles. He never had any children of his own, so he took a kindly, paternal interest in the well-being of other men's sons.

One of the numerous encounters with youths that caused him great concern occurred in March 1921 when he, McCormick and

Johnnie H. Asher moved in on two complete and modern stills that were cleverly secreted in caves excavated in the bluff of the Red River about one and one-half miles north of Bradley's Corner. That place had earned for itself the unenviable reputation of being as wicked as Sodom and Gomorrah combined. It is a fact that Bradley's Corner was a constant and recurring headache for the Rangers and local law enforcement officers in their efforts to bring order to the oil fields of Wichita County. Insofar as Bradley's Corner was concerned, those efforts were not entirely successful. What corrected the conditions there was the eventual end of the oil boom and the natural death of what Gonzaullas called "that festering sore," namely, Bradley's Corner.

The Rangers were prepared for almost any eventuality when they closed in on the river bank caves. They were not prepared to find that the stills were "guarded" by several barefoot boys who should have been in school. The boys made no move to defy the officers, even though pistols, rifles and ammunition were in the caves within easy reach. Gonzaullas admitted to being shaken by the discovery. The boys were taken to Wichita Falls and placed in the custody of local officers, with the hope that through supervision and sympathetic guidance they might be rescued from what would, otherwise, be a life of crime.

The "Lone Wolf" had strong convictions on the subject of crime prevention. They included the importance of adults setting good examples for youths in order to help keep them on the right path. He knew how much he had been influenced by the example set for him by his boyhood hero, Texas Ranger Captain John R. Hughes, the "Border Boss," at El Paso at the turn of the century.

In Gonzaullas' opinion, there were four principal, interrelated causes for habitual criminality. "First," he said, "there are narcotics, which are responsible for three quarters of the total number of law violators." Then he listed liquor, gambling and association with persons of low repute. From his experiences and observations in investigative work, he pointed out that "if boys from good families associate with questionable characters, who are often much older, the boys can be led into wild parties, to drink, to gamble, to use narcotics. We see men gamble, and then steal to be able to continue that vice. We see men and women hooked on narcotics. They rob, steal, even murder, to get money to satisfy their craving for dope. The women 'sell their bodies' as prostitutes. Eventually, such men and women land in the penitentiaries, almost always lost to society as productive citizens. Because of indifference, we all pay a terrible price in those wasted lives and in the financial cost of law enforcement and incarceration."

Gonzaullas asserted that, in order to control and to prevent crime, "it is vital that good people not shirk their duty. When a jury falls down on the job, we are all out of luck!" Another point he frequently stressed was the "lack of active cooperation on the part of citizens with officers of the law. Coupled with this," he said, "is prejudice against officers. Just because your candidate did not win an elective office is no reason for you to fail to give your full support to the man who did win. Yet, we see that attitude far too often. No officer can make good without the full cooperation of citizens. There is too much 'squawking' about officers not doing their duty. If everyone would boost the officers and cooperate with them in every way possible, instead of criticizing, it would help a lot." Although he expressed those views a half-century ago, their basic soundness is as applicable to the field of law enforcement today as it was then.

Those two stills hidden in the bluff of the Red River and "guarded" by the young boys had a combined daily whiskey production capacity of forty gallons. There was also a joint sewage system to dispose of the waste unobtrusively, as the bootleggers used every stratagem to avoid attracting the attention of officers. Taken in the seizure were seven hundred gallons of corn mash ready to run, a hundred gallons of "Choc" beer, twenty-five gallons of corn whiskey, plus a substantial quantity of such miscellaneous items as artificial coloring, corn chops, sugar, hops and yeast.

The team of Gonzaullas and McCormick made a 1:30 A.M. haul at Kemp City (whose name was changed some sixteen years later to Kamay) when they entered a house that had been marked as bootlegging headquarters. They had to lie in wait until that hour before making their move. Going to the house, they knocked and, in answer to a woman who was on the other side of the locked door, identified themselves as Rangers and ordered that the door be opened. In response, the woman said she and her female companion were not dressed, that they would put on clothes before complying with the order to open up. After sufficient time had passed for the women to fully dress themselves and the door still was not opened in line with their demand, the officers broke it down and entered. They discovered that the two women and a man were busily engaged in pouring out whiskey, an operation that Gonzaullas and McCormick brought to a halt.

A search of the house revealed a large quantity of liquor. It was in quart and pint bottles and hidden wherever they looked. The bottles were in storage cabinets, in "secret" compartments under the floorboards, in closets, in beds and in chests of drawers. In addition, the Rangers uncovered some still parts, including "worms," the spiral pipes or coils in which the vapor is condensed, also some copper sheets for use in manufacturing stills. There was no complete still outfit on those premises. Three automobiles were parked in the vacant lot that lay between that house and its near neighbor. One of the cars contained a hundred-pound sack of sugar. In the other two were quart and pint bottles of corn liquor.

Carrying the investigation still further, the house next door was checked. There the Rangers found a complete still in operating condition. Of fifty-gallon capacity, it proved to be the source of the whiskey that was secreted in the first house they entered. And, there was a tank fabricated from copper sheets like those in the first house.

After almost eleven months service in the oil fields of North Texas, Rangers Gonzaullas and McCormick had just about worked themselves out of a job there. During that time, they had derived satisfaction from the knowledge that crime in the region had been drastically reduced to the point that local officers could again handle it without help from the state. The most unpleasant part of their duties as Rangers had been several investigations and arrests, in the multi-county district, of police officers and sheriff's deputies on such charges as accepting bribes to protect illegal establishments or for engaging in illegal activities themselves. At the end of August 1921, McCormick and Gonzaullas were ordered by Captain R. W. Aldrich in Austin to proceed at once to Company "B" headquarters and there receive assignment to duty elsewhere in Texas.

In its comments on the removal of the Rangers, the *Wichita Falls Daily Times* reflected the friendly attitude and respect the citizens of that area had for the men. The paper said,

> Last fall, when this county seemed to be in the grip of a crime wave, Captain Aldrich with four Texas Rangers suddenly appeared at the courthouse. Several more state officers arrived shortly afterward. Sergeant McCormick and Ranger Gonzaullas were two of the company.
>
> Although it required several months time to entirely control the situation in the county, a change was noted imme-

diately after the state officers began their work. The good that was accomplished was commented upon by grand juries and public officials.

All of the company of Rangers were later transferred out of the county to other points in the state and only the two men were permitted to remain.

Both McCormick and Gonzaullas have proven themselves to be efficient, daring and non-fearing officers, and although they made arrests throughout the county and made it a place uncomfortable for all law violators, they will leave for other points with the good will of nearly every resident of Wichita County following them.

III

Even the Cows Were Drunk

"Lone Wolf" Gonzaullas was reassigned to the border region along the Rio Grande, an area he knew like the palm of his hand. He was fluent in the two languages spoken, and he fully understood the nature of the people there. Gonzaullas worked out of Del Rio with Company "C."

There was a swarm of illegal traffic in both directions across the river. A prime responsibility of the Ranger force was to help control the smuggling of liquor and narcotics from Mexico into Texas. The Volstead Act created an atmosphere in which much money could be made by those who were willing to take their chances in flouting the law. Because of the ready availability of good quality liquor in Mexico, and the comparative ease with which it could be obtained in Southern and Southwestern Texas, thanks to their proximity to the border, whiskey making was not the massive problem that existed in the northern portion of the state. It was just easier and simpler to smuggle liquor than it was to manufacture it.

There were two other important responsibilities of the Ranger force on the river. One was to get a control on the practice of lawless elements in Mexico coming across the fordable stream almost at will and raiding isolated ranches, stealing cattle, then racing back with their loot before they could be apprehended. The other key duty was a reverse action. It was to halt the smuggling into Texas from Mexico of fever tick infested cattle. Serious inroads had been made into the cattle population in some parts of the state by death from the fever caused by organisms injected into the bloodstream of cattle by tick bites. Dipping of cattle was resorted to as the only means of ridding the animals of the insects. However, they could be reinfected if ticks were brought into a clean area by the movement of infested cattle.

Along with those duties, there were the normal day-to-day peacekeeping activities. Occasionally, there were local incidents of such bizarre nature as to break any monotony. Soon after Gonzaullas settled down in Del Rio, he became involved in one of those. Captain Frank Hamer was in charge of the company there at that time. He later achieved lasting fame by helping to trap the notorious outlaws Clyde Barrow and Bonnie Parker near Gibsland, Louisiana, and taking part in the shoot-out that resulted in their deaths. In September, Gonzaullas accompanied Hamer, Sergeant John A. Gillon and E. B. McClure to Pinto Switch on the Galveston, Harrisburg and San Antonio railroad (now known as Southern Pacific), twenty-three miles east of Del Rio just across the Val Verde-Kinney County line. Their trip was in response to a report about an extra-gang foreman who was disturbing the peace and making threats of bodily harm to other persons.

In violation of railroad policy prohibiting the use of intoxicants, the foreman had obtained a supply of tequila. He began a drinking bout on Saturday morning, September 17, 1921. By afternoon, he was "wild with drink." That extra-gang foreman obviously had a thing against the work crew cooks and was heartily displeased with their products. He stumbled into the kitchen car where the cooks were preparing the evening meal and, with a string of blue oaths, pitched out onto the railroad right-of-way all of the food he could get his hands on. Then to ensure that they would not be able to duplicate their work, he pulled out a pistol and proceeded to shoot holes in the frying pans and all the other utensils in sight. Following that, he slugged two of the Mexican workmen over the head with the gun and fired random shots. Luckily, he hit no one. One reason for that was the fact that crew members took to their heels and hid in the scrub brush that grew in the pasture just over the barbed wire fence. Satisfied, he staggered out of sight. The crew remained in the brush until a westbound freight stopped at Pinto Switch to drop off two cars loaded with construction material. While the train was stopped, sixteen of the Mexicans climbed aboard the caboose and rode into Del Rio, leaving their possessions in the bunk cars.

Gonzaullas on Texas-Mexico border duty near El Paso soon after his enlistment on October 1, 1920. (Courtesy Texas Ranger Hall of Fame and Museum.)

A night's rest permitted most of the effects of the fiery liquor to wear off; however, on Sunday morning the foreman again hit the bottle and in a short time was in as fierce a drunken rage as he had been the previous afternoon. He vowed to shoot a number of those who remained with the work train, one of them being the wife of the assistant foreman. She had endeavored to calm him, an act he violently resented, so he threatened to kill her as he repeatedly poked the pistol barrel into her abdomen. Neither she nor others whom he menaced knew whether he would pull the trigger. It was a nerve-wracking experience for all. A westbound train was flagged on Sunday and an urgent request sent to Del Rio for help. The uncommunicative Mexican refugees of the previous day had not reported the incident to authorities. As soon as word of the disturbance reached the sheriff's office, the men climbed into a touring car and headed for Pinto Switch over the rocky, bumpy road. The drunken extra-gang foreman was subdued by those arresting him and brought to Del Rio to sober up and face charges. That was the end of his railroad career.

A Dallas traveling auditor who had been working n Del Rio for two and one-half months decided to take a souvenir back with him. So, he purchased a bottle of the ever available tequila in order to, as he expressed it, "show the boys in Dallas one of the principal products of the border." He had made the tactical mistake of boasting that he had bought it over the counter in a Del Rio cafe, a bit of news that reached the attentive ear of Ranger Gonzaullas. The latter was waiting for the auditor at the railroad station when he arrived to board the eastbound passenger train en route home. Caught with the goods in his possession, he was taken before the magistrate, charged and released on bond, but not in time to leave town on that train. The Dallasite departed Del Rio one day late, minus his souvenir. His loose tongue had a spin-off. The cafe operator who sold the illegal tequila was himself arrested and required to post bond, pending arraignment by the federal grand jury.

Although he thoroughly enjoyed his Ranger duties along *El Rio Bravo del Norte*, as the Mexicans refer to the Rio Grande, Gonzaullas' services were needed elsewhere. He had established a widely appreciated reputation upstate for his rare ability to ferret out violators of the Volstead Act. The federal government called him, so he took leave from the Rangers and went into service as a prohibition agent under Director David H. Morris. He was one of four Texans added to the force at that time. The others were W. H.

Myers of Galveston, G. M. Floyd of Madisonville and Fred Wilson of Houston.

Morris optimistically reported at that time that "the boundary situation in Texas has promise of early solution." He recommended federal legislation governing smuggling across the Mexican border which would put rum running on the same basis as merchandise smuggling. The latter was subject to a two-year prison sentence. Morris also touched on the problem of liquor reaching the United States from Canada via Mexico. "Whiskey is shipped from Canada to Mexico as medicine," he said, "and is smuggled into this country for bootlegging purposes. Rum runners travel in high powered cars with women companions, make perhaps several trips before being caught, and then go free by paying maximum fines. This will be stopped by amending the Federal smuggling laws," he said.

As a federal prohibition agent, Gonzaullas entered into that field of service with the same degree of zest that had marked his tenure as a Ranger. Placed in charge of a "flying squadron" of L-men (Liquor-men), he became the scourge of Texas bootleggers, whether importers, manufacturers, wholesalers or retailers. One of the first places to feel the squad's sting was Galveston. Throughout the prohibition period, that city was a funnel through which a great volume of intoxicants flowed into the state from overseas. Stopping the traffic at sea was outside the jurisdiction of the "Lone Wolf" and his men, but they did their part in dealing misery to those who made whiskey and related liquids available to the thirsting public. Galveston was a hotbed of defiance, so it was a prime target for the agents.

Gonzaullas was a careful man. He made sure there were sufficient facts in hand when raids were conducted, so he could file charges that would stick. An intensive undercover investigation over several weeks had resulted in incontrovertible proof of guilt, whereupon he was ready to act. The flying squadron arrived in the island city along with the new year of 1922. Seven resorts and so-called soft drink stands were visited in the first raid, one result being confiscation of a large amount of liquor. Eleven men and three women were arrested and charged with violation of the Volstead Act. They spent the remainder of that night in the county jail. All those charged waived examining trials when they were haled before United States Commissioner Charles G. Dibrel, and made bond. When the L-men swooped down on the first resort, patrons there were detained for a short time so word of the presence of the agents would be concealed from their next intended stop.

Skipping over the state, the L-men went quickly to Austin where evidence had been secured linking eight deaths to the sale of denatured alcohol mixed with soda water and grape juice. Gonzaullas and Agent Bassett Miles stood in the place for nearly a quarter of an hour and watched liquor sales being made before they arrested the two Negro operators. It was an interesting case in that two Austin police officers, Chief Sam D. Griffin and Sergeant R. E. Nitschke, had obtained full evidence concerning what was going on. Despite diligent efforts, they had failed to persuade previous prohibition agents to enter the case and make arrests, it being the agents' contention that such sales were not in violation of the Eighteenth Amendment for the reason that denatured alcohol was not considered to be an intoxicant.

Gonzaullas did not subscribe to that view and, along with the Austin police, concluded that it was a direct violation. Confirmation of that opinion was received from Washington. In addition, it was shown that not only were such sales prohibited by that amendment but also that they were considered to be criminal offenses under federal statutes already on the books when prohibition took effect on January 16, 1920.

Most of the Austin victims had been Negroes, though a few Mexicans also died from consuming too much of the poisonous liquid, which is slow in manifesting its deleterious effects on the human body. Chief Griffin pointed out that by selling such a potentially lethal concoction to an unwary person, the seller was just as much a murderer as if he had used a pistol and taken the other man's life. Denatured alcohol can still be used as fuel or for other industrial purposes but, by the addition of unwholesome substances, is rendered unfit for human consumption and can be lethal if taken in large quantity over a period of time. In a public statement, Griffin said, "People who patronize present day bootleggers should take warning, for they take their lives in their own hands when they drink any of the preparations which are being sold promiscuously at present. The police department will do all in its power to aid the prohibition officers in their efforts to stamp out this murderous practice." But, so insatiable was the general public's craving for alcohol that his warning fell on deaf ears in the capital city. It was received with a similar degree of indifference elsewhere in Texas, for that matter.

It was to be argued by many that, instead of the Eighteenth (prohibition) Amendment having a wholesome effect on the habits of the American people, just the opposite was true. Without majority public support, enforcement became increasingly difficult. Public resentment began to flare and the law came to be treated with disdain. Before prohibition, women would avoid even walking in front of a saloon. They would use the other side of the street, though it meant going out of their way. They were never to be seen inside a saloon. That was considered unthinkable. The 1920s changed all that. It became fashionable to flout the law. Women joined men in going to "speakeasies." While they were about that, they became sufficiently daring to smoke in such places, though not yet in "polite society." Those defiant attitudes were in their barely perceptible beginning stages of development when the "Lone Wolf" signed up as a prohibition agent.

In the meantime, men of the flying squadron were busy. From Austin, they made a pop call at Beaumont and picked up five operating stills on a farm near the city. The farmer declared to Gonzaullas that he was astonished to learn of their presence! Next, the city of Port Arthur was the scene of sixteen fast raids on Procter and Houston Street establishments, as well as one on Eighth Street. But, Galveston was not to be neglected. Ten additional raids on resorts there scooped up a great quantity of assorted liquor, together with sixteen men who faced charges of possession and sale of intoxicants. Another flying visit gave many Galvestonians a further understanding of what the Eighteenth Amendment was all about. Hundreds of quarts of whiskey were confiscated and arrests made. As had happened in previous visits by the "sponge squad," patrons of the establishments were detained to keep the alarm from spreading. At one spot, they were still there into the early hours of the morning, making the best of their situation by eating and dancing. Telephones were put out of order by the L-men and parking lots blocked to prevent cars from leaving.

The worst news for Galvestonians was the official word from Austin that the island would be dry for the upcoming 1922 bathing girl revue. A statement was made by Louis B. Manss, head of federal prohibition agents in Texas, at the conclusion of the latest raids in Galveston, that "officials of Texas are tired of seeing Galveston the laughing stock of the whole country in regard to enforcement of the prohibition law and it is the intention of this department to dry up the town and keep it that way." Nevertheless, saying and doing were two different matters. Crime syndicates had become financially involved in liquor traffic. There was big money to be made. The L-men worked valiantly to keep the bootleggers hopping, closing one resort after another. But, additional resorts sprang up in the style of the mythical nine-headed Hydra battled by Hercules. When he cut off each of the Hydra's heads, two more appeared in its place. There was nothing mythical about Galveston's speakeasies, but they proliferated like Hydra heads. A concentrated drumfire of raids and arrests finally began to have noticeable effect. Although the place was not shut down as Manss' statement implied would be the case, liquor soared in price and was harder to obtain while "Lone Wolf" Gonzaullas remained in prohibition service.

From Galveston, the next hop was to Mexia. "Well, I have seen horses, mules, hogs and men drunk," the "Lone Wolf" commented, "but this is the first time in all my life that I have seen cows drunk!" He was alluding to an incident in Limestone County where he and his flying squadron led a series of fast raids, working hand in glove with Sheriff W. S. Loper. The areas hit were principally in and around the oil field boom town of Mexia and the county seat, Groesbeck.

The incursion met with signal success. It was kicked off by the officers' movement into wooded and brushy country near Rocky Point. Gonzaullas' usual advance surveillance had disclosed the presence and activity of moonshiners there, but the results obtained exceeded expectations. Still number one was found one-half mile back in the woods. From that point, the agents followed a well-worn path that led them consecutively to four additional stills, all situated a half-mile apart. They were so carefully hidden in the brush that men in reconnaissance planes could not spot them.

It was at the third still that Gonzaullas and his men came across the drunken cows. Although the barrels of corn mash had been covered with wire mesh to keep animals out, the determined cows had forced the protective netting aside with their muzzles and then had freely eaten. One had almost completely passed out and was lying on the ground feebly kicking and unable to rise. The other was near that state but still on her feet, though she was having difficulty untangling her legs. She was staggering drunk and bellowing piteously. Such heavy indulgence could be expected to result in the death of animals, whether bovine, equine or porcine.

The location and layout of the five stills indicated to Gonzaullas that the bootleggers had a broad trade territory. All still parts were standard and interchangeable. When the L-men and sheriff arrived, two of the stills were in full operation; one was cooling, and from its coil fresh-run corn whiskey was still slowly dripping. The remaining two outfits were in "go" condition. When sufficient evidence was set aside, the stills were completely destroyed by the wielding of heavy axes, liquor poured out, the mash and chops strewn over a wide area so they could not be retrieved.

At one Limestone County farmhouse, they never could discover the still they reasoned must be there somewhere, but took possession of a large quantity of corn mash, which was ready to be used. Such a situation was annoying to them. Search at the second farmhouse turned up still parts and, after much manual labor with spades, a valuable cache of corn whiskey. It was buried, well camouflaged and found only through extensive digging.

Next they went to a third farmhouse. The "Lone Wolf" declared that if the operator of the secreted still there had used the same degree of energy and cleverness in a legitimate enterprise, he would surely have become comfortably rich and within the law. At the farm near Kickapoo, an intensive, detailed search was made, at first without result. The fact that evidence indicated liquor was being made on the place kept the squad following every possible clue. At length, their attention was focused on the smokehouse. It was innocent enough in outward appearance. A check inside revealed nothing out of the ordinary, at first. However, in one corner a feed trough was noted. One doesn't expect to find feed troughs in smokehouses, so it was moved. Underneath there was nothing but soil. Yet the presence of that feed trough was suspicious in itself. Why was it there? It is on just such a bit of carelessness that most criminals trip. A spade was brought and shoved into the dirt. It struck something hard. When the soil was removed, there came into view a wooden trapdoor and, upon its being lifted, a ladder was seen leading down into stygian darkness. A lantern was obtained and, with the men squatting around the hole, lowered into the pit. The prize came into view in a cellar that was approximately twenty feet square.

It was in that underground room that the whiskey-making operation was conducted in a fine quality still. The smoke from the fire was carried out of the cellar through a conduit that was vertical at first, then turned near horizontal but ran at a rising angle until it surfaced right beside a large black pot in the yard. It was the type of black cast-iron pot that was utilized in that era for boiling clothes, also for making hominy. The pot, which stood on short legs, was heated by a wood fire burning under and around it. That was a perfect cover for the smoke from the still fire, as it would be wafted to the heavens along with that from the constantly burning pot fire. The operation was carried on by a man and his young son.

The flying squadron ended that particular visit to Limestone County by going into Mexia, raiding several liquor-selling places and making arrests. Altogether, the squadron took possession of thirty-eight hundred gallons of mash, eight complete stills, two Studebaker wagons (one of which was loaded with sugar and the other with corn chops), an enormous quantity of whiskey and various manufacturing accessories. At the time, the "Lone Wolf" remarked that enough copper tubing was collected to make an arch completely over the Littlefield Building, then Austin's tallest skyscraper.

IV

Indicted for Murder

After the Limestone County raids, the "Lone Wolf" turned up in San Antonio bent on cleaning out the liquor handlers. He meted out trouble to them, as well as to narcotics pushers. One quart bottle of whiskey confiscated in that city was the single clue that led to the uncovering of a liquor conspiracy involving more than a dozen men who were engaged in smuggling through New Orleans and into Southern, Central and Northern Texas. Federal L-men and Texas Rangers worked together on the case compiling evidence.

Following the seizure of the steamship *Olga* and her cargo at Port Lavaca, Texas, a millionaire rancher in Victoria County was arrested and arraigned before the United States commissioner on charges of violating federal tariff and prohibition acts. Charges were also filed by the state for violation of Texas' own prohibition law. Two other Victoria County residents were arrested and charged. Additional arrests followed over the state. The Associated Press, reporting from San Antonio in connection with the rum running, said, ". . . an entire truckload of goods was captured by the State Rangers at the same place [the residence in that city where the telltale quart was found]. The load, more than 300 bottles of bonded liquor, was disguised under camping equipment. Next came the seizure of 235 quarts of bonded goods at another place. The liquor was in a box labeled 'shoe polish.' "

Subsequent investigation proved that the operation was tied in with rum running activities through Savannah, Mobile, New Orleans and Galveston. The case soon launched the "Lone Wolf" on extensive undercover work aimed at developing facts on the vast contraband movement from the Bahama Islands to the United States.

In his career as a prohibition agent, Gonzaullas noted that a favorite practice of bootleggers was the hiding of stills in cellars, to which entrance was gained by a trapdoor. It was about as ineffective a method of concealment as is secreting an entrance key under the door mat, or putting a wallet beneath a mattress. In Calaveras, then far beyond the outskirts of San Antonio, he and flying squadron agent William M. Thompson followed a service car filled with merrymakers bent on celebrating San Jacinto Day. The car pulled in front of a house, and the driver went inside. He came out a few minutes later with a supply of whiskey, whereupon Gonzaullas and Thompson moved in. Under the dirt floor of the barn they found the old familiar earth-covered trapdoor that led to a cellar. Down there they came across what they termed the best quality corn whiskey they had ever seen, and they had confiscated much very good liquor, as well as "rotgut." In addition, there were ten gallons of grape wine and some corn mash, hardly a major haul, but it resulted in another bootlegger being put out of business, at least for a while.

Then, it was back to Beaumont for an intensive series of raids, during which the "Lone Wolf" was at the head of one of the largest forces of dry raiders that had ever been assembled in the South or Southwest. The visit to that Southeastern Texas city led to an incident that eventually was to cause a change in Gonzaullas' activities. In performance of their assigned duties, he and companion agent W. A. Nitzer were at the entrance of a liquor-selling recreation hall when they were challenged by a local official. It was on a Saturday night late in July 1922. In the ensuing altercation, during which he threatened Nitzer with bodily harm, the official started to draw a pistol and, according to eyewitnesses, had it halfway out when he was shot by Gonzaullas and killed on the spot. A noisy local commotion erupted, with an element of the populace making threats to lynch the two L-men.

Gonzaullas was arrested, taken before a justice of the peace, charged, refused bail and placed in the Jefferson County jail pending a grand jury probe. With something of a record for speed, the jury returned an indictment of murder against Gonzaullas and, to the amazement of many, also indicted Nitzer. He, too, was placed in jail. As might have been expected, federal authorities rose to their defense. State Prohibition Director David H. Morris, Legal Advisor C. A. Warnken, Federal Agents W. C. Guinn and M. A. Moore, two federal attorneys and United States Marshal Phil Baer came to their assistance. In addition, Gonzaullas' close personal friend and attorney, Fletcher Jones, arrived. It was pointed out that a federal officer charged with an offense while discharging his duty may not be tried before a state court or held in jail by state officers. Jurisdiction was transferred to the court of Federal District Judge William Lee Estes, who released the men on bond of a thousand dollars each. That was Gonzaullas' second term in jail in as many years.

Upon release and pending trial, Gonzaullas and Nitzer went back into the fulfillment of their assigned duties as prohibition agents, heading for Dallas. In that city, residents on Alton Street were roused from sleep by the sound of glass being broken, followed by the strong odor of corn liquor. A cache of 135 half-gallon jars of corn whiskey had been confiscated and was being destroyed. With other Dallas raids under their belts, they moved on to new fields elsewhere in Texas, but they were back in two weeks to make a rich haul of red and of white corn whiskey, as well as rye and Scotch whiskey. The containers were drained into a gutter as passersby viewed the proceedings with pleasure or anguish, depending on their personal attitude toward strong drink.

Sweeping around the state, prohibition agents showed up at Pioneer in southwestern Eastland County, where much evidence for raids and arrests there had been gathered by Edith Zutler, a woman secret operative in federal service. Participating in the raids were thirteen L-men "with small arms and with short rifles, spurs and boots and 21 Federal search warrants." The reward for the agents' work was huge, numbering thousands of gallons of whiskey, gin, beer, brandy and various other popular liquors. The "Lone Wolf" had posed as a tool dresser when doing advance investigative work. He wore large dark glasses and greasy, dirty clothes, so he passed unnoticed while he garnered additional evidence. He and Miss Zutler had been in Pioneer for about ten days.

The bootlegging situation in the Pioneer oil field area had been the subject of numerous complaints, especially from nearby Abilene, whose citizens have long been known for their "dry" sympathies. The trigger for the raids had been a complaint voiced by the district judge. It had been publicized in the *Dallas Morning News*. It pointed to the unsavory conditions in the oil fields of his district with the sharp comment that "the governor knows of it but has done nothing." His intentions were the best, but the judge actually performed something of a disservice to the cause of liquor control there. The publicity he received, combined with a charge to the Eastland County grand jury the first week in September, gave fair warning of what might be expected to come. As a result, a number of the liquor sellers were wise enough to close shop until the storm could blow over. They thereby escaped arrest and confiscation.

The *Pioneer Oil Herald*, whose office was on the ground floor of the Wright Hotel, commented that the building was sandwiched between two great piles of broken bottles. The editor observed that as liquor was confiscated, it was brought in containers to the rear and sides of the hotel where the bottles were smashed, leaving "an awful stench or smell."

The raid was a complete surprise to the civil authorities of Pioneer and of Eastland County, as well as the deputy district prohibition agent at Abilene.

Gonzaullas later stated that it was difficult for anyone to conceive the extent of vice in the Pioneer community. In his investigation, he found that extortion schemes were widespread and far more lucrative than outright holdups.

Throughout Texas it was an unending, repetitious story . . . 5,000 gallons of mash seized here . . . 150 gallons of whiskey confiscated there . . . stills destroyed . . . arrests and more arrests. But, the "Lone Wolf" loved the chase and was especially delighted when big-time operators were caught. One such event occurred in Dallas on December 21, 1922, just in time to ruin the Christmas holidays for a great many whiskey drinkers. He and two other L-men were at a garage on Wood Street just ready to go in and search the place when a new Cadillac drove up. The man they sought was at the wheel. Checking the car, they found the back floor and seat loaded with liquor.

In the garage itself, while looking for more liquor they felt sure was somewhere in the place, they noticed that a window frame appeared to be loose. Seized and pulled, the frame board readily gave way. Beneath it was a rope tied to a sash weight. Nothing strange about that, except that the rope was under no tension. They yanked on it and right before their eyes a secret panel opened, revealing a great stock of choice liquors which it was later proved were smuggled into the state by rum runners operating through Galveston. "It was a regular 'open Sesame,' " the "Lone Wolf" said with a grin. "The stock consisted of such items as Gordon gin of 'avant la guerre' vintage, old-time Johnny Walker in non-refillable bottles, and other quality liquors." A truck was brought and the goods loaded aboard to be taken to the Federal Building, where they were locked in a vault.

The "Lone Wolf" had become so popular that he was even brought into newspaper marital advice columns. In the "Letters to Mrs. Wynne" of the old *Dallas Dispatch*, his helpful and understanding nature was given a boost. One such letter read,

> Dear Mrs. Wynne: I have been married nine years and have three children, all under eight years. My husband is kind and loving, except when drinking. Then he scolds, fusses and even kicks his little children. I know who is giving him whiskey and home-made wine. I want to report it but do not know how to go about it. How should I do so, and would I have to give my name? If my husband were caught there, would he be arrested? Would I do the right thing to report it?
>
> "DISGUSTED."

Mrs. Wynne's reply was somewhat in the give-it-to-them-straight style of the famous Dorothy Dix in her popular column of advice to the lovelorn:

> A man who will abuse his babies, drunk or sober, is not a man to be protected.
> Go immediately to M. T. Gonzaullas (Lone Wolf), U.S. District Attorney's office, second floor of the postoffice. You will give your name, but the information will be regarded as confidential and will not be divulged. Should your husband be present when the raid occurs, he will be placed under arrest, but your condition will be taken into account. You can trust the Federal authorities to protect your home and innocent children.

At that time, the L-men were hitting Dallas and all of Northern Texas hard. The attacks on places operating illegally were as steady as machine gun fire, reminiscent of the great offensives mounted in the recently fought War to End All Wars. Taken in one raid on Grand Avenue was a "blue book" listing customers of the place, addresses, telephone numbers, liquor preferences and quantities purchased. It was an eye-opening enumeration. Included were names of some of Dallas' leading citizens, as well as prominent individuals in Sherman, Denison and other nearby smaller cities, even some as far distant as Shreveport and New Orleans. Gonzaullas' wry comment was, "Some of the names in the book would stagger the staunchest prohibitionists!" Newspaper headlines announcing the seizure of that book resulted in great anxiety for many who had reason to believe their names were recorded in it.

A sad duty that Gonzaullas had to perform at that time was the arrest of a former prohibition agent from Titus County on a charge of possession of illegal whiskey. He had become involved with a Dallas man in the sale of liquor and was caught as he left a farm carrying a gunnysack containing bottles of whiskey. On the other hand, some humor was still to be derived from events. There was the case of the submarine whiskey cache operated by a woman and her two daughters. Rather dowdy in appearance, she wore Mother Hubbard type dresses. Like an automaton, she constantly used the back of her hands to shove out of her face wisps of long hair that would not stay in place. By prearrangement, the mother would meet her customers under Dallas' Commerce Street bridge after dark. Mentally keen, she had a knack for sizing up men. It seldom failed her. When they measured up to her standards, she would take them with her onto the Trinity River in a rowboat, a silent, solemn figure handling the oars like Charon, the ferryman on the River Styx. Hers was a hard life, but she concluded that it beat performing menial tasks to keep body and soul together. Upon reaching a certain spot, she would reach down and, with a grappling hook, pull up a sack of whiskey bottles, make a sale, tie up the sack and lower it, then row back to the river bank. Gonzaullas tried to snare her in the act by posing as a customer, but whenever he was in the boat the canny old woman was never able to locate the sack on the muddy bottom of the stream. He surmised that she recognized him, so it was left to an L-man who was a newcomer to Dallas to catch her red-handed.

Encounters with women were increasing for the "Lone Wolf." These were not to his liking but had become a necessary part of enforcement work. A recurring minor problem for L-men in Dallas, and one that caused some public merriment in the city, was an aged woman who had been arrested eight times for dealing in whiskey. Profits were so great that she doggedly returned to bootlegging each time. Gonzaullas referred to her as a "bootleggeress."

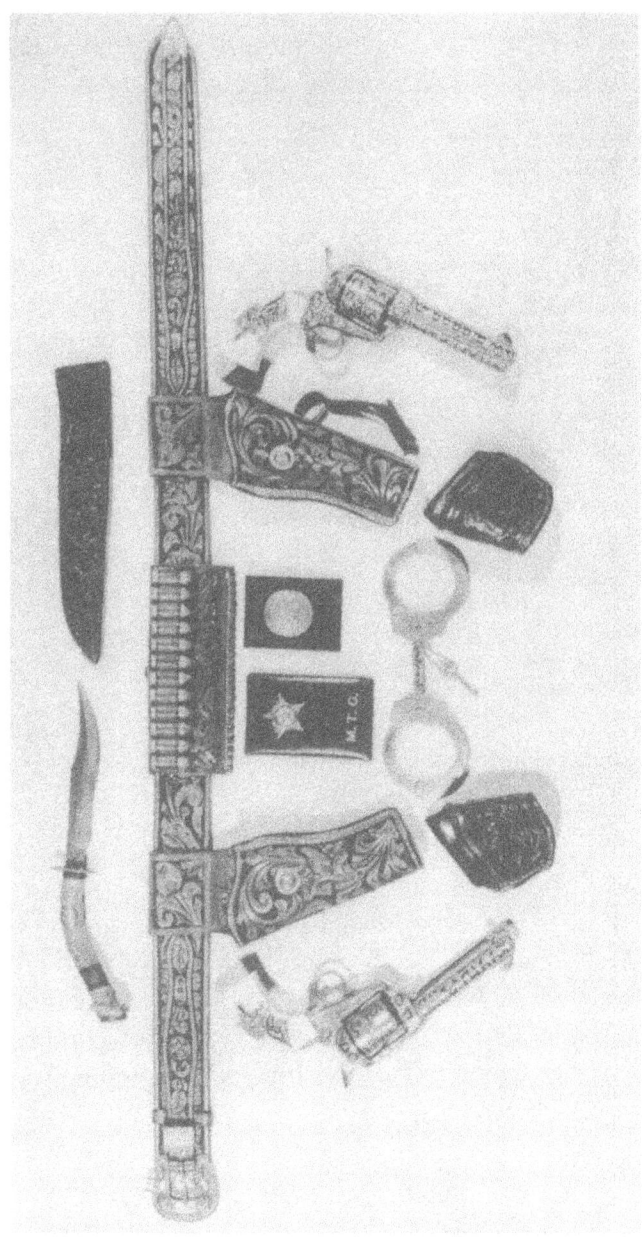

Some of "Lone Wolf" Gonzaullas' personal collection of guns. On both the automatics and revolvers, which were embellished with elaborate gold engraving, the trigger guards were cut away to provide ready access. The guns that he used regularly in his field work were modified in this way, but other pistols were not. (Courtesy Texas Ranger Hall of Fame and Museum.)

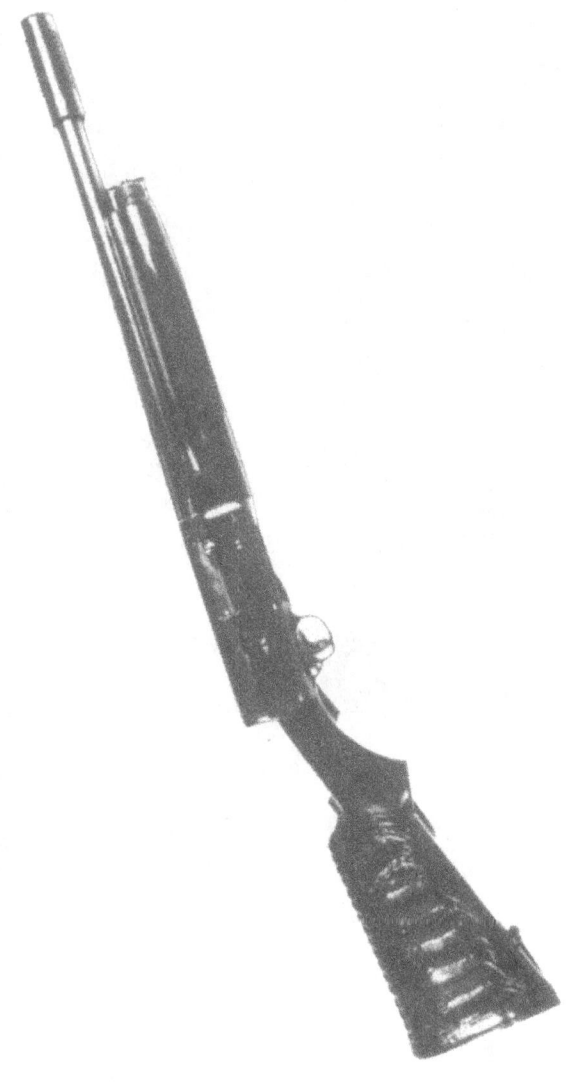

Gonzaullas' field shotgun with silencer sported a hand-tooled leather cover for the stock. (Courtesy Texas Department of Public Safety.)

Six women joined five men in what almost turned out to be a successful effort to permanently rid themselves of their nemesis. The "Lone Wolf," prohibition agent George Webb and H. G. Caldwell, a deputy sheriff, raided a house on Dallas' Gould Street and ran into a veritable hornets' nest of opposition. When the officers went into the house, one of the women started breaking bottles of whiskey to keep them from falling in their hands. That was a standard practice in the trade. Gonzaullas threw his arms around her to stop it. When one of the men came at him with a butcher knife, the "Lone Wolf" was obliged to release the woman and draw his pistol to force his attacker to drop the knife. Just then, he was seized from behind with a headlock and general pandemonium broke loose.

Webb and Caldwell were elsewhere in the house but came running to Gonzaullas' assistance, finding him on the floor in the midst of a seething heap of humanity. During the commotion, Webb was "scratched, pinched, shoved, pushed and much abused," Caldwell's nose was the direct target of a fist and the bruised Gonzaullas was fighting to extricate himself from the clutches of the screaming women and cursing men. Although they were not conducting themselves as ladies, inasmuch as they were also throwing dishes, bottles, lamps and anything else they could get their hands on, the presence of the women kept the officers from using their guns, as they would otherwise have done. The noise from the battle was so great that it attracted the attention of neighbors, who crowded into the street in front of the house to await the outcome and witness the arrival of ambulances and police cars.

Control of the situation was gained by the officers when one of the women fainted in the excitement and the other women, together with two of the men, turned their attention to her in an effort to revive her. The upshot was that three of the men ended up in the hospital and charges were filed against all. The incident was hardly worth the effort, since only two bottles of whiskey were saved from destruction, but these provided sufficient evidence to back up the charges.

And, then there were the women in Oak Cliff.

In rapid succession, three additional raids uncovered more books containing lists of booze customers, adding to the fears of those involved that there might be public disclosure of the names on the lists, with resultant acute embarrassment. Book number four came to light during a visit by the "Lone Wolf" and fellow prohibition agent James Mason to a house in Oak Cliff. There they found

350 gallons of whiskey in quart bottles, more than 800 gallons of mash, four stills and various moonshine manufacturing accessories. Gonzaullas pronounced the mammoth still setup in the attractive bungalow one of the best-equipped whiskey-making devices ever seized in Texas.

The "Lone Wolf" had learned that a man was purchasing 200 pounds of corn chops every night at a grocery store in Cedar Springs. Regular purchases of that size could mean only one thing, so an investigation was in order. He and Mason followed a load of chops to the residence, then watched through the window as the occupants of the house busied themselves around the operating stills. While they were there that first night, an automobile stopped in front of the house; the driver went inside and bought several quarts of whiskey which were placed in a cardboard box. The box was put into the car and the purchaser drove away. For three additional days and nights, watch was kept on the house, as well as the arrival and departure of patrons. It was obvious that this was a profitable operation. The agents observed the house owner making other purchases of such items as sugar and dried fruit. When they were ready to move in, Gonzaullas obtained a search warrant from U.S. Commissioner R. V. Davidson, Jr. Accompanied by two newspaper reporters, he and Mason walked into the house at 10:30 A.M. Two women were there at the time, the man being absent.

They were cordially greeted by the blond, plump young wife, who sensed lucrative business to be transacted. What transpired was not the kind of business she anticipated. Seated in a rocking chair was an old woman who was assiduously knitting. She was tall and thin, her graying hair parted in the middle and skinned back into a small, tight knot on the nape of her neck. Her black dress with ample skirt had a narrow, white collar and white cuffs on the long sleeves. The dress was so old and so frequently washed it had developed a hint of a greenish-black hue. The woman's long, bony fingers deftly handled the needles. During the entire sequence of events that followed, she never acknowledged the presence of the visitors or their activities by raising her eyes or dropping a stitch.

After stepping through the front door, the "Lone Wolf" introduced himself with the terse statement, "I'm Gonzaullas."

"For Gawd's sake," the young woman exclaimed.

"Nice little place you have here," Gonzaullas commented amiably, then noted that she kept glancing toward the bed. Checking the reason for her concern, Gonzaullas found a soundly sleeping two-week-old boy. "Sh-sh," he warned others in the party.

From that time on, all walking in the house was done on tiptoes to avoid waking the infant. The old woman, lips set firmly in a straight line, clicked away with her knitting needles as if she were alone in the dwelling.

As a part of the raid, the L-men not only obtained possession of the blue book but also broke fourteen hundred quart bottles of whiskey against a large stone in the back yard, filling the neighborhood with the odor of fresh-run moonshine. Gentleman that he was, the "Lone Wolf" did not arrest the young or the old woman. The latter turned out to be the mother-in-law of the young blond. He would not take the women and baby to the Federal Building, but waited until the main quarry, the husband, returned. Much of the illegal whiskey that was being manufactured in that era was of poor quality. Gonzaullas pronounced this Oak Cliff product as better than bonded liquor being smuggled into the United States. As it turned out, there was no need to use it, but the "Lone Wolf" had entered the house armed with his new so-called "hand machine gun," an automatic pistol equipped with a large magazine and capable of firing sixty-four rounds.

The fears of disclosure being felt by purchasers of illegal whiskey turned out to be well founded when, on May 9, 1923, the federal grand jury returned indictments of named Dallasites for conspiracy against the United States through habitual purchase and possession of illicit liquor. It was a landmark case, said to be the first of its kind in the nation. United States District Judge William H. Atwell had intimated that such liquor buyers would be prosecuted. The grand jury followed the judge's instructions in returning the indictments. Another step in the government's campaign against violation of the liquor law was the use of injunctions to close places of business where federal prohibition and antinarcotic laws were constantly flouted.

Gonzaullas had been advanced in rank to general prohibition agent. Though he was, to his great amusement, frequently referred to as a "hooch sleuth," he provided further justification for having earned the striking nickname of "Lone Wolf." Evidence of his recent shrewdly handled, and eminently successful, undercover work while acting entirely alone preceded by about one month Governor Pat Neff's fiery speech to members of the Houston Bar Association at a Rice Hotel banquet given in Neff's honor on April 27, 1923. The governor stated, "It is more dangerous for a Texas boy to be a prohibition enforcement officer in the State of Texas than it was to carry Old Glory on the battlefields of France!"

Continuing, the governor told the attorneys, "Half a dozen prohibition officers have been shot in cold blood in this state since I have been governor, and not one of the assassins has ever seen the door of the state penitentiary because those murderers had the protection of the officers of the counties in which the incidents took place." Strong language, that. Then he referred to the work of the Rangers, the number of bootleggers they had captured in pitched battles, and the amount of liquor seized. (Up to 1935, the Rangers were under the direct control of the governor's office.) "They brought the report to my office," Neff said. "I asked them if they had filed complaints, and they told me 'no.' They added that there was not an officer in the county where the battle took place who would prosecute those bootleggers." The governor further charged that assertions had been made in those localities that no bootlegger should be convicted. "In 50 miles from Houston," he continued, "a sheriff stood guard over a bootlegger's den because he had an interest in it. Not a hand was turned to bother it."

In another Texas county, undercover men from the governor's office "bought pure liquor over the bar in between 25 and 30 places in just one town. And," the governor told his listeners, "in one place where they bought liquor, the sheriff of that county, with his badge of office on his coat, sat at the bar while the drink was bought!" Governor Neff continued with the further condemnation that "there are sparsely settled counties along the border of Texas where bootleggers bring their liquor across the line to peddle it over the state, and not an officer in those counties moves to control them. A Texas Ranger who enters those counties does so at the peril of his life!"

Acknowledging the growing opposition to the prohibition law, the governor observed that "the quo warranto law is opposed by two classes of people, namely, bootleggers and those others who honestly believe it is a violation of the local self government theory." The slowly, almost imperceptibly, rising tide of public disenchantment with prohibition would continue to plague enforcement officers until its repeal.

One of the officers entering a defiant county at what the governor said was the peril of his life was "Lone Wolf" Gonzaullas, acting in his federal capacity. Disguised as an oil man, he had gone into Titus County alone to garner evidence on bootleggers and the reported operation of rum runners, who used fast automobiles to transport shipments of liquor to Northern and Central Texas in open revolt against the Eighteenth Amendment. Titus County had earned the unsavory reputation of being an extremely dangerous area for agents. Federal District Judge Atwell of Dallas had said that "hundreds of warning threats" had been made against prohibition agents in the past to stay out under penalty of death. The audacious courage of one man, working alone in that hotbed of bootleggers, completely deflated its image of toughness.

Posing as a lease hound, the "Lone Wolf" took advantage of the oil fever to cover every part of the county, meeting and becoming well acquainted with businessmen and farmers, enjoying friendly meals at their tables, scrutinizing farms in detail, all done with the avowed purpose of "spudding in a well." As usual, Gonzaullas did his work carefully and with painstaking thoroughness.

When he had completed the gathering of facts, the "Lone Wolf" obtained search warrants and, again acting entirely alone without a single man to back him up in a tight spot, arrested a total of 150 individuals and seized 66 whiskey-making stills. Although David Coffman, the assistant federal prosecutor in Dallas, had said that it was dangerous for a prohibition agent even to visit friends in Titus County, the reputation of "Lone Wolf" Gonzaullas so cowed his adversaries that he encountered no difficulty in carrying out his roundup of men and equipment. Bootleggers who had come to know and like him as an oil man were dumbstruck when he flashed his prohibition agent's badge in their faces. All capitulated without a shot being fired.

Beaumont moonshiners were reputedly just as unfriendly toward outsiders as were those in Titus County. It was common knowledge in the Southeastern Texas city that specific areas in the surrounding swamplands were controlled by bootleggers and definitely off limits. That state of affairs was the cause of annoyance on the part of sportsmen who had been accustomed to freely wending their way along favorite sloughs where there were particularly good fishing spots. Waterfowl hunters were faced with the same problems of access during the hunting season.

At intervals, previously available sections of the swamps were arbitrarily sealed off by whiskey manufacturers. Such steps were taken to protect their investment in stills by making it more difficult for prohibition agents to slip up on them. The only means of travel in the swamps was on the water of the bayous, as the marshy, reedy soil effectively prevented movement on foot.

Fishermen and hunters discovered such newly imposed restrictions the hard way but were sufficiently prudent to heed warnings that were given. A typical incident involved two men in a rowboat on the Neches River. They were moving downstream intending to head east off of the river and into a bayou they had fished for years. Upon reaching the mouth of the bayou, they turned the bow of their boat into it. They had progressed only a short distance when they were hailed by two rough-looking men standing on the low bank, each man cradling a rifle in his arms. "You fellers ain't got no business in here, so git!" they were told. The fishermen in the rowboat looked at the guns, noted the malevolent glare in the eyes of their challengers and, without ado, turned their skiff about. Fishing probably was not so good there, anyhow.

In the late spring of 1923, the "Lone Wolf" dropped from sight. He was not seen, nor were reports of his activities received from any county in Texas. It was apparent that he was up to something. Not even his close friends knew his whereabouts, a mystery that bothered hard-nosed reporters who prided themselves on usually being able to ferret out the facts in any newsworthy case. In this instance, they were stymied.

Just as abruptly as he had disappeared, "Lone Wolf" Gonzaullas showed up at the United States district attorney's office in Dallas at the end of July, professing astonishment at the interest in his absence and saying that he had only been "taking a little vacation in the Bahamas." Pretending reticence, he let drop the tidbit that while in the islands he had made a study of the liquor industry there. The economy of the Bahamas was booming, due largely to the tremendous amount of rum running headquartered at Nassau. It was public knowledge that from the Bahamas there was conducted a gigantic operation through which millions of dollars worth of liquor was smuggled into Atlantic and Gulf ports. In Gonzaullas' opinion, the federal government was simply unable to cope with the activities of the smugglers. The situation concerning liquor in those years was comparable to that which prevailed later in the 1970s regarding the smuggling of narcotics into the United States. The scope of the illegal enterprise was so vast, and the U.S. coastline peppered with so many thousands of likely landing spots for fast boats equipped with high-powered engines, that control of the flow was impossible with the force available to do the work. The reporters had hardly turned their backs when the "Lone Wolf" was gone again on another mysterious mission. Again, no one knew his whereabouts.

In October of that year, a Pullman car was chartered by one Jack Murphy from officials of the Louisville & Nashville Railroad for a special party traveling from New Orleans to Mobile, Alabama. The stated purpose of the charter was to convey a party of home seekers and growers interested in establishing orchards of Satsuma oranges. Mr. Murphy himself collected all the tickets and turned them over to the Pullman conductor, a practice that was out of the ordinary, to say the least.

When the train arrived at Mobile at 2:00 A.M., the car was shunted to a location in the railroad yards at a considerable distance from the passenger terminal. Early the following morning, H. C. Geron, the L&N passenger agent at Mobile, made a courtesy call to extend a welcome to the visitors and see to their comfort. However, the Pullman was empty, except for the porter. He was asked where the visitors were and replied that they had left very early, adding that "they sure had a lot of guns for home seekers!" M. T. Gonzaullas and Izzy Einstein were among the "home seekers" on that chartered car. They, their fellow passengers and others who had arrived by different railroads, a total of fifty-two prohibition agents, spread out over Mobile to begin a series of raids that would not only paralyze the illicit liquor business there but also involve prominent citizens, officials and law officers on various charges, including attempted bribery.

Friends back in Texas soon learned that the "Lone Wolf" had been involved in an earlier raid in Savannah, Georgia, where more than two hundred individuals were arrested. Gonzaullas slipped from Mobile to New Orleans where he worked undercover for ten days. To give the appearance of an ordinary tourist who was "doing the town" he was accompanied by his wife while he made a series of inspection tours of New Orleans gambling and illegal liquor-selling resorts. Widespread raids by prohibition agents followed the tour. Leaving the Crescent City, the "Lone Wolf" made Houston his next stop on the cleanup route. Then, it was back to Beaumont and on to Savannah for more work.

Slowing down in Mobile in early May 1924, Gonzaullas testified in the federal court trials of indicted liquor bosses and associates, giving details of their activities, telling how he obtained their confidence and listing "protected" dealers. He presented minutely explicit information on specific events, barroom scenes, dates and individuals involved. He provided the court with descriptions of his relations with offenders, of the intricacies of whiskey traffic operations and bribes paid him on the assumption that he would give federal protection to them. His evidence was one of the key factors in the conviction of many of the 326 who had been arrested during the raids.

55

After concluding his testimony in the Mobile trial, the "Lone Wolf" returned to Texas, heading for Sherman in Grayson County where he and W. A. Nitzer were scheduled to go on trial in federal court on a change of venue from Beaumont, the charge being murder of the Jefferson County official on July 22, 1922. Both officers pleaded self-defense. Nitzer was acquitted on an instructed verdict from the bench. The following day, after deliberating for twenty minutes, the jury acquitted Gonzaullas.

Gonzaullas' bulletproof vest on display at the Texas Ranger Museum in Waco. "Lone Wolf" told the story that the holes in the outer layer were made when he had an associate test the vest by firing at him. (Courtesy Texas Ranger Hall of Fame and Museum.)

V
On Again, Off Again

To the astonishment of many of his friends, and all of the bootlegging fraternity, "Lone Wolf" Gonzaullas submitted his resignation as general prohibition agent on July 1, 1924, effective immediately. The news was like a bolt from the blue and was received with unfeigned joy by the illicit liquor crowd throughout the South and Southwest. At a press conference Gonzaullas stated, "I'm leaving the department of my own accord. I've simply had enough of the service and want to get out in the business world. I've every reason to believe that, if I devote the same effort to business enterprise, I will meet with success in the same degree that I enjoyed in federal service."

Pressed by reporters for clarification of reasons for the abrupt action, he added, "I thought seriously about resigning some time back, but decided to stick it out until after the Sherman trial. I've been acquitted, as you know, and now I'm going into the real estate business."

"Did you say 'real estate business'?" he was asked incredulously.

"That's right," Gonzaullas replied. "Real estate business." His expression was one of complete seriousness.

"You've just got to be kidding us, sir," was the retort of one of the newsmen present. "How come you spent so much time today with Aldrich [Ranger Captain R. W. Aldrich] and Hamer [Captain Frank Hamer]?"

"Just talking over old times," Gonzaullas replied, ending the interview.

The newsmen were right in their suspicions that he was joshing them. On July 2, 1924, M. T. Gonzaullas was reenlisted in Texas Ranger Service by Captain Aldrich.

It is clear that being a man of vision and rare intelligence, Gonzaullas foresaw the inescapable failure of federal prohibition and realized there was no future for him there in a permanent career. He had witnessed the increasing antagonism of citizens toward prohibition agents, who were only trying to uphold the law no matter how unpopular it had become. It was a reason for his pronounced disillusionment with that arm of the federal service. His own views on the importance of American citizens honoring laws on the statute books and standing behind enforcement officers were well known. He believed that even unpopular laws must be enforced. Should they prove to be unwise, then they should be repealed, but until repealed they must be enforced.

An editorial in the *Christian Courier* of January 29, 1925, so aptly expressed his personal sentiments that he cut it out, marked it in red ink and preserved it. Under the headline "THE PLIGHT OF GOOD LAW ENFORCERS," the newspaper announced,

> The *Courier* has no patience with the muckraker, or the yellow journalism that sees nothing but crookedness, graft and incompetence in law enforcement officials; but prevailing conditions are such in this country that certain facts must be faced and properly dealt with, or the Government must go on the rocks.
>
> And, one of the facts is that an honest, efficient officer does not have adequate support in the performance of his duty. For example, party bosses and higher officials often interfere with a law enforcement officer who is catching the criminal higher up. One of the most fearless, faithful and efficient law enforcement officers recently told the writer that he had resigned because his superior officer had objected to his activities when he was just about to complete a chain of evidence and arrest a band of master-mind bootleggers.

Although Gonzaullas did not say so himself, being reticent about discussing any phase of his work through the years, it is possible that the reason he saved that article from the *Christian Courier* and marked it in red ink is that *he* was the officer referred to, who resigned in protest against interference by a superior.

The editorial continued, referring to a different individual,

> Again, the honest official who has played no favorites frequently finds himself without a job, in spite of the fact that he has taken his life in his hands to catch criminals and protect society. Here is an excerpt from a personal letter written by such an officer to a friend: "I have gone through the fire for months. Indeed, I have been in the official harness for 22 years and now I am about to be turned out to root hog or die.
>
> "I have just recovered—rather, I am just up—from an abscess on my lung caused from an old gunshot fourteen years ago, which wound was inflicted by a bootlegger in dry territory down in South Texas when I was the only officer down there trying to enforce the liquor laws of Texas. The good folks were behind me then, but of course they have forgotten me now. I have been a lifelong prohibitionist and have lost several good jobs for voting for the cause and protecting its leaders; but I have no regrets and blame nobody, as I was doing right, though I am now about to be cut adrift without a job.
>
> "I have done my bit toward the advancement of society and protecting it against the criminal element, and will continue the good work somehow."

The *Courier* continued,

> This man is one of the bravest, cleanest and most efficient officers known to Texas people. He has captured some of the most desperate criminals and killed others too desperate to be captured, being wounded several times himself in these gun battles. He is not trained for any other service, and yet, with bootleggers running rampant, highjackers going unmolested, and lawbreakers generally taking things with a high hand, this true and tried officer, as well as a number of others whose names are a terror to criminals, is idle today.
>
> Thus the general public does not give the backing needed by the officers to convict criminals. Good men shirk jury service, or if they serve on the jury they allow maudlin sentiment and prejudice to control their verdict and set free men they know ought to go to the pen or the electric chair.

Upon receipt of his resignation as general prohibition agent, the dismayed Washington chief told Gonzaullas that whenever he wished to return to that service a job would be waiting for him. He was called back late in the following year for urgently needed work which he was best qualified to do. After being assured that he would have a free hand, he did return for an eighteen-month period, during which time whiskey prices in Texas shot up because he closed off the sources of bootlegging supplies.

In the meantime, following the July 1, 1924, resignation from federal service and his reenlistment by Captain Aldrich, Gonzaullas spent his time working on Northern and Central Texas Ranger cases, then again went with the force to the Rio Grande in January 1925. The men were ordered to the border to halt a threatened invasion of that part of the state by rum runners from Mexico. An intrusion had been made into Texas by more than a dozen heavily armed Mexicans who crossed the river north of Laredo, bringing with them several hundred gallons of tequila for delivery in this country. Fears mounted among border residents from Laredo upstream that there might be renewed raids on ranches in isolated regions of Southwestern Texas. The beefing up of the Ranger force along the Rio Grande had the desired sobering effect on any who might have been planning further smuggling or hit-and-run raids on ranches from south of the border. From the Rio Grande, Gonzaullas went back to Mobile for a brief stay to testify in another trial connected with the liquor cleanup there in which he had had a part.

The "Lone Wolf" happened to be at the right place at the right moment in Dallas just after lunch on August 13, 1925. While he was at Worsham Buick, located at Olive and Pacific, he looked up to see a Negro man, pistol in hand, running toward the garage. Thinking that the fellow was fleeing from the scene of a robbery, Gonzaullas instinctively shouted at him to "drop that gun," as he pulled his own weapon. Not knowing who his challenger was, and trusting to his fleetness of foot, the man ignored the command, turned away and continued his flight. Gonzaullas called again, ordering him to stop, but he kept going. At that juncture, the fleeing man was also hailed by W. E. Perkins, who held a special deputy sheriff commission and was employed at Anderson Furniture Company on North Harwood.

"Stay back, or I'll shoot," the suspect yelled at them, whereupon both the "Lone Wolf" and Perkins began firing. At the same instant the man himself fired, but his shots went wild. He ended up in Parkland Hospital with six of Gonzaullas' bullets in his body. Gonzaullas went to the office of Sheriff Schuyler Marshall to explain the circumstances.

The wounded man had been walking on Elm Street and passed a clothing store where Mrs. Nathan Nudleman, wife of the owner, recognized him as the person who had recently given her husband a worthless check. She ran out of the store, grabbed him by the arm and shouted to her husband, "Here's the man!" She was struck in retaliation as Mr. Nudleman came onto the sidewalk in her defense. The suspect then hit Nudleman on the head with a savage blow from a pistol, tore loose from Mrs. Nudleman's grasp and fled across Elm to Harwood straight into the confrontation with Gonzaullas and Perkins.

The "Lone Wolf" apologized for shooting "at" the man, explaining that he "really didn't take good aim but just shot loosely from the hip."

Rangers Gonzaullas, Stewart Stanley and others, working under Captain Tom Hickman and together with Denton County Sheriff Bill Fry, Dallas County Sheriff Schuyler Marshall and several deputies, cooperated on a case that tied together the robberies of area banks by members of a gang and the gunning down by one of them of Denton County Deputy Sheriff H. B. Parsons. A raid on a farm southwest of Denton turned up a large amount of miscellaneous loot, including a handful of unset diamonds, explosives, and several disguises and masks that had been used in robberies. One of the disguises was that worn by a man of small stature who posed as a woman. Company "F," 144th Infantry, Texas National Guard, was called in to guard the farm property and keep intruders away while the extensive search and digging operations were in progress. The National Guardsmen, who were there in a civil capacity, were deputized by Sheriff Fry.

Evidence was found on the farm that solved the robberies of the banks at Krum and Tioga, as well as the attempted robbery of the Sanger bank. In addition, the nighttime break-in at the Valley View bank and the cover-up fire set in that town the previous winter were connected with the gang operating out of the Denton County farm. At Valley View, $12,000 in cash and $100,000 in bonds were taken. Some of the nonnegotiable bonds stolen in that burglary were found on the farm. In the arson fire at Valley View, more than $150,000 damage had been done to property in the business district. Gonzaullas had been gathering evidence on the cases for several months.

Commenting on his own presence in Denton County, Dallas County Sheriff Marshall said, "I don't want to take the attitude of being a roving sheriff and I hope the people will not look on my actions as such." His statement was in answer to some local comments questioning the reasons he had taken part in the farm raid. "I can remember days when sheriffs from one county would go to another and help in the fight to preserve the law and keep order in Texas. I'll say one thing. In the event that I am again invited to come to Denton County, or any other for that matter, I will accept the invitation and take along with me a group of deputies who are able to handle any situation they may come up against!"

It was just before Christmas, 1925, that the "Lone Wolf" was persuaded to return to the federal prohibition service for a short time and again put the bootleggers on the run. He had the utmost disdain for their kind and responded to the appeal with the understanding that he would remain for only a matter of months. He had no intention of staying for an indefinite period.

His new affiliation with the federal service was kept secret for almost three months, while he worked undercover to collect evidence, a job from which he derived great satisfaction. By the middle of March, he was ready to act. Three raids were made in different parts of Dallas County by Gonzaullas and prohibition enforcement officer Bryant Skeen. They turned over to United States Marshal Samuel Gross at the Federal Building a full truckload of liquor and manufacturing equipment. In addition to Skeen, Gonzaullas had four other men assigned to his staff.

He took time off from liquor law enforcement in early April to accompany Dallas County Sheriff Marshall, Pat Lowery, Rube Little, Will Moffett, Hugh Worthington, Bob Alcorn, Captain Tom Hickman, Dave Smith and Mrs. C. M. Isbell to Huntsville. They went to the penitentiary to witness personally the electrocution, on April 6, of two men who had been convicted of killing Dallas Motorcycle Officer Isbell in February 1924, when he stopped them for speeding.

After the murder the men fled the state, going first to Arkansas, where they killed a railroad company special agent at DeQueen. The criminals were tracked and ultimately taken into custody by special investigators Allen Seale and Hal Hood and city detectives John Henderson and Will Fritz when the fugitives called at the post office in Independence, Missouri, for mail addressed to them. The execution had originally been set for April 2 but was changed on a reprieve granted by Governor Miriam A. Ferguson because that day was Good Friday. It was considered indelicate for executions to take place on a religious holiday.

Returning to their "sponge squad" raids in Dallas after the executions, Gonzaullas and his force hit hard at fashionable roadhouses and booze joints alike in "Little Mexico." The "Lone Wolf" and agents L. H. Tyson, A. H. Miller and W. J. Knight found at two places fifteen hundred bottles of beer which were seized and smashed, "leaving an awful mess for somebody to clean up!" From another night spot, prewar vintage liquors were taken, as well as prohibition era moonshine, gin and other intoxicants.

At four tailor shops, which were "fronts" for bootlegging operations, almost four hundred gallons of whiskey, gin and wine were discovered. While the agents were raiding one of the shops, an automobile arrived at the back door loaded with three hundred pints of whiskey and gin, which were added to the prize haul. Gonzaullas and his crew used hammers and pinch bars to check walls and floors as they looked for hidden compartments. One cache, which they had reason to believe existed, almost escaped them. For more than an hour they searched in meticulous fashion, but with no success. Then, Tyson touched the button on an innocent-appearing switch which was supposedly for the ceiling lights. When he pressed it, no additional lights came on but an unseen panel in the wall swung open. Behind it, they found the objects of their intensive search.

Heading for his "old stomping grounds" in Wichita County, the "Lone Wolf" was in familiar territory. Five miles northeast of Thornberry in adjacent Clay County, he and his Texas Ranger friend J. W. McCormick arrested four men on charges of "unlawful possession of utensils designed and intended for use in the unlawful manufacture of intoxicating liquor." They seized a four-hundred-gallon still, six hundred pounds of sugar, a hundred pounds of apricots, eight hundred pounds of barley, a hundred pounds of hops, eight pounds of yeast, and other articles, despite the presence of a large, belligerent German shepherd dog chained to the still for its protection. Gonzaullas turned over to the Wichita Falls municipal welfare board the six hundred pounds of sugar and one hundred pounds of apricots for distribution to the poor. It was always his policy to make available to needy persons seized items that could be utilized for food.

After widespread raids in the twelve-county Wichita Falls prohibition district, the "Lone Wolf" popped up in Dallas again, where more liquor customer "blue books" were taken in hand. To top it off, he had started making it a practice to get the names and addresses of patrons in raided establishments, also their car license numbers. His avowed purpose was to have the information available for use by authorities in serving subpoenas on patrons to appear as witnesses to the sale of liquor. Many hours of sleeplessness were experienced by Dallas socialites who cringed at the thought of again being brought into public court trials.

There was no cessation in the district raids until October 1926, when Gonzaullas and fellow prohibition agents Walter J. Knight, R. C. Van Zandt and W. L. Zent of Fort Worth went with United States Marshal Samuel L. Gross to Texas' newest oil boom town, Borger, located about fifty miles northeast of Amarillo. Borger was only seven months old but had exploded to a population of more than forty thousand. The people and businesses were housed in a motley assortment of tents and hastily constructed, ramshackle wooden buildings, principally on the two-mile-long main street, which was either a sea of mud or an ankle-deep bowl of dust. There was no water or sewage system and there was no drainage. The great oil boom there had drawn the same type of unsavory characters that had plagued the earlier fields in other counties. Law-abiding people also were pouring in to work on the rigs and in other related jobs, but they seemed to be in the minority. At least, they had no voice in political control of the town.

The L-men arrived in town in the second week of October driving a Ford which bore on each side the name of one of the oil companies operating in the area. They were disguised as oil field workers, sporting a week's growth of beard and wearing rough, soiled clothes. They spent two days making two purchases of liquor from each of Borger's many bootleggers. The "Lone Wolf" later remarked that "the only real trouble we had in buying the whiskey was that most of the booze sellers hit us up for jobs with the company whose name was on the car!"

When their gathering of evidence had been completed, they left town, returned the borrowed car, cleaned up and in Claude, which was forty miles to the south, met additional officers who were standing by until evidence was in hand to support the raids. The investigative L-men were joined by three more agents, A.O. Grisham, J.W. Chalk and Charles Becke. Then the entire force of federal narcotic and prohibition agents, together with U.S. marshals and deputy marshals, moved in. They arrived in Borger in two big oil field jitneys and hit the ground running. Their arrival coincided with that of Company "C," Texas Rangers.

Confiscated by all the lawmen were such items as three hundred gallons of whiskey, five thousand bottles of beer and several dozen slot machines, all the latter being pounded to pieces by the wielding of heavy axes and sledgehammers. A lake of liquor resulted from the breaking of bottles wherever they were discovered. The Rangers and Marshal Gross did not consider taking the horde of prisoners to jail because the building was too small to accomodate them. Instead, the officers herded the sullen crowd of men and women into a domino hall and left them under the watchful eyes of United States deputy marshals, each of whom was equipped with a sawed-off shotgun. No attempt to escape was made by any of the prisoners.

As far as the supply of padlocks would stretch, Borger dives were locked up. When the officers' stock of locks was exhausted and they had bought out the Borger stores, the agents used nails to secure the doors. All over town there could be seen prohibition agents and Rangers, with a pistol on each hip, hammering away as they nailed doors shut.

In only one instance was there even a hint of possible gunplay. A man who was toting a .45 he did not care to surrender started to reach for it. The "Lone Wolf" shoved his own gun at him and snapped, "You must think you're tough!"

"I am a little tough," the fellow replied.

"Well, now, I'm tougher than you are, and wire haired, too," the "Lone Wolf" growled. Whereupon the other, noting the proximity of the L-man's pistol barrel to his stomach, shrugged and tossed the .45 onto the ground. The outcome was a disappointment to the watching throng, who thought there might be a bit of action.

Borger prostitutes were not arrested by the Texas Rangers in the raids but were given a limited time to get out of town. They took the hint and departed as quickly as they could arrange transportation. After the town was dried up, the agents returned to their respective headquarters.

During succeeding months, there was a consistent pattern of liquor raids in the prohibition district, a charge against seven Wichita Falls druggists for selling extracts with a high percentage of alcohol, gunfights with moonshiners, and finally Gonzaullas' decision that it was time to go back onto the Ranger force. That would be his last work as a federal prohibition agent. He reenlisted with General Robert L. Robertson on June 10, 1927, and was assigned to Company "B" as sergeant under the command of Captain Tom R. Hickman. He soon faced another challenge.

Pair of Gonzaullas' Colt revolvers decorated with Indian symbols and semiprecious stones. (Courtesy Texas Ranger Hall of Fame and Museum.)

VI

Santa Claus Is a Thief

A short, but potentially violent, flurry of racial excitement gripped Childress, Texas, in August 1927, causing the mayor, Will P. Jones, and the sheriff, John B. Compton, to send a telegram jointly to Governor Dan Moody urgently requesting the help of the Texas Rangers. They were needed to keep the tense atmosphere of confrontation between blacks and whites from getting out of control. In answer to the appeal, the adjutant general's office dispatched the "Lone Wolf" and Ranger C. O. Moore of Waco. On arrival at Childress on Monday, August 15, they found that not only had there been public fights between members of the two races, but also that the authority of local law enforcement officers had been defied by some of the white populace.

Trouble had been in the making for a number of weeks, its origin being blamed on the erection of housing for several black families in a white residential section of the city. That construction work had been done by a local businessman. Tension increased rapidly and fistfights broke out between hotheaded white and black youths. The Negro citizens, a relatively small percentage of the total population, became alarmed over reports of the organization of a "Night Riders" group which they feared would have overtones of Ku Klux Klan–type activities, of which some had vivid memories. In several recent racial encounters, men and boys on both sides had been beaten and bruised, but up to that point no one had been seriously hurt, although knives and pistols were brandished.

Attempts were made by responsible leaders of the two races to resolve the matter without further friction. However, a number of white boys took it upon themselves to, as it was expressed, "run the Negroes out of town." Those whites were arrested and placed in jail, whereupon a mob overpowered the lone jailer, took away his badge and gun, then let the young hoodlums out of jail. That was on Saturday, August 13. Reports were brought into Wichita Falls by travelers that special officers patrolling the railroad station premises in Childress refused to permit passengers to leave the trains when they stopped there during the height of the excitement, fearing that incoming rabble-rousers might aggravate the already taut situation.

It was then that the mayor and sheriff determined that the rapidly deteriorating conditions within the city were on the verge of getting completely out of hand, and that state aid was needed to avoid bloodshed. Dispatch of the telegraphic appeal followed. The circulation of news that the adjutant general had ordered the two Rangers to the city was like pouring oil on troubled waters. Texans, generally, looked upon Rangers with a sense of awe.

Gonzaullas and Moore quickly took charge making swift and thorough inquiry into the situation, after which more than two dozen men and youths were arrested and charged with responsibility in fomenting a race riot. By Thursday, the "Lone Wolf" sent to Adjutant General Robertson in Austin a telegram in which he stated, "Arrested and convicted 25 men responsible for race-riot here. Situation normal. City and county officers capable of handling situation now. They wired Governor to this effect. Request we be withdrawn. Advise."

Relieved that their city and county had been spared the humiliation of a full-blown race riot, Jones and Compton wired the governor expressing on behalf of the city and county gratitude for the services of the two Rangers, stating in part, ". . . We believe their efficiency and endeavor saved the city of Childress and Childress County and citizens great impending embarrassment, for the situation was one that could have easily assumed greater proportions . . . . We desire to commend Sgt. M. T. Gonzaullas and Ranger C. O. Moore for their courteous, efficient and impressive manner in handling the situation, and in their personal conduct." As requested, the Rangers were withdrawn.

Following up a lead back in Dallas, Sergeant Gonzaullas and two federal narcotics agents secured search warrants and paid a visit to a residence on Marburg Avenue. They entered without difficulty and arrested a woman and three men and took possession of capsules of morphine. The officers did not get their hands on all of the capsules in the house at once because one man, in an effort to avoid being caught with them, promptly swallowed seven capsules. Each contained ten grains of morphine, the total of seventy grains being enough to kill him.

Gonzaullas accosted one of the occupants of the house as he endeavored to flee through the back door. He had cause to run, as eight capsules of morphine were found in his pockets. All those in the house were arrested and handcuffed, after which attention was concentrated on the swallower.

There were two reasons for paying particular notice to the man who downed the capsules. One was to save his life. The other reason was the desire to get those items out of him for use as evidence. The "Lone Wolf" telephoned Emergency Hospital and explained what had happened. Dr. H. B. Alspaugh sped to the house in an ambulance and, while the agents sat on the man to keep him still, worked on him with a stomach pump. The capsules were retrieved intact and the subject removed to Emergency Hospital for medical treatment, after which he ended up in the Dallas County jail.

The Christmas season of 1927 was ruined in Cisco by four bandits who robbed the First National Bank on Friday, December 23. A bizarre facet of the case that captured national attention was that the leader of the gang wore a Santa Claus costume. He alone had a semblance of disguise and it was in the form of the white beard that was a part of the outfit. When his identity became known later, it was realized that he was disguised for the reason that he was well known in the town.

Poorly planned and badly bungled, the robbery turned out to be a complete failure insofar as the theft of funds was concerned. The first thing that went wrong for the outlaws was that as they moved into the building two girls, aged ten and twelve, tagged along at Santa's heels. As a result of what ensued, the children's faith in the jolly old elf was badly shaken. With the entrance of Santa, a man walked up to the desk of Cashier Alex Spear, pulled out a pistol and ordered all those in the bank to raise their hands. Thinking it was a joke, the customers and employees were slow to do so, but when Santa Claus drew a pistol and two additional men came in the side door with guns in hand, it dawned on them that this was not a laughing matter.

Those in the building were herded into a tight little group at the rear and kept there while the vault was ransacked. Shoved in sacks was cash totaling $12,200 and about $150,000 in bonds. The latter turned out to be of no value to the bandits, as the bonds were nonnegotiable. Much more cash was overlooked. When they started out the side door, headed for the Buick which was standing in the alley, the bandits kidnapped the two girls, Emma May Robinson and Laverne Comer, also Marion Olson, who had come home to Cisco from Harvard University for the holidays. The girls and Olson were used as shields. In the confusion of the moment, Mrs. B. T. Blasengame fled with her six-year-old daughter, running to the police station, which was one block distant, to turn in the alarm.

Cisco Chief of Police G. E. Bradford and Patrolman George Carmichael ran to the bank and challenged the thieves, who commenced firing. In the subsequent blaze of gunfire, Olson was struck in the right side, Chief Bradford was killed and Carmichael received a bullet in the head. He died later. Two of the bandits were wounded by the officers before they went down. R. L. Day, operator of a Cisco cafe, rushed up to the car and pulled the trigger on his gun, which misfired. A shot from inside the vehicle creased his scalp. Cashier Spear was shot through the jaw, Pete Rutherford in the thigh, Brady Boggs through the leg, breaking the bone, and Oscar Cliett was less seriously wounded. The hostage Olson shouted that he had been struck by a bullet and wanted to get to the hospital. With a gun held on him, he was ordered to shut up and remain seated. Olson defied that command, got out of the car and ran. Miraculously, he was not shot to death.

The outlaws sped from the alley and headed south. Their next bit of trouble came when they were forced to stop about half a mile from the bank because their automobile had a flat tire. There was only one thing to do and that was commandeer a car. They seized one in which fourteen-year-old Woodrow Harris from Rising Star was seated at the wheel. In their frenzy to keep moving, the thieves did not realize that the youth, who fled the scene along with his family, had removed the key before he took off for other parts. That was discovered after they transferred to Harris' car several sacks containing burglar tools, guns and ammunition, the bonds and the $12,200 in cash. They also moved the two children to the other vehicle.

When the car could not be started, they were obliged to get back in the getaway Buick with its flat tire. By that time, pursuit had caught up with them and a battle ensued. In their haste, they ordered Laverne and Emma May to throw the sacks out of the Harris car. They did that, with one exception . . . the sack containing the $12,200. It was a fortunate oversight on the part of the children. Not realizing they had been shortchanged, three of the robbers sped away in the original vehicle, taking the girls with them but deserting one of their number, L. E. Davis, who had been critically wounded. During their flight, they threw out roofing nails to slow the cars chasing them. In the countryside they were forced to abandon the Buick. The terrified girls were left in it, where they were later found by members of the posse.

Davis was taken to the hospital in grave condition. Outside the building people were gathering. Incensed by the murder of the chief and the injury to others, threats of lynching Davis were being made. A call for help had gone out, not only to neighboring counties, but also to the adjutant general in Austin. He ordered Captain Tom Hickman and "Lone Wolf" Gonzaullas to Cisco. They arrived after dark on the twenty-third. Because of the growing mob outside the hospital, and despite the fact that Davis was thought to be near death, he was transferred to a Fort Worth hospital, where he died on Saturday night, Christmas Eve.

The Santa Claus suit was found when Laverne and Emma May were picked up. On it were bloodstains which had come from Marshall Ratliff, later identified as the gang leader and the wearer of the costume. He had been shot in the chin. Prior to the arrival of Hickman and Gonzaullas, orders had been given to members of the posse to shoot to kill in the event the bandits were engaged in another fight. No more chances were to be taken. Men spread through the post oak country of Eastland County in a grim search for the fugitives, but they were not to be seen. Their trail was picked up now and then by means of blood and the indentation in soil of an easily recognizable heel print.

The search continued through the night and the next day. Toward Saturday evening, some of the men returned home to be with their families for the traditional opening of gifts, but hundreds of others stayed with the posse, taking no time out from the hunt. Bloodhounds had been brought from Gatesville but were of little use in following the trail. Hickman went to Fort Worth to secure photographs of known bank bandits from the Bureau of Identification there. These were brought to Cisco so bank employees and others could examine them with the hope of identifying the remaining three who were at large.

During the hunt on Friday, Palo Pinto County Sheriff Gib Abernathy was injured when his gun went off as he was getting out of his car. The blast took two fingers off his right hand and inflicted a serious wound in his right leg. Abernathy was taken to the hospital at Cisco for treatment. He suffered severe loss of blood and required transfusions provided by people from Palo Pinto, Eastland, Stephens and Young Counties.

The three bandits who remained at large had no planned route for escape from the vicinity of their crime. They wandered in an unorganized manner around Cisco, trying to find a means by which they could get some distance between them and the town. While hundreds of men beat the bushes east, south and southwest of Cisco from Friday afternoon through Sunday, the fugitives were never far from their pursuers. At times the hunted and hunters were so close to one another that the criminals heard posse members crashing through the brush within a stone's throw.

Shortly after midnight, in the beginning hours of Monday morning, December 26, the bandits kidnapped Carl Wylie at his home near Putnam, which lay west of Cisco. They weren't interested in Wylie himself but in his car in which he drove home from a late date. As the outlaws took off from the farm home with Carl Wylie in their clutches, his father, R. C. Wylie, came out the door of the residence and started firing at them. The only casualty was his son, who received minor but painful wounds from the gunfire. The weather was bad. A cold norther had blown in accompanied by intermittent rain and sleet.

"They carried me about the country all day . . . there were three in the crowd and two were wounded," he said. "Last night [Monday] we stayed in a pasture eight miles north of Cisco and nearly froze. One of the robbers took my overcoat," Wylie related. "This morning [Tuesday], we drove into the Cisco city limits. One of the robbers scouted around until he found a Ford touring car without curtains. They got into this and left me. I drove into town."

In his recounting the circumstances of the kidnapping itself, Carl Wylie continued, "The robbers came to our place soon after midnight Sunday saying they had a sick man and wanted to borrow a car. My father told them I was away but would return soon. They waited until I showed up at one o'clock. They then pulled their guns and made me accompany them."

After appropriating the Ford touring car, they kept heading north, crossed Stephens County and, by late morning, ran into a roadblock near South Bend in Young County. It had been put in place by Sheriff Jim Foster and his Young County deputies. The robbers reversed direction, and the officers gave chase for about two miles. Seeing they could not outrun the sheriff's car, the outlaws pulled the Ford over and jumped out of it, firing as they ran. The officers returned the fire and one man was brought down with a load of buckshot. He proved to be Marshall Ratliff, the Santa Claus. His companions fled into the cedar brakes and were lost to sight. Ratliff was suffering from five wounds. Three were received in the battle at his capture and two were sustained during and soon after the robbery of the bank. One of the escapees from the fight was known to have been shot in the hand.

Heavy rain that fell during the night obliterated tracks in the cedar brakes, but with clearing weather on Wednesday morning a reconnaissance plane was brought in. "Lone Wolf" Gonzaullas was the passenger who searched the land below and gave instructions to the pilot for maneuvering. It was determined that the two fugitives had crossed the Brazos River in the vicinity of Bunger. A farm boy reported that he had seen two men make their way across a clearing. To him, it appeared that one had a broken or otherwise injured arm. More than 150 men were making an acre-by-acre search in the Goose Neck Bend section of southeastern Young County, but without success, due to the brush that was almost inpenetrable in many places. Aerial reconnaissance continued throughout Wednesday and all day on Thursday.

The end of the chase came as unexpectedly as its beginning. On the morning of Friday, December 30, one week to the day since Santa Claus and his accomplices had robbed the First National Bank in Cisco, two ragged, exhausted and wounded men stumbled into Graham, the Young County seat. They approached a young man on the street and asked for directions to a rooming house where they might get accommodations. He realized who they were but quietly gave them directions, then rushed to report the encounter to the sheriff's office. Everyone was astonished. The criminals were supposed to still be in the Brazos River brush country some seven miles south of Graham.

The officers instantly followed up on the alarm. As they approached them, the two men separated and started a stumbling effort to run. But, they were too weak and feverish to get far. They were taken to the Young County jail, booked and quickly identified by Hickman and Gonzaullas as Henry Helms and Robert Hill, both ex-convicts.

As far as Gonzaullas and Hickman were concerned, that ended their connection with the case. However, the matter dragged on for months that stretched into years, as trials were held, sentences handed down and appealed, and tempers tried. Before the entire matter could be laid to rest, there would be a lynching. To a great many people, Christmas was ruined in Cisco not only in 1927 but also for a decade to follow.

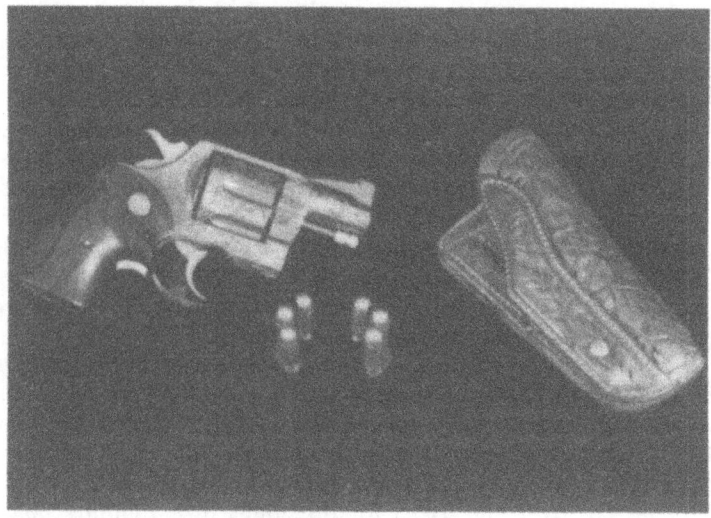

Model of 1917 revolver, specially altered for "Lone Wolf," was chambered to fire .45 automatic cartridges in half-moon clips. (Courtesy Gaines de Graffenried.)

VII

Purification at Borger

When the "Lone Wolf" was ordered to Borger, along with Captains Tom Hickman of Company "B" and Frank Hamer of Headquarters Company and other men of the force late in 1929, three years had passed since he, as a federal prohibition agent, had helped clean up the town. The trouble was that Borger would not stay "cleaned up." There was far too much money to be made in vice, in moonshining and bootlegging, in gambling, in political corruption and payoffs for the place to march down a straight and narrow path.

Behind it all was the great oil field. Flares from "waste" natural gas illuminated the landscape by night, and demonic, billowing dark clouds from carbon black burners dominated it by day. Those dense clouds would frequently blot out the sun and, when atmospheric conditions were right for it, would lie over the town in a greasy, choking, smutty pall. But, the attitude frequently expressed was "What the hell. There's money to be made." When cash flows, humankind will endure conditions that would otherwise be considered intolerable.

The countryside around Borger was heavily forested, not with trees but with wooden oil derricks that extended as far as the eye could see. In the town, the sidewalks were crowded with pedestrians, streets jammed with cars and wagons, with rumbling oil field trucks loaded with pipe. Borger was another world compared to the quiet, peaceful ranching and farming communities of the

Texas Panhandle where wells produced precious water instead of petroleum.

There was as much sidewalk and street traffic at nine or ten o'clock at night as at midday. Stores stayed open eighteen hours, and some never closed. Just crossing the main street without being run down by motor vehicles required agility. Evangelistic preachers stood on wooden boxes at street corners exhorting sinners to turn from their evil ways, but they had few serious listeners. At night the thoroughfare was brightly lighted and was proudly referred to as the "great white way," but side streets were enveloped in darkness. Lurking in the shadows were thugs who lay in wait for newcomers who would be unaware of the danger of walking alone.

Political corruption in Borger had developed into such a lucrative business that many city and county elected and appointed officers became ensnared. What was called "the line" was organized. It held tight control over all activities in the city, legal and illegal. The ever-present slot machines were owned by "the line." Gambling dens, liquor sellers, bawdy houses, in fact almost all kinds of business were required to have one or more for the public to play. All slot machines had to be owned by "the line," and woe be unto any person who tried to get by with having his own slot machine and not paying tribute.

Women in the Dixon Creek area, as the red light district was known, were obliged to turn over a part of their earnings to "the line," else they could not ply their trade in Borger. The same was true of gambling dens and liquor houses. They all paid for protection from manhandling by goons from "the line." No payment, no protection, and that meant visits from the strong-arm squads to rough up the owner and smash his property. The arrangement would have done credit to Chicago in its heyday of crime bosses running roughshod over the citizenry.

By 1929, there had been some physical improvement in the community. Street paving had put in desultory appearance. Masonry buildings were being erected here and there, and concrete sidewalks alternated with the boardwalks that were left from the earlier days. In contrast, the crime rate was infinitely worse than that which the L-men and Rangers had found on their visit in 1926. In the brief life of Borger, twenty-four murders had been reported within the town limits, but there was only one prosecution.

A carry-over from the embryonic period was the practice of expropriation by "the line" of automobiles. During their stay in

Borger three years earlier, the Rangers had restored to rightful owners several autos that had been taken from them by force and without payment. All a "line" associate had to do was express a wish for a car and one of the organization's gangsters would simply take it away from a citizen who was "out of line," so to speak. There was absolutely nothing that the victim could do as far as getting help from local law enforcement officers was concerned. Most of the latter were deeply involved in nefarious activities and would do nothing in response to a valid complaint.

However, radical change was near. Tragically, the triggering action had to be the sacrificing of the life of an official who had not been corrupted by "the line." District Attorney John Holmes was a resident of Borger. He had been in office for about one year and during that time had worked diligently to collect evidence that could be presented to a grand jury, from which he would seek indictments. It was a difficult and dangerous task. Holmes had so persisted in his efforts that he became a recognized threat to the continued dominance of the community by the lawless element. The district attorney had made trips to Austin to confer with state officials, including Governor Dan Moody, and received encouragement to carry his investigation through to conclusion.

Several of Holmes' friends in Borger had warned him about rumors that he was a marked man, but he would not take them seriously. He refused to believe that anyone would attack him, although statements were being made in public to the effect that he would not serve his full term.

On the day of his death, Holmes left his office late in the evening, accompanied by his wife. On their way home, they stopped to pick up Mrs. Holmes' mother. Turning into the driveway, Holmes stopped the car beside the house so Mrs. Holmes and her mother could get out and go into the residence through the back door. The district attorney drove into the detached garage, stepped out of the car and was in the process of closing the garage doors when he was felled by five shots fired at close range and in rapid succession. His wife was in a back room and, horrified, looked out the window just in time to see him fall on his face, at which moment the killer stepped forward, leaned over and touched him. It was later concluded that he was trying to determine if Holmes was actually dead. Then the assassin ran from the backyard, jumped into a car that was waiting nearby, its motor running and a driver at the wheel. On the way to the vehicle, he ejected from his gun the five spent shells. Significantly, the assassination occurred in the evening the day before Holmes was scheduled to meet with the grand jury in Stinnett, the county seat of Hutchinson County, and present his evidence on the crime bosses in Borger.

The arrival of the sheriff at the residence sent Mrs. Holmes into hysterics and she ordered him out, accusing him of obstructing the district attorney's efforts at law enforcement. From among the Hutchinson County official family, only the county judge was asked to serve as a pallbearer. The widow gave as her reason the antagonistic attitude the others had taken toward her late husband's endeavors to clean up the city and county.

Holmes' death, which was attributed to a paid killer, sent shock waves throughout Texas. Governor Moody immediately ordered the Rangers to Borger and followed that by declaring a state of martial law to exist in Hutchinson County. The governor's next step was to appoint his personal friend, Clem Calhoun, to succeed Holmes as district attorney and carry out with vigor the work that the dead man had brought so near fruition.

Brigadier General Jacob F. Wolters, commanding the Fifty-sixth Cavalry, Texas National Guard, reached Borger quickly, along with the large Ranger force. Under martial law, search warrants were dispensed with, making the investigative and enforcement work much easier. The first step taken was to round up the local law enforcement officers and take them into custody, relieving them of badges, handguns and all their other paraphernalia. They were picked up on the streets, in the "49" dance halls, in bawdy houses and gambling dens. "Some of them tried to get smart with us," the "Lone Wolf" recalled, "but we just smacked 'em around and hitched a few to the snortin' pole at the jail. That took the wind out of 'em and they didn't give us any more trouble." The snorting pole was a large, twelve-inch-diameter pole, one end buried deep in the ground, to which those arrested could be fastened by means of chains locked around their ankles or necks.

"You just can't imagine the pile of guns that stacked up as we took them off the Borger officers, plus the run-of-the-mill gun-toters on the streets. It was just unbelievable," Gonzaullas chuckled. "And, you should have seen how those fellows squirmed when the good people of the town came down to the jail to see 'em with the rings on 'em and chained to the snortin' pole. Why, those people laughed and laughed, because they knew that 'the line' had come to the end of the line!"

Again, gambling dens and the illegal liquor houses were padlocked or nailed shut. By 1929, there were so many slot machines in Borger that when they were smashed by the Rangers the coins had to be collected in big galvanized wash tubs. The money was turned over to the few churches in town, all of which were financially anemic, thus providing a welcome transfusion of cash.

Because their "protectors" were disarmed and in the custody of the military government of Hutchinson County and because their own various illegal means of livelihood were being dried up, men and women of the criminal element began packing to leave town in a hurry. They used every available means of transportation: private automobiles, jitneys, wagons, some even carrying their goods by hand or pushing wheelbarrows loaded with personal possessions. At the time, the exodus was compared with the mass migration of the Belgian refugees fleeing before the oncoming German army in World War I.

The Panhandle and Santa Fe Railway Company had built a thirty-one-mile branch line from the town of Panhandle on the AT&SF to Borger in 1926 after the oil field came into production. Borger was the terminus of the stub. Many of those fleeing the town, like rats from a sinking ship, utilized the railroad as their means of exit. When the mixed train pulled out of the Borger station, the passenger car was filled to capacity, people standing shoulder to shoulder in the aisle and on the platforms. Those who could not get in had crowded on top of the box cars and refused to come down, despite remonstrance of the train crew. All were frantically seeking to get out before they were arrested by the Rangers.

The truth of the matter was that the Ranger force was glad to see them go. The bosses of "the line" and their minions had been arrested and placed in jail. They were the principal targets. Mass exodus of the petty criminal element did pose one problem. Some could have served as valuable witnesses against the accused. On the other hand there were law-abiding citizens of Borger who were in a position to testify on the basis of positive knowledge. And, the few ministers in town came forward to valiantly proffer their services, but there was little to which they could swear on the witness stand. Their testimony would have been principally hearsay. As the "Lone Wolf" himself stated at the time, "those ministers don't know first hand what went on in the bawdy houses or in the gambling dens or saloons. They just think they do."

When word of the closing of the net at Borger was spread through law enforcement departments of neighboring states, officers began coming in to check on men carried on their own "wanted" lists. Upon finding them, they initiated steps for extradition. Albert Mace, an ex-Ranger, was appointed chief of police for Borger, and a new force of completely reliable men was recruited to guard the town, which had experienced a drastic drop in population. Borger never again reached the population high point it attained prior to the 1929 cleanup operation. Ranger C. O. Moore was appointed to the office of sheriff for Hutchinson County, and the back of the long-lived crime era was effectively broken. John Holmes would have been pleased to see that what he had so bravely initiated was carried through to a totally successful conclusion by the Texas Rangers, the oldest state or territorial police force on the North American continent.

VIII

Thwarting a Panhandle Mob

His experience in the Northern Texas and Panhandle oil fields was taken into consideration when Ranger Sergeant M. T. Gonzaullas was sent to the new oil boom town of Van in Van Zandt County. The *Van Free State Press* welcomed him with the editorial comment,

> Sergeant M. T. Gonzaullas of the Texas Ranger force, better known as "Lone Wolf," has been assigned to Van to assist Van Zandt and Smith County sheriffs in maintaining peace. "Lone Wolf" is one of the best known and most respected peace officers in the south. He's quick on the trigger and all bad gun men know that, so seldom frequent his quarters. Sergeant Gonzaullas acquired fame when he was a prohibition enforcement officer in this state . . . . Gonzaullas is a fine fellow to know—and respect—and one of the most earnest workers on the Ranger force . . . .

The large oil deposit at Van was under the control of major companies who wisely cooperated by pooling their interests. What was referred to as a "unitized" plan of development evolved. There was not the reckless adventuring in drilling previously displayed by hordes of small independents. That wild situation was to be repeated in the vast East Texas field later in the year.

Van was atypical in another respect, also. The rowdy, wide open, crime-laden booms and busts of the earlier oil fields were not repeated in full at Van. That is not to say that the town did not have crime problems at first. It did have some, but they were kept from getting completely out of control by the "Lone Wolf," working closely with Van Zandt County Sheriff W. P. Nixon. Just after midnight on February 17, 1930, Gonzaullas, Nixon and four deputy sheriffs began a series of raids that continued until thirty-five men and fifteen women were arrested and charged. The raids were the aftermath of actions by a group of toughs who started a string of fights that sent one man to the hospital in Dallas with a fractured skull. The injury resulted from his being struck on the head with a length of pipe that was swung by one of the ruffians. Intermittent trouble followed until the lawmen acted to put an end to the almost continuous disturbance of the peace.

All of the "49"-style dance halls in Van were closed and padlocked. Charges against those arrested included assault with intent to murder, dope peddling, bootlegging, vagrancy and other delinquencies. Bond was made by several, but those who were unable to secure the aid of bondsmen were transferred to Canton for lodgment in the county jail until they could be brought to trial. The effective work of Gonzaullas and the sheriffs of the two counties earned Van the reputation of being the most peaceful oil town seen to that date in the state of Texas. Nearby boom towns that were to develop soon would not be so recognized.

One reason the "Lone Wolf" so thoroughly enjoyed his work was the variation in assignments. There was never any monotony. During the early part of the Depression year of 1930, in response to a personal request made to Governor Dan Moody for investigative aid, Gonzaullas was dispatched to Wichita Falls. He was to check on threats that had been made in an anonymous letter addressed to W. B. Hamilton and left at the door of his residence on Brook Street. The criminal was sufficiently wise not to use the United States mail for the delivery of the threatening message.

Hamilton was a prominent and wealthy man whose principal business interests were investments and oil properties. His family was a ready-made target for any extortionist who could hide behind the mask of anonymity in the hope of frightening the man into a payoff. The threat was judged to be directed mainly against the sons. Kidnapping was suspected as the next step in the campaign of personal terror. To acquiesce in such a scheme would only have brought further threats and more demands, so Hamilton reacted as any prudent man would.

The "Lone Wolf" came to the family, lived in the home and acted in the dual role of bodyguard and chauffeur. He was sufficiently well known in Northern Texas from his experience in the oil fields of that region that word of his presence rapidly spread through the crime world. His presence had the desired effect. The extortionist made no further demands, obviously having considered the risk inherent in an involvement with Gonzaullas. Hamilton wrote to Governor Moody on March 14, 1930, after the matter had been settled. He said, in part, "Mr. Gonzaullas, as is his custom, entered earnestly into ferreting out this situation . . . . I think the State of Texas is very fortunate in having a man of his character, loyalty and ability as a part of this patriotic service. I feel that he will add more glory to the high record of achievement of the Texas Rangers . . . ."

The "touchiness" of citizens and local officials about the presence of Rangers in their community was largely based on a misconception. The very fact that the state officers were there was believed to suggest to the nation that crime was rampant and the local lawmen were unable to handle the situation on their own. State and national newspapers were ever eager to headline the news that Rangers had been ordered to a certain city or town.

The sensitivity of the inhabitants of the city of Ranger had immediately been made manifest on the arrival of a Ranger force there in 1920, a force that had not been requested by local people. It was Pampa's turn to be dismayed when Sergeant Gonzaullas and Ranger J. P. Huddleston stepped off the train on March 30, 1930. They had been seen on that train by a judge who inquired and learned from them that they were en route to Pampa. Their mission was not disclosed. He telegraphed word ahead to the town and started a chain reaction of excitement and rumor that was without foundation in fact.

Because a municipal election was scheduled to be held on April 1, impulsive people in Pampa supposed that the Rangers had been sent in to supervise the event personally. It was known that the presence of Rangers had not been requested. The situation was not helped by the Ranger force's long tradition of being reserved in speech. Gonzaullas and Huddleston did nothing to enlighten the residents as to the reason for their visit to the city. Imagination ran rampant and was almost equalled by indignation.

A citizens' meeting was instantly convened to prepare a protest to Austin. Three Pampa leaders, namely, Judge Ivy Duncan, T. D.

Hobart and the Reverend Mr. T. W. Brabham, were delegated by the group to convey to the office of the governor the distress felt by the residents over the unsolicited presence of the Rangers in their city and what they regarded as the accompanying bad publicity. Like a blazing campfire onto which a bucket of water is cast, the tumult was reduced to wet ashes by word from Governor Dan Moody that Gonzaullas and Huddleston were en route to Stinnett to attend a session of the court and had been instructed to detour from Amarillo to Pampa en route to the Hutchinson County seat. Their visit to Pampa was for the purpose of securing facts for the governor on a matter that had nothing whatsoever to do with the municipal elections.

Governor Moody stated that the Rangers would remain in Pampa no longer than necessary to handle the business assigned to them, after which they were to continue their journey to Stinnett. That was exactly what happened. Shamefacedly, the trio reported the facts to the hastily assembled protest group, whereupon suspicion and latent hostility toward the Rangers evaporated. When their business was concluded, Gonzaullas and Huddleston departed with a friendly send-off by a crowd of red-faced Pampans.

Within three months, the "Lone Wolf" was back in Pampa, accompanied by Ranger W. H. Kirby. They had been ordered there to protect witnesses who had been threatened regarding testimony which those persons were expected to give in a federal liquor conspiracy probe. On that June 30 visit, Gonzaullas issued a stern warning that intimidation of witnesses in the case would not be tolerated. Submissive Pampans made no complaint to the governor that time.

The Rangers had not been dispatched to Pampa in order to take part in the investigation being made by federal prohibition agents. Their presence was simply to ensure the complete safety of the individuals who had been threatened with bodily harm. In a public statement, the "Lone Wolf" said they were in the city to preserve order and forestall any violence "that would reflect adversely upon the good name of the community." Again, as soon as their mission had been accomplished, they departed. But, events soon to transpire would bring a Ranger force back to the area in two weeks.

A serious racial disturbance in the eastern Panhandle was the cause of Gonzaullas' return in July. The motivating force was the brutal slaying on July 11 of the young wife of a prosperous farmer near Shamrock in southern Wheeler County, only fifteen miles from the Texas-Oklahoma line. She had been attacked at her residence by a Negro who admitted that he had attempted to ravish her. He confessed that when she fought back he repeatedly struck her on the head with a piece of iron pipe. She was so severely beaten that her facial features were unrecognizable. The assailant, who had been employed on an adjoining farm, was challenged near the house and recognized by the victim's husband and his thirteen-year-old brother. Then the body was found and an alarm was turned in to the sheriff's office.

When news of the murder and arrest of the suspect spread, threats of lynching were made. Basing his action on rumors that several hundred men were organizing to march on the Negro residential section of Shamrock to wreak vengeance, Sheriff W. K. McLemore soon formed a large posse of Wheeler County men, deputizing many, to render aid in the event of mob action. He feared incidents on the order of those which had just occurred at Erick, Oklahoma, a short distance beyond the state boundary. The victim had previously resided in Erick, where she had been held in high regard. On the report of her murder reaching there, latent hostility surfaced, venting its wrath on innocent people who had nothing to do with the crime.

A mob of approximately 260 excited men assembled in the business district of Erick and began to visit the homes of all the Negro families in the town. The mob was orderly, but uncompromising. "Get out, now," was the message delivered to each terrified family. They were permitted only enough time to grab a few possessions and run. After Erick was emptied of the hapless Negroes, the mob members went to surrounding farms where black families were known to reside and work. They, too, were ordered to leave and not return. Most fled to Elk City, being afraid to stop in the nearby county seat of Sayre.

Sheriff McLemore appealed to Governor Moody for aid, and four Rangers were immediately dispatched. With the rank of acting captain, M. T. Gonzaullas was placed in charge of the group. The others were J. P. Huddleston of Dallas, W. H. Kirby of Abilene and Bob Goss of Honey Grove. The whereabouts of the accused man, Jesse Lee Washington, was shrouded in secrecy. He had been whisked out of Wheeler County. Throughout the five days that he was hidden, mobs combed areas of the Eastern Panhandle and Western Oklahoma where they thought it likely that he had been taken. It had been noised about that he was being kept in the tight security of the Oklahoma state prison at Granite, but no confirmation could be obtained. Had he been there, he would have been beyond the reach of any mob. Strong talk was bandied by two mob groups, one bent on finding and lynching him, the other determined to assassinate him whenever he was brought out of hiding for arraignment. The report was spread through the populace that one of the mobs had in its possession a Thompson machine gun. The "Lone Wolf" said emphatically, "We will protect the life of this Negro from a mob at all costs!"

As it turned out, Washington was right under their noses. He had been spirited around the Panhandle, across the line to Oklahoma and then back to Texas, finally spending most of the time in an undisclosed hiding place in Collingsworth County, not far from Shamrock. The theory under which the officers operated was that the mobs searching for him would not expect their prey to be so close to the scene of the crime. It was a calculated risk, but it paid off. In a cleverly planned and executed maneuver, the prisoner was moved from the hiding place to the Gray County jail in Pampa on July 16. That jail was located on the third floor of the new courthouse, which had been occupied for only about twelve weeks. The spot provided maximum security.

Sheriff McLemore and his prisoner arrived at the Pampa courthouse in a sedan, the accused man being clad in a bulletproof vest and chained. Washington knew of the threats being made against his life and was terrified. He crouched low on the car seat and kept his head down. McLemore was disguised as an oil field worker, wearing greasy clothes typical of that trade and having an old cap on his head. The bill of the cap was pulled down to shield his eyes. He was not recognized even when he walked into the Gray County sheriff's office with his shackled prisoner in tow.

Their watches synchronized with the sheriff's, the four Rangers reached the courthouse a split second behind McLemore, allowing just enough time for him to get inside the building and for Washington to be locked safely in his cell. This timing was intended to mislead those who they knew would be expecting the state officers to have the prisoner in their custody. They tried to further confuse their adversaries by starting the rumor that the man would be brought to the city jail in Shamrock. Some were taken in by that report, but others discounted it, feeling sure that their quarry would not be left in a spot that would be difficult to defend.

Gonzaullas and his associates were prepared for any emergency. Their automobiles contained two machine guns, ten

Reverse sides of richly embellished, gold-plated Colt .38 Detective Special revolvers used by Gonzaullas. The pistols were ornamented with a gold, miniature Texas Ranger captain badge and with emblems of organizations of which Gonzaullas was a member. (Courtesy Texas Ranger Hall of Fame and Museum.)

thousand rounds of ammunition, a hundred hand gas grenades, fifty regular grenades, plus their usual arsenal of rifles, shotguns and pistols. It was a display of armaments sufficient to stay the hand of even the most arrogant mob leader. Thus equipped, they took their stand at the Gray County courthouse to guard the prisoner around the clock. The "Lone Wolf" repeated, for the benefit of all, his previous announcements that he and his men would spare no means to protect the life of the accused man and see that he was given full access to the procedures of the law.

Washington having been indicted by the grand jury in Wheeler County on the morning of July 17, the next necessary step that McLemore, Gonzaullas and the other officers faced was to transport him from Pampa to the district court in Wheeler for arraignment. Arrangements were made with Judge W. R. Ewing for their arrival at the courthouse there precisely at 6:00 P.M. on that same day, July 17. The two automobiles carrying Washington, the sheriff, Gonzaullas, Huddleston, Goss, Kirby and deputies Scott Rheudasil, Herman Wachtendorf and Frank Jordan left Pampa at 4:30 in the afternoon without attracting undue notice. Their destination fifty miles away was known only to them. On the poor roads of that era, driving time between the two towns was about ninety minutes. En route, several cars attempted to pass them but were waved back and ordered to stay behind. The Rangers did not want anyone to go in ahead of them and spread word about their approach with the prisoner so a potentially troublesome mob could gather.

They timed their journey so they reached the courthouse in Wheeler at straight up six o'clock. One of the deputies was left outside to guard the vehicles, and the other officers crowded around Washington to shield him from a possible sniper. Then they moved into the building. The proceedings required only a short time, during which Judge Ewing appointed Miami attorney E.F. Ritchey as defense counsel. The judge was unable to get a Shamrock attorney to accept such assignment. The trial was set for July 28 in the Thirty-first District Court at Miami, the Roberts County seat, with Judge Ewing presiding.

When the party came out of the Wheeler County courthouse following the arraignment, a crowd of a hundred or more had gathered on the sidewalk across the street from the parked cars. Although there were no threatening motions, several of the men did start to cross the street toward the officers and prisoner but turned back upon shouted orders from the "Lone Wolf."

The trial in Miami on July 28 was completed in one day. The Rangers and deputies brought the prisoner to Miami in the morning and placed him in the courtroom before any spectators were permitted to enter. Those who were allowed in were thoroughly searched and only those who could be seated were admitted. No one was allowed to stand. After the judge issued a stern warning against demonstrations, the crowd remained orderly. There was only one brief stir and that was when a man leaned over, ostensibly to tie his shoelace. Gonzaullas grabbed him, took him outside and again searched him from head to toe. No weapon was to be found, but his shoelace was untied, so his act was proved to be legitimate. The officers were taking no chances with anyone. The prisoner was surrounded by Rangers and deputies, who took their position to shield him from any shot that might be aimed his way. As a result, the curious spectators saw little of him.

Jury selection was completed by 2:30 P.M., the defense attorney having questioned sixty-five of the eighty veniremen before the panel was completed. Most of those dismissed expressed prejudice against the Negro race or were opposed to the death penalty. There were no blacks in Miami and the jury was composed principally of farmers and ranchers. The defendant entered a plea of "guilty" and, through his court-appointed attorney, asked for mercy. Testimony was completed before the recess for dinner at 6:00 P.M. Court was reconvened at 8:00 and arguments by the prosecution and defense were concluded by 9:00, at which time the case went to the jury. A verdict of guilty was returned in fifteen minutes and the sentence was death in the electric chair. Two days were allowed for appeal.

Back in jail at Pampa, the convicted man remained under heavy guard until he was transferred to the penitentiary at Huntsville. Events moved swiftly in that period. The doomed man was strapped in the electric chair at 12:11 on the morning of September 8. Eight minutes later he was pronounced dead.

Rangers don't express personal opinions about assignments given to them, but eyebrows must have been raised when they received an order to go to Shamrock and stop a circus performance. Running down bandits was routine. Smoking out bootleggers was "old hat." But, to prevent a circus from playing a one day stand . . . ?

The little city of Shamrock, which had seen a lot of the "Lone Wolf" and his associates in recent weeks, was the stage for a con-

89

frontation between an American Legion post and local church leaders. The Legion was sponsoring a Sunday performance of the Ringling Brothers, Barnum & Bailey Circus in September 1930 as a fund-raising event. To the astonishment of Legion members, a protest was made by some Shamrock churches that the show would be illegal, that it would be in violation of the state's blue laws. Before the storm passed, a barrage of telegrams and long-distance calls passed between Shamrock and Austin. There were calls for the Rangers to be sent for the purpose of stopping the performance, and Governor Dan Moody even threatened to order a thousand Texas National Guardsmen there to assist, if necessary. It was a full-fledged tempest in a teapot. One local wag offered the idea that the governor might also call on the United States Marines for backup. Another suggested that five hundred missionaries be included with the National Guard contingent, while a third thought that the Shamrock Legionnaires should arm themselves with pop guns "to train on the Rangers when they arrive."

Shamrock Mayor G. C. Berkley got into the act, questioning the sending of Rangers, and was challenged by none other than the governor himself. Sheriff W. K. McLemore, who had recently handled the murder case with expertise, was involved in the initial request for the Rangers' presence. Then, he backed away and wired the governor,

> Rush Message—Important! After thorough investigation, it is my opinion that the presence of Rangers in Shamrock, Texas, to prevent performance by Ringling Brothers circus Sunday, September 14, wholly unnecessary expense and unwarranted according to leading citizens and due to fact that local officers have not to this time had opportunity to enforce law in connection therewith. In addition, am advised that both County and District Judges have wired you that presence of Rangers unnecessary and situation still in hands of local officials. Emergency measures unwarranted and you are assured that my department is adequately equipped to take care of situation. My request for Rangers hereby withdrawn.

Governor Moody replied to a message from Mayor Berkley, saying,

> Received telegram signed by sheriff and committee asking me to supply sufficient Texas Rangers to prevent Ringling Brothers and Barnum and Bailey shows from holding Sunday

performance. Replied that the Rangers were available. Do I understand that you endorse the holding of these circus performances on Sunday in violation of the criminal laws of this state, or have you made arrangements to see that the law is not violated or that it is enforced if it is violated?

Upset at the governor's chiding question, Mayor Berkley fired back a message in which he stated,

Do not endorse Sunday performances of circuses and assure you that I will enforce the law to the letter of my jurisdiction. I am informed by the Sheriff's department that they are adequately equipped to cope with the situation. I think the presence of Rangers wholly unnecessary in this case.

Unaware of this exchange of telegrams, the *Shamrock Texan* moved in with its own to the governor inquiring who had requested that the Rangers be sent in the first place. This was a good news story for local consumption. It would also go out from Shamrock to United Press. The governor was glad to oblige with the information. He wired back immediately,

Received telegram signed by the sheriff and other citizens advising that circus was scheduled to hold two performances at Shamrock on Sunday and requested Rangers. The sheriff later withdrew his request for Rangers. I have ordered Rangers to Shamrock to prevent this circus from holding Sunday performances in violation of the laws of Texas and have advised the sheriff that I of course expect him to cooperate with these officers in their attempt to uphold the law and that I do not intend to order the Rangers to turn back unless given satisfactory assurance that the local officers can prevent and will prevent this circus from holding Sunday performances in violation of the laws of the land. It seems that the circus is scheduled to be in Texas on three Sundays. If it attempts to hold Sunday performances at any place in Texas the Rangers will be sent there to prevent any such violation of the law. Upon no basis can a circus be justified in coming into Texas and attempting an open and flagrant violation of our laws. (Signed) Dan Moody.

Following that, the governor fired off another message to the sheriff reiterating his intention to send the Rangers unless McLemore gave assurance that he would enforce the blue laws. He closed his message to the sheriff with "Judge Ewing wires me 'I know nothing of conditions existing in Shamrock. Disregard telegram sent in my name.' "

The Shamrock Legionnaires were incensed. They, too, kept the telephone and telegraph wires hot as they endeavored to secure the aid of state Legion officials, as well as influential persons who might try to persuade Governor Moody to rescind his order for the Rangers to travel to Shamrock. The upshot was that the circus cancelled its performance in that town, as well as in the other two places scheduled to have Sunday shows in Texas. The Ringling Brothers' advance agent notified the Legionnaires that passes which had been issued for use at Shamrock would be honored at the circus performances in Amarillo on Monday, September 15. But, Amarillo was one hundred miles distant and the shows there were on a work and school day.

Following the flap over the circus at Shamrock, the Ranger force was entitled to a bit of fun. It came in the form of a scheduled quarter-mile horse race at the famed Arlington Downs on Monday, November 10. For the members of a law enforcement arm of the state government to participate in such an event does seem a bit incongruous. However, at that time horse racing was legal in Texas. There was no public wagering on the outcome, but some cash was known to have surreptitiously changed hands when the Rangers' race was concluded. The event was a crowd pleaser, so both racing and Ranger fans turned out en masse to take part in the hilarity and to cheer for their favorites.

A "catch-as-catch-can" race in the choice of mounts and saddles, it was not as fast as standard races because of the disparity in the speed of the mounts and weight of the individual riders. The weight differences on the part of the Rangers had a recognized effect on the ranking at the finish line. To lessen the load on their horses, all seven men removed their heavy guns and cartridge belts. The riders were R. G. (Bob) Goss, W. H. Kirby, Captain Tom Hickman, Sergeant M. T. "Lone Wolf" Gonzaullas, E. P. Waggoner, Bill Langley and G. L. Waggoner. At the finish line, E. P. Waggoner came in first just ahead of the "Lone Wolf." G. L. Waggoner was in third place. Following the conclusion of the event, the Rangers strapped on their belts and guns, once more feeling "dressed."

IX

Sherman: The Prisoner Was Roasted Alive

Mob action by a relatively small percentage of the population has brought shame to American communities from the earliest years. That was as true of the seventeenth-century witch hunts in Salem and the 1863 draft riots in New York as it was of the roasting alive of a prisoner when the Grayson County courthouse in Sherman, Texas, was fired on May 9, 1930. Good people always deplore mob rule and later examine their own feelings of guilt to see where they personally failed and what they might have done to prevent it. Then it is always too late.

On that Friday, May 9, a trial was getting under way in Sherman. George Hughes, a black man, was accused of raping a white woman in the Choctaw settlement of Grayson County. District Judge R.M. Carter, presiding, called the case at 9:30 A.M. and the jury was sworn in by noon. So highly charged was the atmosphere that support for Sheriff Richard Vaughan during the trial had been requested from the state. Four Rangers were sent by the adjutant general's office. They were Captain Frank Hamer, Sergeant J. B. Wheatley and two privates. In addition, a detachment of militiamen from Denison had been ordered to Sherman.

In the courtroom, Hughes was being guarded by the four Rangers. Sheriff Vaughan and his deputies were on duty there and in the corridors of the building. Because only persons directly connected with the case were permitted to enter the courtroom and take a seat, it was no more than half full. The prisoner had been brought to the courthouse early in the morning, but even then people were beginning to congregate on the lawn. They later pressed into the building and up the stairs, endeavoring to force their way into the district courtroom, but were kept back by the officers. A substantial portion of the mob was composed of farmers, many of whom were from the Choctaw settlement where the woman was attacked. Making up the mob were men and women, as well as youths (both male and female) in their middle or late teens. Defendant Hughes appeared unconcerned over all the furor and sat with head in hands or looking down. He was not handcuffed. Hughes pled guilty to the charge against him.

When the woman victim was brought to the courthouse in an ambulance during the morning and carried into the courtroom on a stretcher, members of the mob went wild, demanding that Hughes be turned over to them as they shouted, "We want the Negro!" After the first witness, G. M. Taylor, was called and began giving his testimony, the racket in the hallway began to interfere with the proceedings. Judge Carter sent the jury out and ordered the building cleared. Vaughan and his deputies moved the crowd down the stairs but could not keep the milling mass of people outside. It finally became necessary for tear gas to be used. That infuriated the crowd, which renewed the shouted demands for the prisoner. When those in the mob forced their way back upstairs and into the courtroom, Hughes was taken to the office of the District Clerk and locked in the thirty-foot-square steel and concrete vault. That action was intended to protect him. It actually led to his death.

Captain Hamer told Judge Carter that in his opinion, the trial could not be continued in Sherman without blood being shed. By 1:00, the judge went into conference, declaring it was likely that a change of venue would be ordered. When word of his comment reached the mob, pandemonium ensued. The members feared that the man they sought would slip from their grasp. Shots were fired over heads in an effort to keep the frenzied throng at a distance, but that action had the opposite effect. At that point, Hamer received a message from Governor Dan Moody which Hamer said told him to "protect the Negro if possible, but not to shoot anyone." The captain was quoted as having stated to Judge Carter, "This means the mob will get the Negro." The content of the message later became a disputable point, with the governor saying he had not ordered Hamer not to shoot anyone, but by that time it was a moot question. The mob leaders heard about the message and decided that the alleged instruction to Hamer would apply with equal force to the National Guardsmen. It was concluded that no matter the extreme to which the crowd might go, no one was in danger of being shot. That was judged to have been the turning point in the whole ugly affair.

Tear gas was again used, the only result being to further enrage the mob. What followed was believed to have been prearranged. A woman threw a large rock through a window of the tax collector's office and broke the glass, whereupon two youths of high school age dumped five gallons of gasoline through the opening. It was ignited with a roar, to the cheers of the seething mass of humanity watching the unfolding events.

The Grayson County courthouse had been built in the 1880s. Although the exterior walls were of masonry, all the interior was of frame construction. The wood was old and dry. When the blaze exploded, an alarm was turned in and the twenty-one-man fire department responded with every piece of equipment in Sherman. To help those trapped on the upper floor make their escape, ladders were placed against the building. Judge Carter and others scrambled down. When the county auditor stepped away from the ladder down which he had come, a mob member attempted to stab him but was held back by others.

As fast as a hose was laid and water turned on at the hydrant, the hose was slashed. The fire burned so furiously that, even though the courthouse stood in the middle of a city block, flying embers began to ignite buildings on the north side of the square. Mob leaders permitted firemen one sound hose to turn onto those structures, but warned that if the jet were turned toward the courthouse the line would be cut.

When the blaze erupted, Sheriff Vaughan and most of his deputies were out of the building endeavoring to quiet the mob and disperse its members. The four Rangers were seen fleeing the flames, but it was noted they did not have Hughes with them. The screaming throng took that to mean that he had been spirited away without their spotting the act. However, in the tumult that accompanied the roaring flash fire, it was not possible to open the vault and let George Hughes out. He was doomed to suffocate and roast in that oven.

An enormous crowd milled about the courthouse grounds. Included were women and small children who strolled in the streets and on sidewalks watching the flames and later the smoking ruins of the courthouse itself. In an attempt to move the crowd away, the National Guard unit from Denison marched in formation with bayonets fixed, but the mob did not disperse. Emboldened by their conviction they would not be fired on, the crowd turned on the militiamen, throwing bricks, bottles and slabs of wood. The guardsmen did not fire but were forced back to the jail where they had maintained their headquarters since arrival.

Word of the extreme gravity of the insurrection brought a contingent of fifty men of the 112th Cavalry, Texas National Guard, from Dallas by interurban train. Colonel L. E. McGee was in command. Other officers were Major S. J. Houghton, Jr., Captain Tilton D. Stafford and Lieutenant Louis A. Beecherl. The men were selected from A, B, E and Headquarters Companies. On arrival in Sherman, they fared little better than their counterparts from Denison.

The mob soon rumbled over the question of whether Hughes had been removed and hidden or actually was in the scorched steel vault that stood, ghostlike, within the teetering walls. They had to find out but could not until the embers had cooled. The arrival of the 112th Cavalry rekindled the hostile attitude of the crowd. Colonel McGee and his officers conferred with Sheriff Vaughan and the Rangers on a plan of action. Armed, but without fixed bayonets, the National Guardsmen were deployed around the building ruins and began to move the throng slowly outward to the sidewalk and street, though they were greeted by hoots and catcalls. It appeared there would finally be submission. Suddenly a group of teen-agers started an uproar which was instantly taken up by others. Cursing and shouts of "get his gun" and "get some bricks" increased in intensity and more missiles started flying.

Forced back almost against the dangerous walls, the guardsmen fired shots over the heads of their attackers. They were further assaulted with a storm of bricks and bottles, pieces of wood and anything else on which the attackers could lay hands. The mob was reassured by the cavalrymen's action that they would not have rifles aimed at them. The firing into the air was judged to be a bluff, whereupon there was a rush that pushed the guardsmen to the corner of the square. One private's rifle and ammunition belt were snatched from him, to the exultation of the mob, and an intense barrage of flying objects repeatedly filled the air. Broken noses, cuts and bruises resulted not only for the military but also for mob members caught by faulty aim.

The crowd was correct in its assessment of the military's position acting under orders. Rather than shoot into the menacing mob, the militia retreated to the jail. It was reported that leaders yelled, "We've got 'em on the run, boys!" Guardsmen dug in for an anticipated mass assault. Threats to rush the jail and dynamite it were heard. All lights were turned off except those of the interior rooms where there was no opening to the outside. A call went out for reinforcements. Governor Moody ordered 225 additional men to Sherman. They were under the command of Colonel Louis S. Davidson and left Fort Worth and Dallas about midnight on special interurban cars. Among the units dispatched were the 124th Cavalry and Company H, 144th Machine Gun Corps. Local peace officers from other nearby counties were called in. Pickets were set up around the jail and men took stations on the roof.

Then came the ultimate horror. With the officers and guardsmen out of their way, mob leaders directed their attention toward getting into the steel vault to satisfy themselves whether George Hughes was there. A light rain had cooled the ashes so approach could be made. Acetylene torches were used to cut openings large enough for sticks of dynamite to be inserted. When they were set off, the vault door was breached, and to the surprise of some, George Hughes' body was found inside the vault.

As his body was roughly thrown out just before midnight, the vast crowd cheered and shouted. After the morbidly curious, which included women with exhausted children sleeping in their arms, had an opportunity to stare at it, the corpse was dragged to the street and placed on a truck bed. A procession of an estimated two thousand or more yelling rioters followed the truck as it headed toward the Negro section of Sherman about ten blocks distant. Upon reaching a large brick building, locally known as the old Frisco Hotel, the parade stopped in front of a Negro drugstore.

Throughout the day the crowd had been clamoring to get their hands on Hughes so they could lynch and hang him. Now he was in their possession, though dead from suffocation and the furnace-like heat of the courthouse destruction. That did not dissuade them from their intention. A noose was formed on the rope that had been brought. It was fastened around the neck of the dead man. The other end of the rope was thrown over a lower limb of a large tree that stood in front of the building. The body was hauled up with loud cheers of mass approval.

But, that was not enough. Incendiary material was collected and placed in a huge pile beneath the corpse that was slowly swinging like the pendulum on a great clock. When the pile was set afire to cremate the body, the mob was not satisfied but, instead, was spurred on. The building itself was the next target. Soon it was an inferno. Control of the blaze was beyond the power of the fire department, which was without sufficient hose to reach the site because of the slashing of lines during the conflagration at the courthouse in the afternoon. Nine fires were set on Mulberry Street in the Negro section and one was attempted at the schoolhouse, but by that time 124th Calvarymen under Colonel L.S. Davidson had rushed to the area from the interurban, from which they had descended only moments before. They quickly dispersed the group, taking several into custody.

Hughes' charred body was cut down from the tree by the Guardsmen and lowered to the ground, where it was closely guarded to prevent further violation. Colonel Davidson ordered the Grayson County undertaker to prepare it for burial, which was handled at county expense. It was noted that members of the cremation mob had stripped from all other low limbs of the hanging tree leaves which they carried home as souvenirs of the grisly event.

The Guard units that arrived from Fort Worth and Dallas on the interurban in the small hours of Saturday morning had brought with them, in addition to their regular arms, thirty-two automatic rifles and four machine guns. Those weapons were set up around the jail.

Additional military units, including the 114th Infantry, were being readied to head for Sherman. Four more Rangers were dispatched. They were Captain Tom R. Hickman, Sergeant M. T. "Lone Wolf" Gonzaullas and Privates W. H. Kirby and R. G. Goss. (This assignment came between Gonzaullas' first and second visits to Pampa in March and June.) On Friday night, Governor Moody had publicly deplored the earlier actions of the mob (that was before the vault had been blasted open) and emphasized that reports to the effect that he had forbidden shooting were not correct. The duty of "Lone Wolf" Gonzaullas and his fellow Rangers was not only to aid in maintaining order in the city but also to investigate the events and apprehend mob leaders. They began making arrests on Saturday. The denial by Governor Moody of a "don't shoot" order had a salutary effect. It clearly placed the offenders on the defensive.

Statewide public outrage followed receipt of news on Saturday morning of the series of events at Sherman. Demands were being made that immediate steps be taken to bring the situation under control. Judge Carter, plus other Grayson County and Sherman officials, joined National Guard officers in requesting that the government institute a state of martial law. A large group of businessmen met Saturday afternoon, agreeing to the necessity of such action and passing their recommendation on to the governor. He was not in his office that day, being in Dallas, but kept in close touch with the situation by telephone and telegraph. The order was finally issued. He signed it in the evening, making it effective at 10:30 P.M., Saturday, May 10. However, it did not reach Colonel McGee until about 2:00 on Sunday morning, coming by telegraph from Austin. He was appointed supreme commander.

After martial law was declared, Colonel McGee stated that the military force in Sherman had increased to 42 officers and 377 men. By Sunday morning, he transferred his headquarters from the jail to a frame building on the same block. It was customarily used as a jury room. McGee also made arrangements with the Grayson and Williams Hotels for quarters for the men under his command. They had been sleeping on the floor of the jail.

Uneasy quiet had been restored to Sherman the middle of Saturday morning, but it was believed attributable to a steady downpour of rain rather than any disposition of the mob and their leaders to cooperate. Rumors were flying through the city that further depredations were being fomented. National Guardsmen constantly patrolled in the black section. Unless valid reason could be given for entrance to the area, automobile traffic was forbidden.

When he signed the order establishing a state of martial law in Sherman, Governor Moody had a few things to say about the situation. Calling the rule of a mob the rule of crime, the governor said, "The action at Sherman was equivalent to war on the constituted authority of the state and on an organized group of a detachment of the United States Army." He added, ". . . Men committing crime in a mob are just as much criminals, and are more cowardly than a single individual who commits a like crime."

Acknowledging that the crime "for which the Negro was lynched [sic] at Sherman was a brutal and atrocious one," he went on to point out, "The intimation of the mob by its act that he would not have been speedily tried and legally executed under the orders of a constituted court is a libel and a slander on the citizenship of Sherman and of Grayson County." In addition, he called the mob action "treason."

Reflecting the attitudes of Texans over the state, Governor Moody added, "The action of the mob in undertaking to set aside the laws of the country and constituted authority, and making of itself a group of murderers by burning the courthouse in order to kill the Negro, is a shame to Texas. It is an evil day when any group of persons combines to override the law and add to the crimes of murder and arson the offense of attacking soldiers of their state and their country." He announced his "determination to throw all the state's power to assist in the prosecution of the assailants."

When the telegraphic message was received regarding the declaration of martial law, Colonel McGee moved quickly to implement the order. He designated Colonel L. S. Davidson as provost marshal. Assistant provost marshals named were Majors Earl Crowdus, S. J. Houghton, Jr., and John W. Naylor. Next he established a court of inquiry with Davidson, Crowdus and Naylor appointed to handle the investigations. McGee, Davidson and Crowdus had seen martial law duty at Galveston in 1920 during the longshoremen's strike and at Mexia in 1922. Of the National Guardsmen stationed in Sherman, Colonel McGee stated that seven officers and seventy men had been on duty at Borger in 1929 when martial law was in force there.

The "Lone Wolf" was busily engaged in tracking down information on leaders and instigators of the riot. His skill in the field was responsible for putting the finger on several who might otherwise have escaped charges. His work tied right in with Colonel McGee's expressed aim. The latter had been quoted as saying, "What we want is arrests. Order has been restored and will be maintained. We want the leaders in the mob that burned the courthouse with the Negro in the vault and set fire to the property in the Negro district." For the first time, mob leaders and participants began to recognize the folly of their acts. In an effort to remove some of the stain that had come on the city, Mayor J. S. Eubank said, "The mob that set fire to the courthouse and burned Negro buildings was not a Sherman crowd but recruited from rural communities and from Oklahoma!" He averred that nine-tenths of the rioters "lived outside Sherman." Referring to the National Guardsmen who took such abuse at the hands of the milling mass of people, the mayor observed that "good judgment was used in not firing at the crowd. It was made up of many women and children and innocent persons would have been killed and wounded." Some citizens thought the last part of his statement would have been better left unsaid. How could he claim that anyone who was in the clamoring crowd would be considered an "innocent" bystander, was the question repeatedly asked.

District Judge R. M. Carter commented that "lack of city and county peace officers to cope with the situation was responsible for failure to check the outbreak, and not laxity on the part of authorities. Our officers did all they could without causing heavy loss of life. We needed three hundred men or more." He had a valid point. County officers totaled six and the city police force had ten men.

On Sunday, May 11, which was Mother's Day, pastors of Sherman churches built their sermons around the events of the two previous days. The Travis Street Methodist pastor, Dr. A. N. Evans, pointed the finger of blame for the mob actions on lack of proper training in homes. His words were especially harsh to the ears of listening mothers in that Dr. Evans maintained that if the mothers of the men and women and teenage youths who led or participated in the affair "had instilled respect for the law, and decency, into them the riots would not have occurred." His expression was a part of the community's guilt-ridden self-examination, which came too late.

That Sunday afternoon, the downtown streets of Sherman were packed solid with hundreds of automobiles. Many thousands of people had driven there to view the ruins of the courthouse and to watch the National Guardsmen on duty. The curious spectators came from all parts of Northern Texas and Southern Oklahoma.

When the military court of inquiry proceedings began on Monday, May 12, attention was turned first to the prisoners who were being held in the county and city jails, charged with such crimes as arson, inciting a riot and assault with intent to kill. As the investigation continued, the inquiring military officers questioned others brought in by the Rangers and local peace officers. When the work of the court was completed, its recommendations were made to the civil courts for prosecution of the charges. The intolerance and impetuous action of the accused had come back to haunt them.

Writing in the *Sherman Democrat* of February 20, 1977, just one week after the death of "Lone Wolf" Gonzaullas, columnist Jasmine McGee recalled the role the famous Ranger played in the investigative process following the riot and fires. She quoted some Sherman residents in their recollections of the captain during that time. She wrote, "Mrs. C. V. Adamson remembers Ranger Gonzaullas well. Her son, now 48, was one year old at the time. Stray bullets broke out a window in her home with shattering glass cutting her son's arms and legs. A neighbor, Mrs. Fred Willis, told the Ranger, when he came to the Adamson home to question them, that she had just as soon be dead as scared to death. The handsome Ranger solemnly said, 'Lady, there's a world of difference!' "

Further on in her column, Jasmine McGee said, "Some of the small events local folks recall were related to the poor economy at the time. Mrs. Carter said Judge Carter had a new Stetson hat and did not forget it even in his hurried exit from the burning building. White-haired Mrs. Carter also remembers that a loud bully trying to incite trouble was winged by Ranger Gonzaullas."

This .38 caliber Colt revolver was confiscated from the car of Clyde Barrow by Sheriff Rufus Pevehouse. According to Gonzaullas, the revolver had been stolen from his car during the time he worked in the oilfield boom towns of East Texas. (Courtesy Gaines de Graffenried.)

X

Boom in East Texas

Earlier oil booms with which the "Lone Wolf" had been associated in his capacity as a Ranger were nothing when compared to that which followed the discoveries in East Texas. Kicking off the boom was the strike by C. M. (Dad) Joiner in his No. 3 Daisy Bradford near Henderson. Based on entries in Joiner's logbook, historians set the discovery date as September 5, 1930, but a month passed before pipelines were laid and storage tanks completed so the well could be brought in and production could begin.

Following that came the discovery of oil at Kilgore when No. 1 Lou Della Crim blew in near the end of December 1930, just in time to assure a merry Christmas and a happy new year for the Crim family. The third significant well, No. 1 Lathrop, was brought in near Longview on January 26, 1931, the three proving beyond dispute that an ocean of oil in one field had been tapped.

The 1930 census had given Kilgore a population of 590. It was so small it was not even listed in the atlas census tabulations. No. 1 Lou Della Crim, coupled with the two other big producers, changed all that. Thousands of people poured into Kilgore, scouts, lease hounds, drillers and all the others who flock to a gigantic new discovery. Within two months after oil was brought in there, the hamlet of Kilgore, already boasting some ten thousand inhabitants housed in all manner of hurriedly erected buildings, was incorporated. J. Malcolm Crim, the son of Mrs. Lou Della Crim, became the first mayor of Kilgore when incorporation was made official on

Following the mud and mess of the East Texas oil field discovery boom, Kilgore evolved into a modern city with paved streets, parking meters, and almost as many oil derricks as shade trees. (Courtesy *Kilgore News Herald*.)

February 20, 1931. Kilgore was the hub around which the spokes of the vast East Texas oil field radiated.

Insofar as would be possible, it was vowed that Kilgore would be a law-abiding oil town. That was an ambitious goal. To reach it, constant, dedicated effort on the part of local law enforcement officers and the Texas Rangers would be required. On February 2, 1931, the "Lone Wolf" rode into town, accompanied by his longtime associate J. P. Huddleston. Clad in an olive drab suit, khaki-colored shirt, black tie, boots and wide-brim hat, Gonzaullas made an impressive appearance. He and Huddleston stood out in any crowd. Most of the townspeople were pleased to note their arrival, but the same could not be said about the lawless element, which was growing as fast as Kilgore itself.

Shortly after reaching town, the two Rangers visited the business section to greet old friends in the oil business and to pass on to the parasites, whom they also knew, stern warnings to get out. Some did so immediately. Those who failed to heed the advice were caught up in the enforcement net. Because the crude jail was too small to accommodate the number arrested, the "Lone Wolf" brought out what he called his "trotline." It was a long, heavy-duty chain, onto which trace chains were securely fastened at intervals. At the outer end, each trace chain had a padlock that could be used to fasten it around the ankle or neck of the prisoner. That was before the days of E.R.A. so male and female prisoners were treated differently. The trace chains were locked around the neck of the men and around an ankle of the women, a mark of courtesy toward the latter.

Concluding a public statement as to the reasons the Rangers had been sent, Gonzaullas said, "Crime may expect no quarter in Kilgore. Gambling houses, slot machines, whiskey rings and dope peddlers might as well save the trouble of opening, because they will not be tolerated in any degree. Drifters and transients have their choice of three things: engaging in a legitimate business, getting out of town or going to jail!" Despite the admonition, crime control was not going to be all that easy. The trotline was kept near or at capacity most of the time.

From a humanitarian standpoint, the "Lone Wolf" had to find a building that could be used to house the prisoners fastened to the trotline and get them in out of the weather. He came up with the old First Baptist Church that had been abandoned by the congregation because it had become infested with vermin deposited there by transients who were sleeping in it at night. The long trotline was fastened at each end to the floor and the prisoners allowed to sit or lie on the pews, if they wished. Pointing to the primitive conditions existing at the moment, Gonzaullas reminisced, "When they needed to go to a restroom there wasn't any, so they just passed the bucket." Shotgun-carrying guards, policemen from Chief P. K. McIntosh's force, were on duty twenty-four hours of the day.

As a temporary jail, the old church with its trotline security system was something of a deterrent to wrongdoing, but many among the criminal element assumed the natural human attitude that it could not happen to them and took their chances. Most of them lost their gamble in the long run. Those on the trotline were not only extremely uncomfortable, they were humiliated when people looked in the windows and jeered at them. After a while, the prisoners would plead for their release, promising to leave town and never return. If they were being held in security for petty misdemeanors, they would be freed to run for it, thus making space available on the chain for their successors.

That situation prevailed for a month, during which time the "Lone Wolf" and Huddleston busied themselves in the collection of evidence that would soon be used in the arrest and prosecution of additional violators of the law. At 1:30 on the afternoon of March 2, Captain Tom Hickman and eight Rangers came quietly into Kilgore for the purpose of following the leads that had been secured by the two men. It was the first widespread cleanup in the history of Kilgore. By supper time, around four hundred men and women had been rounded up and arrested. They were marched down the street, which was the Henderson highway, headed toward the jail in the old Baptist Church. The street was lined with spectators to watch the parade pass, their judgment being that it was the most amusing they had ever seen. In the church-jail, all of the prisoners were fingerprinted and charged. Other raids followed until Kilgore was temporarily purged of crime. Captain Hickman and his men withdrew after three days, leaving Bob Goss to replace Huddleston and work with Gonzaullas. Those two men continued the crime control work with such effectiveness that at the beginning of April, a citizens' meeting was held in the schoolhouse to commend the Ranger force publicly "for work they have done here in suppressing crime and protecting citizens from the disreputable element usually associated with oil fields."

Later in the month, the "Lone Wolf" and Goss popped in at Longview, the Gregg County seat. Assisted by the sheriff's department, they seized twenty-five gallons of whiskey and arrested three men, charging them with violation of the Dean Law, Texas' own prohibition act. The whiskey had been concealed in an air pressure tank, which was pronounced to be "one of the most intricate devices for hiding liquor discovered in some time."

Considering the amount of rain that fell and the consequent deplorable condition of streets and roads, it is little less than a marvel that the "Lone Wolf" could maintain his usual neatness and splendor. That he managed to do so was attested by the duly impressed editor of *Gargoyle* magazine, who wrote,

> The niftiest dresser in the Ranger Service is, without a doubt, Sergeant Gonzaullas, who also has the reputation of being one of the nerviest and quickest on the draw. We happened to meet him up in Kilgore, where he is stationed to keep the oil-boomers in hand, and let us tell you his raiment is splendid.
>
> His smooth-shaven, round young face is topped by a big faun-colored Stetson. His olive drab shirt is no humble flannel, but very excellent serge. Its snug collar is pinned beneath an excellent cravat with a long bar-pin. His ornate cowboy boots were shining. Around his waist, on a heavy belt held by an enormous emblem-buckle of gold and silver, hang his most cherished possessions, a pair of the most amazing Colt Automatics you ever saw. This, in itself, is news. The traditional gun among the Rangers was the single-action .45. But that, like other things, has yielded to Progress. He insists the pistols are "a pair," because their ornate bone handles are decorated with the carvings of (respectively) a boy and a girl. He wears the girl on his left hip, closest to his heart. All of the steelwork on the pistols, clear down to their amazing muzzles, is inlaid with gold in intricate patterns. And underneath each, just ahead of the trigger, is his motto—"Never Draw Me Without Cause or Shield [sic] Me With Dishonor."
>
> The sergeant smiles charmingly—he is an altogether delightful fellow when there isn't business to do—when you mention being quick on the draw, and starts talking about his partner, Ranger Goss, who is the finest pistol shot he ever saw. He doesn't think there are half a dozen better shots than Mr. Goss in America. When you go over to Mr. Goss and start talking about that, he shows you his silver saddle. It is all inlaid with silver.

In reporting a June raid on a gambling casino near Kilgore, the *Dallas Times-Herald* caught the reader's attention with its lead, "A teaming company's harness rack was demolished and small trees and shrubbery were trampled down as approximately 500 persons, the majority of them negroes, ran over them in the darkness in an attempt to escape when Rangers and police raided an open-air gambling arena . . . at midnight, where officers found a large assortment of gambling equipment and liquor." The stated total was a slight exaggeration, as the raiding officers estimated the number to be about four hundred.

The "Lone Wolf," Ranger Bob Goss, Kilgore Chief of Police P. K. McIntosh and five of his officers (U. S. Huntsman, Emmett McFall, Kent C. Perry, Howard Wooton and Marvin Wooton) joined in moving on what was called the "Monte Carlo" of the oil field. That term might have been justified insofar as size was concerned, but not for elegance of the gambling quarters.

Even though they were tipped off by a disgruntled patron who had his pockets emptied at the gaming tables there, the officers were not fully prepared for the great number of participants they found in the field casino. The operation was set up in the open air in a three-acre grove at a remote location near Laird Hill about two and one-half miles from Kilgore. It was evident that the management felt secure, because the place was well lighted. Beef, veal, pork and fish were being barbecued over a long pit, the tantalizing odor filling the air. Illegal whiskey and beer were offered in quantity. The estimated four hundred men and women, both black and white, were busily engaged in the various forms of entertainment when the lawmen arrived near midnight.

Upon the alarm being sounded, a rout ensued to the accompaniment of shouts and screams. In panic, more than half of the gamblers rushed off into the darkness like fear-crazed soldiers of a defeated army. Their disorganized flight resulted in many minor injuries as they crashed into tree trunks, the long harness racks and unseen pieces of oil field equipment scattered about on the ground. Most of those who took to their heels managed to get away, some with broken noses, skinned arms and legs and lacerated scalps. The officers did corral 123 people, of whom 23 were women and 10 were white men. They were searched and relieved of such miscellaneous items as knives, straightedge razors and a few handguns. The gambling equipment was completely wrecked before departure of the raiders, the beer and whiskey containers smashed. Those arrested were finally turned over to Sheriff Bill McMurray of Rusk County at about five o'clock in the morning.

It was becoming evident that matters were going downhill because many in the criminal element were not taking seriously the warnings against plying their trade in the East Texas field. Reports

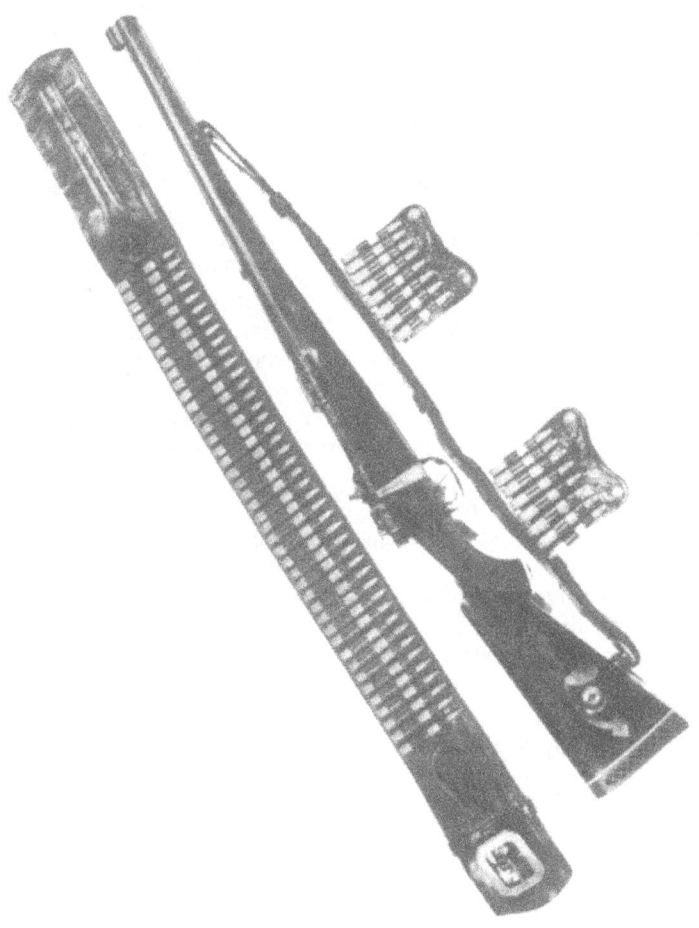

One of Gonzaullas' rifles believed to be a 30-06 Mannlicher-Schoenauer. The cartridges with darker tips probably are tracer bullets. (Courtesy Texas Department of Public Safety.)

were coming in of freewheeling operations in several communities, so the "Lone Wolf" and Goss laid plans to cooperate with county and municipal officers in clamping down on the illegal activities. Longview was the first target with a raid on a music studio on Fredonia Street, where eight and one-half pints of whiskey were seized and two men arrested. A popular roadhouse on the Marshall highway was hit next, arrests of the patrons, the operator and employees were made and an assortment of liquor confiscated. Gregg County Deputy Charlie Gant worked with the Rangers when the roadhouse was entered. After that, a place called the Palace Royal Dance Hall on Ware Street was invaded at 11:00 P.M. by the "Lone Wolf," Goss and deputies on Sheriff Martin Hays' staff. Dressed in civilian clothes and wearing caps, the men were able to gain entrance to the building and seize the guards before a warning buzzer system could be set off. They found that a portion of the dance hall was partitioned off and used for gambling. Arrests of seventy-three followed and weapons were removed from them. Those weapons consisted of thirty-six pocket knives of various lengths, three straightedge razors and two pistols. Before leaving the building, the officers completely destroyed the interior of the gambling hall, along with its equipment.

Gladewater was also on the Rangers' list. Seven arrests were made and a quantity of whiskey seized at a hotel by Gonzaullas, Goss and Gladewater police. A wholesale spree of robberies that occurred in the Kilgore area at the end of June ended with the arrest of two men by the Rangers and Constable Jess Floury. One of those arrested had on his person a wallet belonging to a victim. At a pipeline camp west of Kilgore, twenty-one men were taken into custody on the charge of gambling. The situation was rapidly becoming reminiscent of Wichita County and Borger field lawlessness.

The saddened Gonzaullas and Goss absented themselves from Kilgore long enough to attend the funeral in New Boston of Ranger Dan L. McDuffie, who had been caught in gunfire and accidentally killed by a ricochet bullet in Gladewater on July 7. McDuffie was a passenger in a car driven by the Gladewater chief of police, ex-Ranger W. A. Dial. The shot had been aimed at Dial by an ousted subordinate but struck the steering column of the automobile and glanced off to mortally wound McDuffie. Dial then leaned out of the car and fired, instantly killing the assailant.

McDuffie's death by a quirk of fate was a distinct loss to the Ranger force. He was a thirty-year veteran of law enforcement work and a man with an impeccable record as a peace officer. Forty-eight years old at the time, McDuffie had been closely associated with Gonzaullas in their parallel careers. The "Lone Wolf" was shaken by the tragic event. He, himself, had always exercised the utmost caution in fulfillment of his dangerous duties as a Ranger. When he went into a situation, he planned his actions carefully. He considered what exigencies might arise and what he would do if he were in the other man's boots. His attention to detail in planning gave Gonzaullas the upper hand in situations, but the death of McDuffie was a sobering reminder to him, and his fellow officers, of how continuation or end of life could hang on a freak circumstance. He turned back to the work at Kilgore with increased vigor. The happening at Gladewater had brought back memories of the murder of his brothers.

Gonzaullas and Goss had hardly renewed their campaign against activities around Kilgore when they were ordered by Governor Ross Sterling to join in the "War of the Bridges" on the Red River just north of Denison. In company with two other Rangers, they were to protect employees of the state's highway department when they replaced wrecked barricades at the south end of a new free bridge that had been built as a joint project between Texas and Oklahoma. In addition, they had instructions to prevent a return "invasion" by Oklahoma highway workers, who had smashed and removed the first barricades on orders issued by Governor William H. "Alfalfa Bill" Murray.

The structure had recently been completed alongside a privately owned toll bridge. Owners of the toll bridge asserted that in 1930 the Texas Highway Commission had agreed to a financial arrangement that would provide reimbursement for their now-outmoded bridge, plus other costs. When the time came for placing the new one in service and no payment had been made to the Red River Bridge Company, that firm went to court and secured an injunction which prohibited the opening of its rival until the controversy could be resolved.

That irritated Oklahoma's colorful Governor Murray, who stepped in and endeavored to force the issue, saying that the federal court injunction was issued in Texas and did not apply in Oklahoma. He also asserted that the terms of the Louisiana Purchase in 1803 made the right bank of the Red River the line between the two now-existing states. Both arguments fell on deaf ears. Murray had already tried to bulldoze his way through when he ordered the highway department workers to come to the Texas end of the new bridge and destroy the barricades that had been set up by Texas in line with the court order to prevent crossings until the legal knot could be untangled.

When the Texas Rangers arrived, Murray had the north approach to the toll bridge torn up so it could not be used. An injunction was issued in Oklahoma but was not enforced. He ignored it, declaring martial law along the river and sending in the Oklahoma National Guard. There was little for the Rangers to do except make their presence visible. They spent much of their time in target practice, obviously impressing viewers with their superb marksmanship. Too, they enjoyed the nationwide publicity which pointed up the fact that only four Texas Rangers were needed to handle the Oklahoma National Guard. Much banter passed between the two groups, all the members of which were on amicable terms. Near the end of July, the financial fight was settled. The injunctions were dissolved and the free bridge opened on the twenty-fifth. On that day, the "Lone Wolf" and Goss went back to Kilgore and the mud.

By July 1931, hundreds of oil wells had been drilled within the city limits of the town alone. Mrs. Lou Della Crim, who owned a large amount of property in and near Kilgore, even had some in her yard. Gonzaullas stayed in her home, referring to her as "Mother Crim" and "a very fine lady." In his room there, he kept a minimum of five pairs of boots so he could be sure to have a cleaned, polished pair available at all times, despite the mud of Kilgore. Mrs. Crim's gentle kindness toward him was something he never forgot. He also remembered that she was such a deeply religious person that she would not accept rent payments on Sunday. "You'll have to bring it back tomorrow," he quoted her, "I don't take money on Sunday." He laughed, "She wouldn't accept it but her son, Mayor Malcolm Crim, would take it when she wasn't looking."

The extraordinary amount of drilling activity with its attendant hauling of oil field materials and heavy equipment kept the streets in a deplorable state, even when dry. Following the frequent rains, streets and roads became so bad they would defy description. Even wooden sidewalks in front of store buildings would be caked deep with mud tracked onto them by tramping feet, so they would have to be scraped. Cars, trucks and wagons would become hopelessly mired, most having to remain in place until dry weather conditions returned. The tumult of drilling went on around the clock. Residents had to become inured to the roar and rumble, else there could be no sleep. As was the case with the people of Borger and the carbon black smoke, the citizens of Kilgore could put up with any amount of mud and noise as long as it meant money flowing into their pockets. Within only five years after the discovery well blew in, the East Texas field sprouted 17,500 oil wells. In the city limits of Kilgore alone there were some 700 derricks. The spring fragrance of honeysuckle that once filled the East Texas air was completely blotted out by the smell of oil. Even bacon or ham and eggs frying seemed odorless unless one's nose was right on top of the pan. Clothes reeked of oil, towels and sheets smelled like oil. One longtime resident commented, "It's a wonder our very blood hasn't turned into oil!"

A second widespread series of raids got under way in the Kilgore area in August, when a force of Rangers led by Captain Tom Hickman of Company "B" swooped down on liquor sellers, dance halls and tourist camps, as the crude motels were called in that day. Because of frequent complaints, the captain issued an edict that there would be strict enforcement of the Texas blue law prohibiting dancing on Sunday. That was the same law that kept the circus out of Shamrock. Hickman had brought with him to Kilgore Rangers Stewart Stanley, W. E. Young and M. "Red" Burton. They, plus Gonzaullas and Goss, picked up suspicious characters for questioning in connection with oil field crimes.

At that time the Texas Railroad Commission was trying to enforce a system of production proration on the East Texas field. The commission's effort had begun in earnest during April 1931 but had met with little success. By August it was clear that the commission was powerless to control the unbridled production, as the price of oil dropped to ten cents per barrel at the well. It was a ruinous situation that required Governor Sterling to declare a state of martial law. Foreseeing the problem, Sergeant Gonzaullas had already worked with Colonel H. H. Carmichael, assistant adjutant general, earlier in the month to locate a suitable site on which the Texas National Guard could encamp if necessary. Ultimately it took several years of great turmoil in the oil industry in general and the East Texas field in particular before federal intrusion brought order out of chaos.

The "Lone Wolf" continued on varied assignments in that part of the state as he went about his law enforcement duties. In a whirlwind follow-up on a reported $407 robbery of the cashier at a Kilgore theater in December, Gonzaullas, assisted by Kilgore Chief of Police McIntosh and Officers Marvin Wooton and U. S. Huntsman, had the case wrapped up within two hours. But the arrest of two men in a south Kilgore rooming house had some unanticipated side effects.

At about 9:00 on the evening of the fifteenth, a short, heavyset man without a disguise walked up to the ticket window of the Texan Theatre, poked a pistol at the cashier and demanded the contents of her cash drawer. She complied with his request without hesitation, after which he got into a waiting car and sped away. When the alarm was turned in, the "Lone Wolf" and his companions made a tour of suspected rooming houses where unsavory characters were known to hang out. In one of the houses, they found a man who answered the description of the robber, and a companion. A brief search of the quarters disclosed not only a large amount of cash but also several jewelry items wrapped in a handkerchief and hidden in the tank of a toilet. Of interest to the investigators was the fact that the handkerchief had two holes cut in it, indicating that it had been used as a mask. Questions were raised by the discovery of a black Sam Browne belt, five pistols, two holsters and an assortment of cartridges.

The arrested men were taken to the theater by 11:00 P.M. and one was positively identified by the cashier as the man who had robbed her. They were taken to the jail, charged and locked up, following which a more thorough search was made at the rooming house. Upon examining a small touring car which the men had been driving, the officers found a gold-plated badge inscribed "Louisiana Highway Police. No. 65."

The next morning, communication with the Louisiana Bureau of Identification at Shreveport revealed that the badge belonged to a highway patrolman who had been robbed a month earlier. He was parked at night when two men came up to the car, got the drop on him, robbed and then forced him out of his patrol car. It was an obviously painful experience for the Louisiana officer. The matter had been suppressed in that state but after it became public knowledge following the arrests in Kilgore, the patrolman declined to discuss it, even hanging up on a *Shreveport Times* reporter who was endeavoring to question him on the telephone. The "Lone Wolf," Wooton and Huntsman followed leads that connected the two men to a series of robberies in Eastern Texas and Northwestern Louisiana, also to the rape of a young woman and the beating of her escort.

A high-water mark in the life of Gonzaullas came in February 1932 when he took delivery from George D. Wray, Inc., the Shreveport Chrysler dealership, of a new, specially tailored

On February 21, 1932, the "Lone Wolf" took delivery of this gleaming new 1932 model Chrysler coupe, equipped with a swivel-mounted machine gun in front of the passenger seat. It was used as his scout car.

Chrysler eight-cylinder coupe. It was not only equipped with bulletproof glass but also with a machine gun mounted on a swivel base. In that car, the "Lone Wolf" drove to Fort Worth to join Captain Hickman and Ranger Stanley in a gambling raid on two hotels. One was in the 1000 block of Main and the other was at Seventh and Commerce. In the first raid, on Main, six men were picked up and charged. The other was much more interesting to the Rangers. It came about because an anonymous letter writer had complained to Adjutant General W. W. Sterling in Austin that a gambling operation was being conducted at the Seventh and Commerce address, and further, that Hickman knew about and was protecting it.

Knowing the fallacy of the second accusation, Sterling forwarded the message to Hickman. The latter, Gonzaullas and Stanley strolled into the lobby shortly after noon. The "Lone Wolf" was able to enter the room and actually take part in the crap game without being recognized. However, when Stanley came in a few minutes later, he was recognized and the nine men left $772 unclaimed as they rushed to the door. There they were met by Hickman who quietly herded them back inside, aided in his persuasion by a drawn pistol. After the players were taken to the district attorney's office and charged, Hickman and his fellow Rangers turned their attention to the destruction of the wicker furniture, the big banking table and the water cooler in the room. Hickman smiled as he wielded an axe, saying, "I'm not mad, I'm just rough! Someone told Sterling I was protecting this game and I just wanted to show that I am not!"

Following the imposition of proration on the East Texas field, the problem of "hot oil" became acute. One of innumerable instances occurred at Gladewater, where a celebration of the discovery of oil was under way. There, a twenty-five-man Ranger and National Guard net was closed on eighteen men charged with stealing more than a million barrels of oil in that field alone during the preceding seven months. Persons charged included not only oil field workers but also a railroad agent and a supervisor for the Texas Railroad Commission. Most of the oil was stolen from individuals, but the First Baptist Church of Gladewater also had been defrauded. The "Lone Wolf" was in charge of the detail of Rangers participating in the sweep.

Rangers continued to pursue their work vigorously in the Gladewater area, as well as throughout the East Texas field. However, their work and presence were not fully appreciated by all. At the end of September, the American Legion post joined with the Gladewater city commission in resolutions requesting that Governor Ross Sterling withdraw the Rangers. The request was made on the grounds that "arrests of alleged workingmen on vagrancy charges had a disturbing effect on local mercantile trade." The two groups asserted that citizens of the town desired to have their own officers enforce the law. They stated that the governor had been misled and that Gladewater was "practically free from vice and crime, considering the oil activities in the vicinity." Further, the town was considered "the quietest and most peaceful oil boom town ever known."

Governor Sterling was not impressed. He tartly replied to Mayor A. J. Wood, "This is not borne out from information I am receiving from there every day. Texas Rangers are selected from the best citizenship and they have a reputation throughout the entire nation as peace officers. They are peace officers for the entire state, and if every community in Texas would take the position that Gladewater is taking, concerning the Rangers being in your midst, there would be no place in Texas for them to stay. If Gladewater, as your commissioners seem to think, is a law-abiding community and a fine place in which to live, then I am sure the Rangers will not in any way disturb your law-abiding city."

An entirely different kind of confrontation turned out to be highly amusing to the "Lone Wolf" when a group of late celebrants showed their true colors by turning tail and running. Gonzaullas was in a Tyler hotel trying to get some needed rest just past midnight when his sleep was interrupted by a great amount of commotion below. There was loud talking, raucous laughter, boisterous yelling and general racket. Thinking it would soon cease, he laid a pillow over his head, but that had little deadening effect. When it became evident that there would be no immediate letup in the noise, he got out of bed, went to the window and stuck his head out of it, calling to them to "pipe down." Because of his impatience, he was sharp in tone.

That did it. Members of the group were incensed that anyone would have the gall to admonish them to be quiet. One of them snarled at him to "mind your own business." That was no more acceptable to Gonzaullas than his complaint had been to them, so he carried the matter a bit further by offering to come down and force them to stop.

In a bellicose manner, one of the group shouted, "You don't have to come down here. We'll come up there." So, up the stair they tramped in a body and commenced banging loudly on the door to his room. He opened the door and admitted them, whereupon one of them did a double take and recognized him. "My God, boys," he shouted, "it's the 'Lone Wolf.' Let's scram," and they did just that. The silence that ensued was total.

Gonzaullas at his desk as superintendent of the Bureau of Intelligence in 1937. In this position, as head of DPS detectives and plainsclothesmen, he directed all undercover investigations. (Courtesy Texas Department of Public Safety.)

XI

First of the New-Type Rangers

The Ranger force was approaching a turning point in its long and valiant history. Although there was an unwritten rule against engaging in political activities, the Rangers made no secret of their support of Ross Sterling in his 1932 campaign bid for nomination by the Democratic Party to a second term. His principal opponent was Miriam A. "Ma" Ferguson. Although she led in the primary, a majority was lacking so a runoff was necessary. The runoff total gave Mrs. Ferguson a narrow margin over Governor Sterling, a bitter disappointment to the men of the Ranger force.

In the general election, Mrs. Ferguson won over her Republican opponent, Orville Bullington of Wichita Falls. Bullington received the largest number of votes a Republican gubernatorial candidate in Texas had ever received, 198,000 to Mrs. Ferguson's 328,000.

The die was cast. Captain Hickman and Sergeant Gonzaullas were in the escort as the new governor moved to the platform to take her oath of office on January 17, 1933. The next day they and most of their associates, from the adjutant general down to privates, were on the street with honorable discharges from the service!

There had long been complaints in Texas over the fact that the Rangers were under the direct personal control of the governor. Some prominent Texans had promoted the idea that appointment to the force should be made solely on the basis of experience and training, a merit system so to speak. It was suggested that in no case should political favoritism play a role in naming men as Rangers. When Governor Ferguson made public her appointments to fill the vacancies, a howl of criticism mounted against a number of those whom she and her husband-adviser had picked. The controversy continued on and off throughout the two years of her administration. It was not resolved until the Department of Public Safety was created under the leadership of Governor James V. Allred in 1935 and the Ranger force placed under its jurisdiction. Even that did not please everyone.

Some members of the legislature opposed the creation of the DPS, arguing that the Ranger force would lose its identity and that the new organization would encroach on the rights of local officers. Another strong opinion was that there already were "too many governmental boards, bureaus and departments."

Departure from the Ranger force did not mean that Gonzaullas was to be out of work for long. He was employed as chief special agent for the Atlas Pipe Line Company and Spartan Refining Company, assigned to the familiar East Texas oil field. He extended a helping hand to friends. On his recommendation, eighteen other ex-Rangers went to work as pipeline guards.

Frequent references were soon being made in the press to the deterioration in crime control that occurred in the months following January 18, 1933. The achievements of Gonzaullas and his Ranger associates were compared with conditions later in 1933 and in early 1934. Only three weeks before the notorious Clyde Barrow and Bonnie Parker came to the end of their trail near Gibsland, Louisiana, a prophetic letter was published in the *Dallas Morning News*. It was written by Evans Smith of Kemp, Texas. Smith's thoughts, which were similar to those being expressed all over the state, appeared on May 4, 1934:

> If criminals such as Clyde Barrow and Bonnie Parker are to be caught and placed behind the bars, the state must have a Ranger force that is adequately mobilized and armed. The men on this force should be men who have little of that quality known as fear, and a lot of manhood, love of right, courage and the knowledge that their state government is ready to stand behind them in any and all crises.
> Give Texas more Rangers of the caliber of "Lone Wolf" Gonzaullas, and the crime wave we are going through will not be of long duration. Arm these men with the criminals' own weapon, the machine gun, and give them orders to get

their prisoner dead or alive, and we will find that Texas crime will take a very decided drop. We will also find the law-abiding citizen without the constant fear that his property will be purloined and his life jeopardized.

It is said that an ounce of prevention is worth a pound of cure. Let Texas use this ounce of prevention by training men in the way of the law and through the Boy Scout movement, but also let Texas have her pound of cure ready for those persons who persist in breaking the law. This cure, as I see it, is in the enlarging of the Ranger force, the highway patrol and a closer banding together of the law enforcing bodies of Texas: the establishment of a central office at some strategic point where criminal records, fingerprints and other material of a like nature could be used by all forces, and where a competent corps of specialists in this work could help any sheriff, police chief or officer, or any private citizen who is trying to help the officers of his state, county and city in the "depression" of a criminal population.

Let the people of Texas rise up and call for a united effort on the part of the governor, the county judges, the county sheriffs, and themselves, to do away with this dark spot that is being formed on the white pages of Texas history.

Smith was speaking with the voice of the near future.

As oil company chief special agent, Gonzaullas' permanent residence had been in Gregg County for fifteen months. In April 1934, at the urging of well-meaning friends, he decided to have a fling at politics and announced his candidacy for the office of sheriff, running against the incumbent, Will H. Hayes. Gonzaullas conducted an active campaign but lost to Hayes. He declared, after the vote count, that his one experience in running for elective office was enough to last him for a lifetime and that he could be counted out of future races.

He continued as chief special agent until January 1, 1935, when he went to work as chief investigator on the staff of District Attorney Claude A. Williams of Longview. Williams and Gonzaullas made a good team. In his own campaign for office, the new district attorney had pledged to "clean up the disgraceful situation regarding law violators." The "Lone Wolf" was equally dedicated to his assignment. Results began to flow almost immediately. By January 4 a Longview racehorse bookie, who had been enjoying a flourishing business, was arrested along with fifteen others. By the ninth, injunctions had been secured in district court to shut down a gambling house and to stop the movement of 860 cases of liquor out of warehouses in Longview where, it was stated, they had been stored in violation of the Texas liquor law. Prohibition was dying hard in Texas and in its last gasps caused difficulty for persons who knew its end was near but tried to jump the gun. The Twenty-first Amendment to the federal Constitution had become effective on December 15, 1933, repealing the Eighteenth, or prohibition, Amendment. However, the Texas prohibition law remained on the books until its repeal was ratified by voters in August 1935. Until that date arrived, state officers kept hammering away at moonshiners and bootleggers.

As it turned out, the "Lone Wolf" had been biding his time. He intended to be ready when things opened up again in Austin. The end of the Ferguson administration and the inauguration of James V. Allred as governor in January 1935 held promise of better things to come.

With enabling legislation passed by the Forty-fourth Legislature, Governor Allred's favored Department of Public Safety was established effective August 10, 1935. It was a merger of the Texas Rangers and the Highway Patrol into a unified policing body. Funding was scheduled to begin on September 1. L. G. Phares, chief of the 120-man Highway Patrol, was named acting director of the Department of Public Safety. When recruitment for staffing the divisions, or bureaus, had been completed, announcement was made by Public Safety Commission Chairman A. S. Johnson, through Phares, that Tom Hickman would be in command of the Ranger force with the title of senior captain. In addition to his own new title, Phares continued to command the patrol division, which post he had held since its organization in 1930.

C. G. McGraw of Beaumont was picked to head the Bureau of Identification and M. T. Gonzaullas was brought from Longview to be superintendent of the Bureau of Intelligence. Homer Garrison, Jr., assistant director of the department, was placed in charge of the Bureau of Training and Education.

The "Lone Wolf" was admirably suited to carry out the responsibilities of his new assignment. In it he became the Department of Public Safety's head of detectives and plainclothesmen, directing all investigations of an undercover nature. The Bureau of Intelligence was charged with accumulating and analyzing information on criminal activities in the state, all to be done in full cooperation with county and municipal law enforcement agencies. That included the taking of fingerprints of criminals and victims,

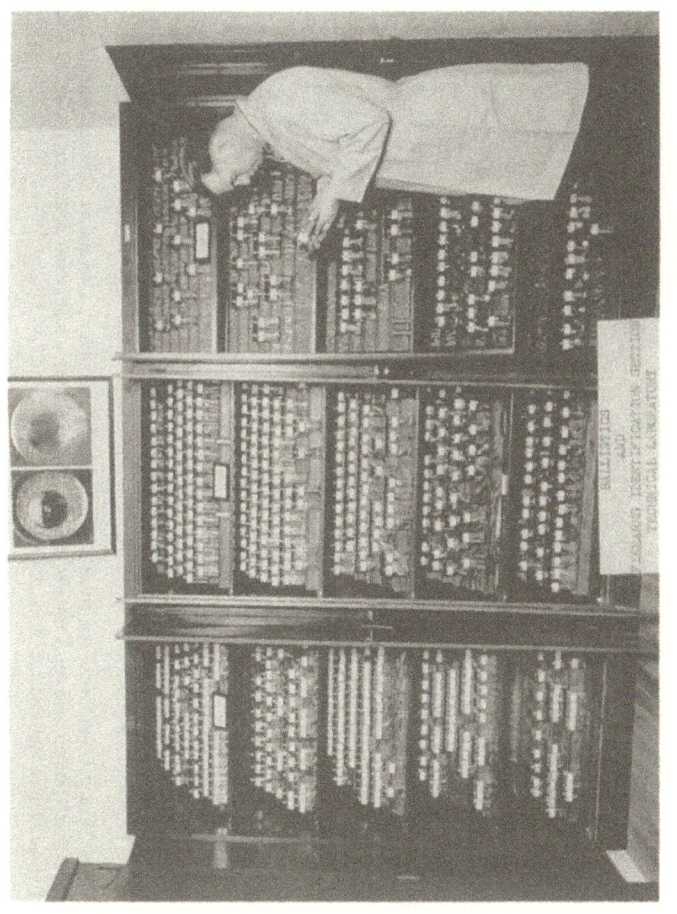

Gonsaullas in the DPS Bureau of Intelligence gun room in 1938. (Courtesy Texas Ranger Hall of Fame and Museum.)

Crime section laboratory of the Texas Department of Public Safety. Gonzaullas, although trained as an "old style" Ranger, was an early advocate of scientific methods of crime detection. (Courtesy Texas Ranger Hall of Fame and Museum.)

the prints being referred to the companion Bureau of Identification for examination. Ballistics tests would be made and, when the occasion warranted, handwriting would be analyzed. Gonzaullas had received intensive training in those fields at Washington and New York during the time he was an investigator for the United States Treasury Department in and after World War I. That schooling had enabled him to achieve his outstanding record as a Ranger while investigating crimes and tracking down the perpetrators.

With establishment of the Department of Public Safety, it could be said that law enforcement in Texas had made the transition from "horse and buggy days" to the modern world in crime prevention and control. In praising the appointment of Gonzaullas to his new post, the *San Antonio Express* commented, "Mr. Gonzaullas was the first of the new-type Rangers—as quick on the draw as the old, but a terror to the evildoers, even more for his knowledge of criminology, his skill in reading finger prints and identifying handwriting or in tracing the killer by the bullet fired from the pistol and his ability in deducing important facts from the slenderest clues. A long list of solved crimes and captured fugitives stands to his credit. His nickname 'Lone Wolf' suggests keen efficiency when alone on the criminal trail, yet the new chief has demonstrated capacity for working with other men."

Although the Rangers and Highway Patrol retained their identities, there was grumbling among some segments of law enforcement groups in the state who took the attitude that the coordination of the two bodies downgraded both. That belief was dispelled as the advantages of the new Department of Public Safety became apparent, even to the most obstinate opponents.

Phares pointed to some of the advantages of the change when he said,

> Until the Texas Rangers were transferred to this Department, they made up the law enforcement agency of the governor, under the direction of the adjutant general, and with every change of administration they were subject to change. Working under these conditions hampered their chances of accomplishing the best results in return for their efforts. However, the Rangers are now under an overlapping Commission and their worries in that connection can be removed and they can devote their entire time to their work without giving undue thought to ways and means of holding their positions with a change of each administration. The

Rangers will continue to work under the direction of captains and will be assigned to certain companies, as they have been in the past. With the inauguration of the new Safety Department, Rangers assigned to the various companies will have certain territory to work in and, unless an emergency arises, they will be required to confine their work to that territory to prevent a duplication of effort and time. This particular division of the Safety Department will remain as the principal criminal law enforcement organization; however, the other divisions of the Safety Department will always be ready and willing to cooperate with the Rangers in any way that they can . . . .

Recognizing the importance of good public relations, Phares observed that the goal was to develop a department as famous as the Rangers and as polite as the men of the Highway Patrol. Speaking of the past, he commented, "Fee-grabbing officers had prejudiced motorists against every man on a motorcycle. The motor patrol, on its establishment, was instructed to be helpful and courteous, while firm. Today motorists welcome them." He pointed out that much the same situation had existed concerning Rangers. "Axe-swinging raids have created ill-feeling. Local officers resented their [Rangers'] appearance . . . . I know of only two conditions that justify sending Rangers into a community. One is when local officers ask for their aid and the other is when local officers refuse to act." A new era had, indeed, dawned.

The Bureau of Intelligence had its first real test of proficiency when its services were requested in the solution of a crime near Clifton in Bosque County. A Clifton man was cut to death with a knife and axe, after which his body was dumped on the GC&SF railroad tracks so it would appear that the victim had been run over by a train. The preliminary setback for the two murderers was the alertness of the locomotive engineer on the next train that approached the spot. The engineer saw the body on the track in the distance. Because the train was moving at a less-than-normal speed, he was able to bring it to a halt just short of the scene.

The crime had been committed on the very day that the "Lone Wolf" assumed the superintendency of the bureau. After local work proved fruitless, District Attorney Penn Jackson of Meridian requested the help of the Department of Public Safety. Working under the guidance of Gonzaullas, bureau investigators J. N. Thompson and John T. Cope pieced together circumstantial evidence that led to the arrest and conviction of the knife and axe wielders. One of the murderers received a sentence of fifty years, and the other was sent to the penitentiary for forty years. The handling of the case was an auspicious start for the brand new bureau.

Within the first ninety days of its establishment, there were referred to the bureau thirty-four felony cases, of which twenty-seven were completely solved in that time. Fourteen of those cases involved murder. The bureau's advanced methods of investigation and solution intrigued Texans. Included in the precise, scientifically based work were such activities as the examination of documents, development of obliterated data on metal (such as motor serial numbers), scrutiny of gunshot and knife wounds on murder victims, analysis of blood stains and of hair, of textile fibers and of flesh, all done in the laboratory. There were scientific checks of glass fractures, firearms (including ballistics tests and comparisons), traces of gunpowder on hands, and numerous other chemistry-based investigations. In the matter of fingerprinting, bureau members would not only take rolled impressions but also lift latent prints by composition and photography. Such things were no longer mere science fiction, they were procedures being utilized in the everyday work of law enforcement in Texas.

The work and responsibilities of Gonzaullas' Bureau of Intelligence and McGraw's Bureau of Identification were so interlaced that in some instances it was difficult at first for county and city officers to fully distinguish between them. The personnel and equipment of the scientific crime-detecting laboratory were used by both, and the meshing of their programs made it increasingly difficult for crimes to be committed without speedy solution and consequent apprehension of those involved. Early in 1936, Governor Allred spoke of the marked reduction in the crime rate, pointing to the fact that the effectiveness of the Department of Public Safety's program had resulted in a migration of major criminals from the state.

During the 1936 Texas Centennial Exposition in Dallas, Gonzaullas (*left*), then chief of the DPS Bureau of Intelligence, looks on as C. G. McGraw (*right*), chief of the DPS Bureau of Identification, fingerprints FBI Director J. Edgar Hoover. (Courtesy Texas Department of Public Safety.)

XII
Science Against the Criminal

Fort Davis, Texas, was the focus of the spotlight of public attention in April 1936 during the trial of a Kermit man on a charge of killing deer out of season. Gonzaullas' Bureau of Intelligence provided the unusual bit of evidence that convicted him. During the previous season, deer hunting had been restricted to the period between November 16 and 30 in that section of the state. On December 8, the carcasses of eight freshly killed does had been found on a ranch in the vicinity of Fort Davis. Game Wardens Ray Williams and Curtis McElroy reached the reported location and found much of the venison was missing. However, one carcass was whole. From it, the wardens removed a .25-35 caliber bullet. Determined to run down the culprit, they started with a list of 265 names and, by the process of elimination, worked down to a small group of hunters who, it turned out, had actually been in the area at the approximate time of the killings. They further learned that the members of the hunting party were still in the Davis Mountains.

On meeting the hunters in what was made to appear a casual encounter, the wardens noted one of the men had a rifle of the caliber in question. Without their purpose being suspected, they borrowed the gun and fired a bullet from it, later retrieving that bullet. They sent it and the one they had removed from the carcass to the "Lone Wolf" for scrutiny. Under microscopic examinations, markings on the two bullets were seen to be identical, thus tying that rifle to the illegally killed deer. Gonzaullas sent a bureau representative to the trial at Fort Davis. He was armed with photographic blowups of the two bullets with their telltale identical markings. Upon the introduction of this irrefutable evidence, the jury was convinced. The hunter was convicted and fined. It was the first case in Texas in which a ballistics test had been used to pin guilt on a man charged with illegal slaying of a protected animal.

About this time, the Rangers began using airplanes to patrol the mountainous country of far Western Texas in the never-ceasing battle against smugglers and outlaws crossing the Rio Grande from Mexico. The "Lone Wolf" was not directly involved at the time, but he watched with interest this new advance in methods to apprehend criminals in that remote region.

Flying over and around the majestic Chisos Mountains, gliding into the canyon defiles and skimming the lower mountain masses and valleys, the Rangers tied air reconnaissance to ground pursuit by men in automobiles and on horseback. That first Ranger air patrol team consisted of Pete Crawford and Levi Duncan. In five hours they could cover an area that would require thirty days to comb thoroughly by ground alone.

Before they turned to the planes, which were made available to the Rangers and to Customs agents and the Border Patrol by the air arm of the United States Coast Guard, days or weeks had been required to track down smugglers and outlaws. The number who escaped that slow coverage was a factor in bringing the Ranger force to this revolutionary phase. Because radio communication was still in its infancy, written messages would be dropped from the plane to ground personnel, who would be stationed at strategic points with horses. Trucks to pull horse trailers were coming into general use, thus expediting the movement to spots where the ground patrol could mount and begin their pursuit in the incredibly rough country. As Border Patrol planes do now, the Ranger plane would circle the quarry, keeping the ground teams in full knowledge of the whereabouts of the objects of the chase.

Horses and pack mules were still indispensable to the Rangers along the river, because few roads penetrated the rocky, deeply eroded landscape. Use of the planes by rifle-equipped officers discouraged intrusion into Texas but by no means brought it to a halt. Smugglers and outlaws were obliged to change their tactics. Because of air reconnaissance, they found it advisable to move at night and try to conceal their daytime hideouts. Sometimes they succeeded, but more often they failed.

Ballistics tests were employed by Gonzaullas to pin down the guilt of a Waco man who was accused of firing five shots into a residence where his ex-wife was staying. He was said to have been aiming at the bed on which he supposed she was lying. The fact that she had fled into another room of the house saved her life. When arrested, he denied the charges.

Officers secured some of the bullets that had lodged in the room. Then they obtained a .38 caliber Smith and Wesson revolver belonging to the man. Two bullets were fired from it and they, together with those that had been taken from the room, were sent to the "Lone Wolf" for examination.

In the Fifty-fourth District Court at Waco, Gonzaullas set up his double microscope. A bullet retrieved from the bedroom was placed under one lens; another bullet, test fired from the accused's gun, was placed under the second lens. The members of the jury carefully examined the bullets through the microscope, seeing for themselves how the markings were perfectly matched.

The defendant, overwhelmed by the weight of the scientific evidence that had been brought to bear against him, took the witness stand and, on advice from his attorney, admitted that he did fire the five shots into the house where his now-divorced wife was living. But, he assured the court, he was only trying to frighten her and had no intention whatsoever of bringing bodily harm to her. The fact that three of the bullets penetrated the mattress on her bed was claimed to have been purely accidental. The jury was not impressed by what he called "a little joke" and returned a verdict of guilty. As in the case of the illegal killing of the deer, denial by the culprit was of no avail in the face of incontrovertible evidence. To the jury, the Waco man's change of story emphasized the tremendous importance of scientific proof. Gonzaullas' presentation was called "magic" by an impressed newspaper reporter.

Gonzaullas' skill in sifting through conflicting data was brought into play when the Bureau of Intelligence was called upon to conduct a postconviction investigation. The case involved a Mexican national, Antonio Carrasco, who had received a death sentence in a trial for the murder of fifty-eight-year-old Mrs. Riley Smith in Culberson County at her home fourteen miles southeast of Van Horn, Texas. Mrs. Smith's death, along with that of her husband, age sixty-two, had occurred on June 2, 1934. The district court trial ended with a sentence of death by electrocution. That conviction was upheld by the court of criminal appeals. The attorney for the sentenced ranch hand claimed racial discrimination in the original investigation and in the trial procedures, the latter insofar as selection of a jury was concerned. The appeals court had ruled that the record showed no discrimination against Mexicans solely because of race, "which must be proved to sustain the allegation."

For their part, some southwestern peace officers were not convinced in the early stages of the matter that all angles of the case were clearly solved. On request, the Rangers had conducted an inquiry into the possibility of a conspiracy but found no evidence to support that theory. After the trial, verdict and rejected appeal, a relative of the Smiths advanced the belief that valuable papers and money they were understood to have possessed motivated the slayings. It was at that point that the "Lone Wolf" began the detailed postconviction investigation.

The murders of Mr. and Mrs. Smith had created a sensation in Western Texas. Following the deed, their ranch house was set afire. The bodies, which were in the residence, were burned almost beyond recognition. The news first reached Van Horn at about 11:00 P.M. on June 2 when Carrasco, the Smith's thirty-eight-year-old unmarried ranch hand, came to town in a light truck to notify the sheriff. That officer was out in the county in company with a highway patrolman investigating an automobile accident. In his absence, Carrasco went to the constable, to whom he stated that he had found the Smiths' house ablaze and feared they were trapped inside. He told the officer that he went first to the Garren ranch, about four miles east of the Smiths', but found no one there, so he came to Van Horn.

Several townspeople went with the constable and Carrasco to the Smiths' ranch, where the ashes of the house were still smoldering. Highly respected citizens of the community, the Smiths also maintained a residence in Marfa, so Mr. Garren, who had come with the group, returned to Van Horn and telephoned L. C. Brite at Marfa to determine whether the Smiths might be at their home there. They were not. The couple had extensive holdings in investments, cash, land and bank stock. The ranch, which was regarded as one of the best in the area, contained about forty-five sections, a total of approximately twenty-nine thousand acres.

It was noted that both of the passenger cars belonging to the Smiths were in the detached garage. A pickup standing outside showed evidence of having recently been washed. Suspicions were aroused when bloodstains were noted on a metal wheelbarrow and on sacks of feed in the corral. Fragments of skull bone were discovered there along with bits of brain matter.

During questioning, the ranch hand explained that he had killed a sick calf in the corral on the previous day, after which he loaded it into a truck and took it to a distant spot where it was dumped. When he was taken to the place where the calf was allegedly thrown out, no sign of the animal could be seen. He suggested that coyotes must have dragged it off. A short time later he was placed under arrest and, on Sunday morning, was transferred to the county jail in El Paso.

There then followed a series of contradictory signed statements by Carrasco. First he said he discovered the ranch house ablaze when he returned from working in a nearby pasture. In the second, and more involved, statement he said,

> I hit Mr. Smith over the head with a board after he fired two shots at me. He was angry at me because I wouldn't gallop my horse while rounding up about 30 head of cattle. When I got to the corral, he drew a gun and said, "I'll kill you, you _____." Then he fired at me. I finished rounding up the herd and then got a piece of wood.
> I met Mr. Smith in the yard, walked up to him and struck him on the head. He staggered into the house. Mrs. Smith came running at me with a butcher knife. In self defense I struck her over the head. She fell to the floor. Mr. Smith had fallen onto the floor of the same room. I felt hungry, so I went to the kitchen to get something to eat. I poured some gasoline into a wood stove. There was an explosion and flames seemed to be everywhere and there was no chance to get Mr. and Mrs. Smith from the burning house. I am sorry that all this happened. I guess I'm lost.

In his third signed statement, the man asserted that the fire began when Mrs. Smith was attempting to light a gasoline lamp and it exploded, igniting her clothing.

The investigation was made by Culberson County officers and later corroborated by the Ranger inquiry. It was concluded that the Mexican national had killed Mr. Smith in the corral and then had gone to the house and murdered Mrs. Smith, after which he returned to the corral. It was deduced that he placed Smith's body in the wheelbarrow, rolled it to the house, placed the corpse inside the building, which was set afire. Blood was found on a shotgun in the bunkhouse the man occupied. Near the gasoline pump there was evidence of recently burned clothing. In addition, bloodstains were noted on the nozzle of the pump hose. It was further observed that efforts had been made to remove bloodstains from the corral by scooping up sand and hauling it in the truck a distance of about six hundred feet, where it was dumped.

After daylight on Sunday, June 3, the remains of the Smiths' bodies were found in the house ruins, as were articles which were recognized as having been pieces of her jewelry. Accompanied by J. D. Neill, Assistant District Attorney John W. Penn and Special Investigator Roy Chitwood of El Paso were at the ranch to make photographs of the ruins and bodies, the wheelbarrow and other objects for investigative use.

Then, another statement came from Carrasco. In it, he said that he killed Mr. Smith with a blast from the shotgun and that Mrs. Smith had possibly witnessed the act. He asserted that she helped him carry her husband's body to the house, where it was placed on a cot in the kitchen. He said he became overcome with fear, so he killed Mrs. Smith by striking her on the head with a piece of stove wood.

Robbery was dismissed by Culberson County investigators as a possible motive when the jewelry was found in the debris of the residence. A paramount question was why the man had not immediately fled the short distance to the Rio Grande and made his way across the river to sanctuary in Mexico. He did not confirm it, but the theory was advanced that he thought the crime was completely covered and, further, because he had worked for the Smiths for a number of years and had outwardly good relations with them during that time, he believed he would be remembered in their wills, hopefully with a bequest of the ranch itself. The Smiths had no children.

Sitting in the El Paso jail and realizing the hopelessness of his situation, Antonio Carrasco made a will on the Tuesday following the death of the couple. In the will, he left his automobile, saddle, bridle, boots, spurs and other personal effects to his "old time cowboy friend K. C. Shannon, deputy sheriff of El Paso County." He asked that the items be picked up at once from the bunkhouse on the ranch and delivered to Shannon at Ysleta. He was fatalistic about the outcome of his trial.

When the case came before the district court in its October term at Van Horn, the defendant pleaded "not guilty." A jury could not be obtained in Culberson County so a change of venue was granted, moving it to adjacent Hudspeth County. The trial was held during March 1935 at Sierra Blanca, resulting in a verdict of guilty and sentence of death in the electric chair.

The Department of Public Safety became involved in April 1936. Following an exhaustive inquiry into all facets of the murder and the trial, Gonzaullas announced that he was satisfied that "there was no accomplice or conspiracy in the crime." Commenting on the thorough working of every angle of the case, he noted, "If there are any papers or money missing, we do not believe they had any connection with the killings. The investigation did not reveal any valuable papers that had not previously been found and were a matter of record."

The "Lone Wolf" also stated that he attached no importance to the fact that the convicted murderer had refused to talk since his incarceration in the jail at El Paso subsequent to the conviction. The ranch hand was not tried for the murder of Mr. Smith. At his trial for the slaying of Mrs. Smith, the state advanced as a motive that "she was killed to do away with the only possible witness to the death of her husband." In affirming the conviction, the appeals court held admissible testimony concerning Mr. Smith's death on the grounds that "the crimes were inter-mixed and blended with one another and so connected that they formed an indivisible criminal transaction." The court also found no merit in a defense objection to the introduction of a statement that Carrasco had made and later repudiated. In it, he had pleaded an alibi.

Back in Austin, the ugly head of discord surfaced in the ranks of the Rangers as a group of county sheriffs expressed vocal antagonism toward L. G. Phares. The pot boiled over in May 1936. The departmental difficulty came to public notice when Senior Ranger Captain Tom Hickman was ousted. That precipitated a legislative investigation. It reached white heat when Phares was named permanent director of the Department of Public Safety by a two-to-one vote of the commission. The dissenting member, D.D. Baker, resigned in protest and Governor Allred appointed W.H. Richardson of Dallas to succeed him. Phares submitted his resignation "in the best interest of the Department." It was finally accepted with reluctance by the Public Safety Commission.

Following Hickman's removal, his successor as senior captain, J. W. McCormick, made known his intention to resign, but the governor persuaded him to remain. The commission advanced H. B. Purvis at Lufkin to the captaincy of Company "A" on the recommendation of Phares, as one of his final acts before stepping down as director. Phares became head of both the Highway Patrol and the Drivers License Bureau. Colonel Horace H. Carmichael was appointed as director of the department to succeed Phares. Chairman Johnson remarked, "He was drafted for this position just as Mr. Phares had been previously drafted. Col. Carmichael was not an applicant and did not even know he was being considered." During that turnover, M. T. Gonzaullas made no comments that are of record. He had enough of politics and would not be drawn into a discussion of the situation.

The fires of the controversy were still cooling when the "Lone Wolf" was selected to join Phares and Purvis in reinforcing President Franklin D. Roosevelt's Secret Service staff when the chief executive visited Texas in June 1936. Although his visit was part of a broad tour, its emphasis in Texas was to coincide with the celebration of the centennial of independence from Mexico. The trio met the president's train at Texarkana upon its arrival from Arkansas and stayed with the party until departure into Oklahoma. Governor and Mrs. Allred, together with United States Senator and Mrs. Morris Sheppard, also entrained at Texarkana.

On August 24, 1936, the *Dallas Morning News* paid editorial tribute to the Texas Ranger force:

> It is fitting in more ways than one that the Texas Rangers should be given a high place of honor at the Texas Centennial. Since the days of Stephen F. Austin, the Rangers have faced everything from the poisoned flints of the Comanches to the machine guns of the modern gangsters. If they have faltered a few times, it has been because they are human. On the whole, their record extending through a hundred years is equaled by few if any similar bodies of law enforcing officers.
>
> The Rangers have given the people of Texas protection from redskin, Mexican raider, frontier robber and desperado, mob violence and the more modern forms of defiance of law and order. They have not done so without leaving many of their comrades on the field of battle. Their record has brought glory not only to the Rangers themselves but to all of Texas. The Ranger has become symbolic of the heroism with which Texas has been carved from the wilderness. For these things, the Ranger deserves the high place of honor given him.
>
> At the same time, the Ranger deserves recognition because the organization is Texan by birth and growth. It is thoroughly indigenous . . . . Even the application of the name seems to have come by common consent rather than by desig-

nation by statute. The Texas Ranger came into existence and remained in existence because there was peculiar need for him. He made the record that he did because the service for which the Ranger was needed offered opportunity for the spirit of daring and defiance of hardship that characterized the vanguard of Western civilization.

Through a hundred years they have fought, as Senator Sheppard said, "to give our turbulent young Lone Star State the life whose anniversary we celebrate this year." Like the State, the Rangers face their second hundred years. Their record will be what they make it. A good start will be to follow the admonition of Albert Sidney Johnson, chairman of the Public Safety Commission, which is "no politics."

The success of the Bureau of Intelligence under the direction of the "Lone Wolf" was indicated in the first annual report made to DPS Director H. H. Carmichael. It covered the period from September 1, 1935, to August 31, 1936. In that time the bureau completed 140 out of 142 cases referred to it, including 56 murder probes. Its staff participated in offense solution work throughout the state, covering almost every type of criminal law violation. Branching into the ever-expanding use of scientific developments, the bureau used electrical equipment to retrieve evidence that was under water. On eleven occasions in that first year, sound equipment was brought into play to gather additional evidence. Those extensions illustrated the progress that was rapidly being made in detection, investigation and enforcement. It was a new science and the "Lone Wolf" was utilizing it to the fullest. Gonzaullas commented that "scientific methods are proving to be more effective than any 'third degree.'"

He again demonstrated the significance of the startling new methods when he was called to the stand in the San Antonio trial of a man accused of the murder of a Public Service Company bus driver. Gonzaullas testified in connection with ballistics tests on the .38 caliber bullet that had been removed from the body of the driver and on one fired from a pistol that had been found in the possession of the accused man on the night of the murder. He stated that both bullets passed through the same gun barrel.

"Then, in your opinion," the assistant district attorney asked, "the bullet which killed Forbes came from that gun?" pointing to the exhibit.

"There is no *opinion* to it," Gonzaullas replied. "It *was* fired from that gun."

Microphotographs of the two bullets were furnished to the members of the jury. That scientific evidence played a significant role in the jurors reaching their verdict of "guilty" and the assessment of punishment in the form of death by electrocution.

In another scientific step, the first paraffin test ever made in Austin was handled by the "Lone Wolf." Its purpose was to show whether the hand of an accused man held the pistol from which a fatal shot was fired, taking the life of a woman. Even scrubbing one's hands with soap and water would not remove telltale traces of exploded gases and gunpowder from the skin of the hand that held and fired a pistol.

Along with ballistics checks, paraffin tests became routine with the Bureau of Intelligence, the results of both types circumventing contrary claims made by individuals being investigated. Most of the time those tests brought voluntary confessions, but when they did not, the proof they offered was invariably convincing to jurors. No longer could criminals maintain innocence by lying and get away with it. The tests caught them. Gonzaullas made a thought-provoking statement. "The more careful a criminal is," he said, "the more likely he is to be apprehended. The most difficult problems are offered by casual, unpremeditated crimes!"

Studying new developments and improving old scientific methods absorbed Gonzaullas' interest. Shortly after the New Year of 1937, he accompanied DPS Director Carmichael on a two-month tour of the Northeastern United States and Eastern Canada. There they delved into advances in crime detection methods so that the Texas Department of Public Safety would keep abreast of progress in this field. In part as a result of that study, the department could boast in 1938 that its Crime Detection Laboratory was second in the United States only to that of the FBI in Washington. "And that's just because we haven't as much money as they have," the "Lone Wolf" commented!

Then came a blow to the department and to Gonzaullas personally. Colonel Carmichael was stricken with a heart attack as he was driving his car in Austin in late September. He died immediately. To continue the strong leadership that Carmichael had given to the Department of Public Safety in the two years he had served as director, the commission named Colonel Homer Garrison, Jr., to succeed him.

Near the end of 1938, Gonzaullas pointed out that on evidence furnished by the DPS laboratory, fourteen men had been sentenced to the electric chair and that "prison terms aggregating 4,800 years have been meted out to those convicted on scientific evidence in the past three years."

Gonzaullas commented also on the expanded role of Highway Patrolmen. "When the patrol was under the Highway Department," he said, "patrolmen only had criminal jurisdiction within the boundaries of the state highways, streets and roads. Their police powers ended at the curb. You can see how effectively they were hamstrung." Pointing to their current efficient operations, he commented, "That was changed in the reorganization process when the DPS came into being and the Legislature gave the Highway Patrolmen powers similar to those of the Rangers. That was a realistic approach to the problem."

As 1939 slid into the new year of 1940, M. T. Gonzaullas was becoming increasingly restive. He was bored, and that was an emotional condition he could not tolerate. His record as Superintendent of the Bureau of Intelligence was superb, but there were few challenges left. The bureau was well organized and it was staffed with competent employees. It was his feeling that he was now excess baggage, that the bureau could continue to run efficiently even if he were not there. Gonzaullas had worked doggedly to reach that goal, but now that it had been achieved he felt the need for a change of direction in his life. Like a bloodhound sniffing the trail, he knew where he wanted to be—back in Ranger service, out in the field matching wits with those who connived to outsmart the law.

The subject met with something less than enthusiasm on the part of his superiors, who would have been pleased for him to forget all about that and remain where he was doing the good job for which he had become noted. Gonzaullas was respectful but adamant in his desire to be transferred back to the Ranger service, "when it should become feasible," as he expressed it.

Laura Gonzaullas viewed the requested change in assignment with the same lack of enthusiasm as that expressed by Department of Public Safety officials. They stated it openly. She would have little to say and certainly would not discourage him if a return to Ranger service was what he really wanted. His contentment had always been her primary concern.

Nevertheless, she dreaded such reassignment. For almost five years, Laura had enjoyed peace of mind in the knowledge that her "Manny" was at home with her in the evenings and not out chasing criminals. His expressed wish did not take her unawares. She had seen it coming for more than a year, but had no means at her command to divert it. If he did go back into Ranger service, and she knew that he surely would, she would accept it with resignation and with complete trust in God to continue to keep His hand on the shoulder of her husband. The faith that He would do so made the future easier to face.

For his part, Gonzaullas' wait was mercifully short. On Valentine's Day, 1940, Department of Public Safety Director Homer Garrison, Jr., announced changes in personnel and bureau organization following a lengthy meeting of the commission. Effective on February 26, 1940, Gonzaullas was appointed captain of Company "B" with headquarters in Dallas. That city would be home for the remainder of his and Laura's lives. "Perhaps," she mused to a friend, "it is for the best after all."

The "Lone Wolf" changed places with Captain Royal Phillips. It was further announced that the Crime Detection Laboratory would be merged with the Bureau of Identification and Records under Joe S. Fletcher, chief. Captain Phillips' duties as chief of the Bureau of Intelligence were to be principally concerned with the maintenance of records on criminal activities and the consolidation of crime reports.

Gonzaullas was back in his element and supremely happy once more. Ahead for him were exciting times and narrow escapes. He would go down in history as the first American of Spanish descent to achieve the rank of captain in the Texas Ranger force.

XIII

Sixth Sense at Work

Captain Gonzaullas, together with Company "B" Rangers Ernest Daniel and Bob Crowder, responded to a request from Lamar County for help. Deputy Sheriff George Robertson was missing, along with two suspects he had picked up for questioning. The local officers had reached a dead end. Just before the Rangers arrived in Lamar County, the body of the deputy was found in a remote spot. Then, the energy of all was turned to the search for the two young men with whom he was last seen.

On September 10, 1940, fifty-four-year-old Deputy Robertson had gone with Sheriff J. H. Ratliff to Carpenter's Service Station on Lamar Avenue in Paris, in answer to a telephone call advising that two men were trying to sell a tire for a low price. The station operator suspected the tire had been stolen. He delayed them long enough for the officers to arrive. Ratliff and Robertson talked to the men for a few minutes, then the sheriff decided they should be taken to headquarters for further questioning. Regrettably, neither the youths nor the car they were driving were searched. Robertson got into the back seat of a 1939-model green Ford two-door sedan, placing the two on the front seat where he could watch them. Sheriff Ratliff returned to the patrol car and led the way. That was just after 2:00.

The vehicles became separated in a traffic snarl at Twenty-third and Lamar, and Ratliff was unable to keep his eye on the Ford for a few minutes. When the traffic cleared and the sheriff looked into his rearview mirror, the green car was not to be seen behind him. Supposing that Robertson must have directed the driver to turn off on a side street in order to bypass the jam, the sheriff continued to the courthouse to wait for them. After sufficient time had passed for the other vehicle to arrive and it had not, he became concerned and a general alarm was spread.

Residents on North Twenty-third Street soon reported that they saw two men fighting in a green car that passed them. As it went by, they heard several gunshots. Following that lead, officers traced the car's movement to Hinckley. Then it was reported that a car fitting the description had been seen near Grant.

A massive manhunt spread out over that portion of Northeastern Texas and was later extended into Southern Oklahoma. Red River bridges were blocked and manned by officers. Volunteers by the dozen came to assist in the search. Added to that number were the men of the local National Guard unit. Lamar and neighboring counties were combed all Tuesday night and on Wednesday without finding a clue. Eventually, one came late Wednesday. It served to narrow the search. A resident of the countryside east of Powderly, just south of the Red River, told how two young men were walking in the area about 3:00 on Tuesday afternoon. They stopped and asked him for directions to the home of a man of whom he had never heard. That night he told his wife he suspected the men were running from the law. It was not until he learned of the search for Robertson that he reported his contact. It had been feared that Robertson was trussed and abandoned. He had to be located. By 9:45 P.M. Wednesday the missing green car was found in dense brush by men using powerful flashlights. When the car was approached, the deputy's body was seen lying on the rear seat. There were three bullet wounds in the chest and one in the jaw. In addition, there were cuts and bruises.

Nothing was touched on the car until fingerprints could be lifted by Gonzaullas. Good prints were obtained on the rearview mirror and right door vent glass. In the car, the Rangers found a bloodstained ice pick, Robertson's blood-soaked handkerchief and his empty wallet. There were also blood-spattered articles of clothing the criminals were wearing at the time they were taken into custody at the service station.

In the meantime, it had been determined that the men were T. R. Fowler and C. M. "Buddy" Acker, both ex-convicts and both twenty years of age. The car had been stolen. A pickup order from Houston was out on the vehicle, based on its theft and the further fact that the pair occupying it had committed a robbery in Huntsville. The victim there secured the license number. The officers were aided in their identification when a young woman appeared at the sheriff's office in Paris to report that she had been hitchhiking and had caught a ride with them from a point west of Memphis. The route taken by the green Ford was traced from Huntsville through Louisiana and Arkansas and on to Paris, where they let the woman out. "They were very polite and well behaved," she noted.

The search for the fugitives was expanded and joined by members of the Texas and the Oklahoma Highway Patrols. The Rangers continued their intensive work on the case and, by September 16, Captain Gonzaullas announced that Fowler and Acker had left Texas the day of the abduction of Deputy Robertson. He declined to elaborate. The Highway Patrol members returned to their home stations. Later developments proved the accuracy of Gonzaullas' statement.

A month later, the break came in the case. Acting on a tip, Walker County Sheriff C. L. Mitchell and San Jacinto County Sheriff Si Hoguet led a group of officers to a shanty hideout between Oakhurst and Willow Springs. There they found the fugitives sleeping. On being awakened, Acker shouted, "They've got us," and surrendered. Fowler fled into the brush, despite the fact that warning shots were fired in an attempt to force him to stop. Bloodhounds were brought from Wynne Prison Unit to join a dozen officers in the search. Two days later, early on Sunday, October 13, Fowler was captured at New Waverly.

The story of how they eluded capture for a month came to light when the "Lone Wolf" revealed that after abandoning the car with Robertson's body, the pair crossed the nearby Red River before roadblocks were set up and hopped a freight train in Hugo, Oklahoma. By a circuitous route, they made their way to Phoenix, Arizona. From that city they went to Mexico, finally getting back to Houston and then to the spot where they were surprised by the officers.

Fowler had hidden his gun in the vicinity of the discarded green Ford. When they returned to Lamar County to face charges, he led officers to the spot and the pistol was recovered. Acker left· his in a boxcar when they jumped off the freight train at Phoenix. They recounted that when Robertson was in the car with them and they turned north on Twenty-third Street in Paris, Fowler pretended to drop a package of cigarettes on the floor. On reaching down to retrieve it, he took out a pistol hidden under the front seat.

Captain Gonzaullas on Charcoal at Texas Ranger encampment near Marshall, Texas, in early 1940s. (Courtesy Texas Department of Public Safety.)

At that instant, the deputy was ordering them to turn back toward the courthouse. It was in the ensuing scuffle that Robertson was fatally shot.

In succeeding months, miscellaneous activities occupied Gonzaullas' time. He was sent to Paris to investigate the employee strike at a furniture manufacturing plant. He directed a nine-man Ranger force in the pursuit of four Army deserters from Camp Wolters, who were finally captured near Cross Plains. At New Boston, Gonzaullas and Rangers Ernest Daniel, Dick Oldham, Stewart Stanley and C. G. Rush, along with Deputy Sheriffs Frank Davis and Floyd Moore, provided body protection during a highly emotional trial to a man who was charged with rape of a young girl. There was confiscation of more than fifty slot machines in Denison, and so on, ad infinitum. Then, in January 1943 he came within a skin's thickness of a shot that was meant to kill him.

The encounter was at Gladewater on the Gilmer road. It involved several law enforcement officers and two escaped convicts, Robert Lacy and Cleo Andrews, who were regarded as extremely dangerous. Lacy, who was also known as Robert Lacy Cash, was an escape artist par excellence. He had escaped from custody on four occasions and was determined not to be captured again. In prison on a murder conviction, he first broke out on October 16, 1938, during a prison rodeo. A few days later he was caught by Sheriff Smoot Schmid and his deputies while hiding in a haystack near Arlington. The authorities had calculated that he would go to visit his wife, which he did, and he was found in the stack by bloodhounds. His wife later divorced him.

Returned to prison, he escaped for the second time only a week later and remained at large until he was picked up in Arizona on December 10, 1939, on a charge of forging a check on his ranch employer. Brought back to the Dallas County jail, he was in a prison car being transferred to Huntsville along with two others. One of the prisoners managed to slip out of his handcuffs and then slugged the penitentiary agent who was driving the car. The three made their getaway, but Lacy was picked up at Boulder, Colorado, on March 18, 1940.

On being returned to confinement, he was kept in hand until January 21, 1943, when he made his fourth escape, that time from the Retrieve Prison Farm blacksmith shop in company with Cleo Andrews. They left in an automobile owned by a government employee. In the car there was a .32 caliber revolver, a handy tool for their use. Lacy was considered to be one of the most spectacular outlaws since Clyde Barrow.

Gonzaullas figured the men would return to their haunts in Northern Texas, where they might find shelter. Then he used the "sixth sense" that served him in good stead throughout his career. He knew a first offender in the area who was out on parole from Retrieve Farm where he had been befriended by Lacy and Andrews. "They did that so if they should get out again and needed help they could turn to him. He was completely taken in by their 'friendship' in the prison," Gonzaullas remarked later.

The "Lone Wolf" talked with that man, who admitted that the escapees had telephoned him from Houston. He was told to get specified weapons and ammunition. They would pick up the rifles and cartridges from him at a selected spot in Gladewater at a set hour on Monday, January 25. He was threatened with death if he did not follow their instructions. That was all the information Gonzaullas needed. A trap was set. It was manned by him and by Rangers Dick Oldham and R. L. Badgett; Gregg County Sheriff Lonnie Smith, his deputies Harry Dawson and F. P. Leach; Upshur County Sheriff Gordon Anderson, his deputy Carl Trice; Gladewater Constable J. H. Leach, and Louis Grigsby, investigator for the Gregg County district attorney's office.

The weather turned extremely bad. A cold, wet norther blew in. Sleet mixed with freezing rain was falling and the roads were beginning to ice over when, at 8:45 P.M., the escaped convicts' car skidded from the Bozman Corner road onto the main highway leading out of Gladewater to Gilmer. It swung about in a circle and then stopped. The officers were ready. Concealed behind automobiles and in buildings at the intersection, they called to the two men to come out with their hands up.

Gonzaullas said, "We called on them to surrender, but they decided to fight." The two escapees had secured another pistol somewhere en route. When challenged, they opened fire, obviously not realizing how outgunned they were. The officers answered with a barrage of rifle and pistol fire. Lacy, after opening the door on the driver's side to make shooting easier, fell out of the car onto the pavement, his body riddled with bullets. Andrews was on the floor with his head near the steering column.

Reacting to the silence from the car, the officers started toward it, walking cautiously. Sheriff Anderson approached the driver's side, where Lacy lay on the roadway. Gonzaullas and Sheriff Smith came to the passenger's side. Just as the "Lone Wolf" started to open the door, Anderson shouted the warning, "Look out, Cap, I think he's playing possum!" Gonzaullas instinctively ducked. There was a flash from Andrew's pistol and a bullet tore through the left shoulder of Gonzaullas' suit coat. His skin was only grazed. Had he not ducked at the warning, the bullet would have struck him in the chest. Gonzaullas was carrying a pistol in his left hand and reacted by pumping five slugs into Andrews.

Subsequent examination of both bodies at the mortuary revealed thirty bullet holes in that of Lacy. Andrews' body had five holes, from those shots fired by the "Lone Wolf." The men were astounded to see that when Andrews fell to the floorboard, he had miraculously escaped the hail of shots aimed at the car and was untouched until Gonzaullas killed him.

Although the sedan was "shot up like a sieve," no machine guns had been used, as Evans Smith had suggested in his letter to the *Dallas Morning News* back in 1934. Not one of the officers was wounded, except for that nick in Gonzaullas' shoulder. In the automobile were "A" and "B" gasoline rationing coupons and a quantity of ammunition. Bullets had smashed the ignition coil and sheared off a spark plug. The dash was ripped and the front seat riddled. Some of the officers had had instructions to train their fire on the engine in an effort to put the car out of commission in the event the occupants were not captured. They had done their job well.

Captain Gonzaullas described the encounter as "the culmination of an intensive man hunt . . . . Every officer risked his own life to capture these two. Each man was on his toes and did his part. It couldn't have turned out better unless the convicts had chosen to surrender instead of shoot it out." In noting that no money was found on the persons of the dead men, the "Lone Wolf" commented, "It wouldn't have been long before they would have robbed someone or some place to get the cash they needed to keep going."

Gonzaullas was not wearing his regular Ranger attire. To avoid attracting public notice when he made contact with the ex-convict turned informant, he had donned a new tweed suit and a snap-brim hat. The "Lone Wolf" was so close to Andrews when he fired the five shots his prize suit was splattered. He described the result as "just like busting open an overripe watermelon. I got splashed all over and was a mess with brains and blood all over me." After the encounter, to all intents and purposes the suit was ruined, not only from the hole Andrews' bullet put through the shoulder but also from the stains. "It never could be restored to its original condition," the captain grumbled.

A chase that would have done credit to anything Hollywood could dream up brought more than fifty Dallas area law enforcement officers together when the three men involved were taken into custody on June 5, 1943. It ended a thirty-day crime spree over a broad region of Northern Texas. The affair actually had its beginning with the escape from Retrieve Prison Farm in Brazoria County of C. M. Mershon and Walter LeMay on April 18. The number of escapes from Retrieve was beginning to lift official eyebrows. At the time the chase began, the men were being sought in connection with a series of robberies and safecrackings. They were responsible for burglaries of more than fifty stores, for having stolen several automobiles plus a large amount of merchandise, some diamonds, narcotics and at least three thousand dollars in cash, and for having slugged two night watchmen.

Earlier in the week of the chase, Gonzaullas and Dallas Detective Inspector Will Fritz had laid plans to trap them, believing that their targets would be stores in Dallas. A tip had been received that the men actually were in Dallas and would, sooner or later, be found at a house on Michigan in Trinity Heights. Fritz and Gonzaullas, or some of their associates, had been keeping the house under surveillance for two days. Just before noon on Saturday, June 5, the convicts' maroon two-door sedan stopped in front of the place. Fritz and Detectives J.T. Luther and Leon Mash started toward it, but the two men, plus a companion named Steve Roberts, took off in the car with the tires burning rubber on the pavement. The detectives gave chase.

The convicts headed for Lancaster Road, with the officers right behind them. The route led over Michigan, Alaska, Lancaster and other streets as the fugitives, with the accelerator pushed to the floorboard, endeavored to outrun their pursuers at speeds that occasionally reached nearly a hundred miles per hour. They made breathtaking turns on two wheels in a futile effort to shake the officers. Getting close, Fritz and Luther fired at the rear of the fleeing car with rifle and pistol shot. At a high rate of speed, the escapees tried to turn off Lancaster Road onto Ledbetter Drive but were going too fast to make it. The car went out of control, narrowly missed the corner of a building, jumped a ditch and came to rest in a patch of neckhigh Johnson grass. Luther, Fritz and Mash opened fire and both Mershon and Roberts surrendered. LeMay ran off into the tall grass and was lost to view. A resident, Louis Manchen, tried to stop LeMay by seizing him, but the convict tore loose from his grasp and then could not be found anywhere in the acreage.

In response to radio calls that had gone out during the pursuit, other police were speeding in that direction. When the ride ended and the location was given, in just a matter of minutes a swarm of officers in twenty squad cars converged on the scene and spread out to surround the area in order to prevent LeMay from slipping through their grasp. Three planes from nearby Curry Field were called in to circle in an effort to spot the man. Ten men on horseback and numerous other armed volunteers from the neighborhood joined the officers in combing the area inch by inch. Fritz sent to Fort Worth and Chief Deputy Sheriff Bill Decker sent to McKinney for bloodhounds, but they did not need them. After a little while, "Lone Wolf" Gonzaullas arrived, in company with Rangers Bob Crowder, Tully Seay and N. K. Dixon. He looked things over quietly and carefully, then picked up LeMay's trail.

LeMay had made his way to the garage of a residence on Burnside. The family members were not at home. He climbed into a large storage closet, got on the top shelf and piled in front of himself such items as gallon cans of paint, a wastebasket and boxes. LeMay pulled the closet door closed and lay down securely hidden, he thought. While the others were beating the grass and bushes and searching buildings, the "Lone Wolf" working by himself slowly made his way toward that garage. When he got there, he looked it over and walked to the storage closet with his gun in hand. He opened the door and ordered the unseen man to come out. The dejected LeMay scrambled out from behind the barricade. Gonzaullas fired two shots into the air to summon others to the spot.

When the car in which the convicts were riding was hauled to Dallas police headquarters, examination revealed that during the wild ride seventeen buckshot had struck the back but did not penetrate the metal. Two bullets fired from Luther's rifle did pierce the car, but none of the three convicts was injured. In the automobile were thirty-two chisels, five hammers, three pistols and nine rifles, plus 150 shoe ration stamps and gasoline ration coupons for over a thousand gallons.

The men had almost a thousand dollars in cash on their persons, most of it being in twenty-dollar bills. They were not only "patriotic" but also wise investors. In a house where they had been staying, they had secreted a thousand dollars in United States War Bonds. There was one bond for five hundred dollars, another for a hundred dollars, and sixteen for twenty-five dollars, all purchased on May 3 with some of their ill-gotten gains.

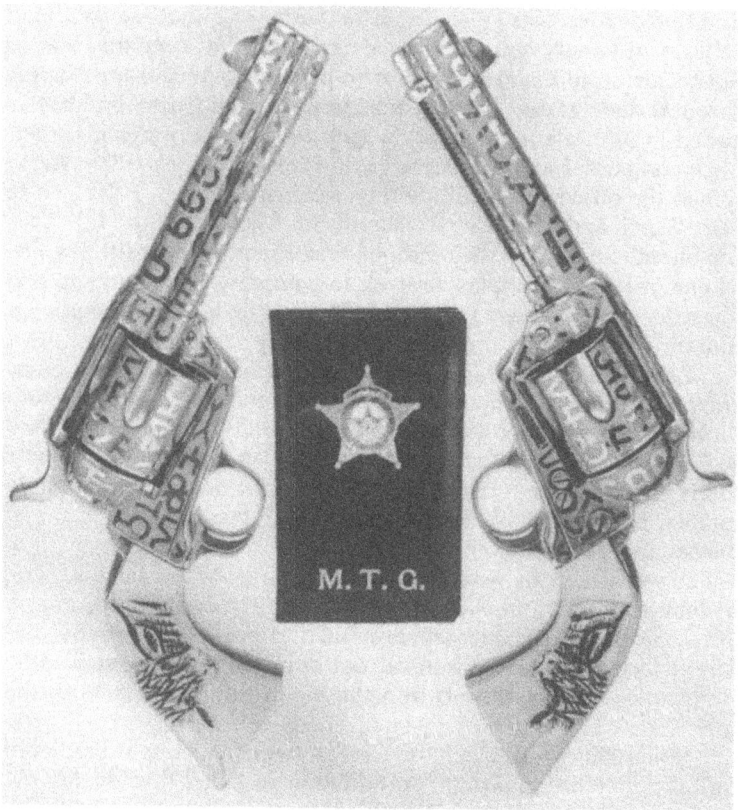

Ornamented Colt .45 revolvers. Famous Texas cattle brands, the seal of the State of Texas, and a miniature Texas Ranger captain badge appear on the grips. The five-pointed gold badge on the leather case has a diamond mounted in the center. (Courtesy Texas Ranger Hall of Fame and Museum.)

XIV

Martial Law at Beaumont

The first intimation of trouble in Beaumont reached the ears of Chief of Police Ross Dickey near midnight on Tuesday, June 15, 1943, when a breathless officer reported that Main Street was packed curb to curb with men headed toward the city jail. No one had to tell him who they were or what they wanted. Most were from the Pennsylvania Shipyards and he knew they would be seeking a Negro man who had reputedly attacked the young wife of a construction worker during the middle of the afternoon when she was in her residence with three small, sleeping children.

When word of the alleged rape spread through the shipyards that evening, hundreds of men working there walked off the job and began to congregate in angry groups. Eventually, spurred by urgings from a militant few, they assembled and started the march on the city jail with lynching as their aim. The man they sought was not there. He had not been apprehended though an intensive search was underway. The chief realized it would be his own responsibility to convince the approaching crowd that that was the truth of the matter.

Before he could get to the entrance door of the building, the vanguard of the mob had swarmed in, making loud demands for the alleged assailant. Chief Dickey was unable to turn them away with words. He was obliged to take a deputation through the jail quarters so they themselves could see and report to the shouting crowd that the fellow was not being held. While the jail tour was being made, an innocent Negro, who was passing on the street, was grabbed by the threatening mob, whereupon Dickey went out to endeavor to protect him. In the melee, during which the man was beaten, Dickey was bruised and received a badly sprained arm.

Next, the throng rushed to the county jail, making the same demand. Jefferson County Sheriff Bill Richardson, seeing that he and his deputies were overwhelmingly outnumbered, took the same sensible approach and escorted some of the leaders through the jail so they could look at the prisoners there. But, there was loud grumbling outside. Why should they take the word of the police chief and the sheriff? Shouts were heard asking how the assembled men could be sure that one of those in the jails was not actually the attacker for whom they had come.

Sensing an assault on the jails, which could only have bloody results, the officers quickly brought the woman victim to both places. She went through, scrutinized each prisoner, then came out and told the mob that the Negro who had allegedly ravished her was not there. She had to be believed, but there were agitating shouts from the crowd. They had not come to town for nothing! Spurred on by strident voices, the mob split into smaller groups and blindly turned their wrath on the Negro community in general, notwithstanding that a great many of the people living there were their own fellow workers at the shipyards. They roamed the areas, pulling Negroes out of cars, beating them and setting fire to the vehicles. Following that rampage, they smashed windows, looted Negro business establishments and put the torch to residences and stores alike. The Gladys and Forsyth Street regions of the city were hit especially hard. Beaumont firemen fought blazes throughout the night.

At the time the roving, incendiary-minded mobs were getting under way, Sheriff Richardson had a band of men searching a wooded area off Eleventh Street where the suspected rapist was believed to be hiding. When the rioting and burning exploded, Richardson was obliged to pull his men off the search and use them in a cooperative effort with city police to try to restore order. In that they failed. When it became apparent that they could not contain the raging mobs, they called on 150 Beaumont Texas National Guardsmen, under Major Fred Stone, to help them.

Around midnight, about fifty of the mob raided the bus station where a group of Negro draftees was being loaded to go to an Army processing center. A terrible scene ensued, with mob members dragging the draftees off the bus and beating them. As would be expected, the black youths fought back in vigorous self-defense, and three of the whites were hurt. The draftees were on the losing end, as several were more seriously injured. After daylight on Thursday, one was found lying unconscious behind the bus station with severe cuts on his neck. The interior of the bus station was almost totally wrecked by the unbridled white gang.

During the rioting on Tuesday night, John Johnson, a forty-four-year-old Negro man, was shot to death and Ellie Cleveland Brown, a fifty-five-year-old white man, was attacked by three black men and beaten. He died about 11:00 A.M. on Wednesday from a fractured skull. When Negro workers at the shipyard left the night shift at 7:00 A.M. on Wednesday, June 16, they were escorted to their homes by local National Guardsmen. No blacks reported for the day shift, and so few whites came on that the Pennsylvania Shipyards were forced to shut down.

With the full realization that the critically serious situation could not be contained even with the help of Beaumont National Guardsmen, city and county officers sent a call to the state for aid. Eight carloads of Texas State Highway Patrolmen from cities as far distant as Fort Worth and Wichita Falls headed for Beaumont. Texas Rangers were also dispatched. They included Captain M. T. "Lone Wolf" Gonzaullas of Company "B" at Dallas and Captain Hardy B. Purvis of Company "A" at Houston. The state's next step was mobilization of specified Texas National Guard units to be held in readiness for quick movement to the riot-torn city if martial law were deemed necessary.

On Wednesday morning, the sixteenth, all public swimming pools and playgrounds were closed. Some of the city's normal services were halted when orders were issued by police to Negro drivers and workers not to make their usual rounds. It was a safety precaution. The jail areas were sealed off by barbed wire barricades. During the day, reports reached Beaumont that mobs of men were on their way to the city from Orange and other towns in the vicinity. Reacting to the rumors, officials ordered that roadblocks be set up and manned by officers with machine guns and tear gas. Cars or buses transporting Negroes were not allowed to pass through Beaumont but were routed around the trouble centers. Instances of waylaying and beating of Negroes by roving white gangs continued through Wednesday morning. When the Rangers and Highway Patrolmen arrived to begin making arrests, defiant gang members assumed a scornful attitude until face-to-face encounters with the officers materialized.

153

News came from Orange that black employees were being turned away at the entrance to shipyards in that city. The reason given was that it would lessen the likelihood of trouble erupting on the job there. All liquor stores and beer parlors in Orange County were ordered closed.

Governor Coke Stevenson was on his way to Washington by train, but he kept in telephone communication with Acting Governor A. M. Aikin, Jr. At 5:55 P.M. on Wednesday, Aikin declared a state of martial law to exist in Beaumont. The National Guard units being held in readiness speedily moved in from distances up to a hundred miles. When they arrived, the city was guarded by a total of twenty-four hundred Guardsmen, Rangers, Highway Patrolmen, local police and sheriff's deputies. Lieutenant Colonel Sidney C. Mason set up his headquarters in the police station and patrols moved out into the city. A military pass was required for civilians to get through the barbed wire barricades around the jails. By order of Major General Richard Donovan, Eighth Service Command at Dallas, the city of Beaumont was placed off limits to all military personnel.

The rioting had the effect of closing down practically all Beaumont businesses that depended on public assembly, such as motion picture theaters, or on Negro help, such as restaurants. All beer parlors and liquor stores were closed. It became practically impossible to purchase a meal in the city on Wednesday. Although they opened that morning, department and most other stores closed within a few hours. Buses stopped operating at 7:30 P.M., and an hour later a curfew was established. It was not completely effective at first. On Wednesday night, patrols of Rangers, Highway Patrolmen and National Guardsmen kept a tight watch over the city. The Negro sections were constantly patrolled as a security measure. The officers accosted small groups of men who gathered in defiance of the curfew. And they disarmed and arrested men occupying cars in which guns were found when they were searched.

Soon after his arrival earlier in the day, the "Lone Wolf" walked up to a cluster of nine men who glowered at him. "Where do you boys work?" he inquired pleasantly.

One replied, "Out at the yard."

In further questioning he determined that at that particular hour they should have been on the job. "What are you doing here on the street? Why aren't you on your job?"

Another of the men snapped, "We took off to come to town so we could protect our families from them _____."

At DPS headquarters, Camp Mabry, Austin, August 4, 1943. *Left to right*: Captain Manny Gault, Captain Gully Cowsert, Captain Ernest Best, Captain M. T. Gonzaullas, Captain Hardy B. Purvis, and Captain Fred Olson. Colonel Garrison was the Director of the Department of Public Safety at this time. (Courtesy Texas Ranger Hall of Fame and Museum.)

Gonzaullas pursed his lips and nodded as though in agreement with the principle of safeguarding the home and family, then he peered around the men on all sides as if he were looking for something. "I declare," he commented quietly, "I don't see your families. Aren't they with you?"

"Naw," he was told, "they ain't here. They're at the house."

The "Lone Wolf" narrowed his eyes as he looked them over. "So, they are at the house and here you are on the street, and you expect me to swallow that line about protecting them?" Next he asked for and was given their names and residence addresses, which he wrote down.

"Now you boys go on home and you stay there until you make up your minds to go back to your jobs where you belong. If you don't get off the street in five minutes I'm going to run you in and lock you up. Now, git!" They did.

He repeated that basic approach many times during the day, ever quiet, ever firm. Other Rangers and Patrolmen used similar tactics and secured equally good results. The street loiterers, who were acknowledged sources of potential trouble, were not as inclined to defy orders given by state officers as they were to openly protest those of local police.

The street loafers had good reason to believe they would be placed under arrest and jailed. It was common knowledge in the city that a stockade had been set up at the fairgrounds. Men who were taken into custody were being kept in confinement there until their cases could be handled. Throughout Wednesday, there were instances in which both white and Negro men were ambushed and beaten, shot or knifed. The crimes were being perpetrated by small gangs such as the ones "Lone Wolf" and his fellow officers were breaking up.

On Thursday, Colonel Mason, in command of the state troops and enforcement of martial law, announced that a military court of inquiry would be held for both whites and Negroes accused or suspected of having taken part in the riots. By that time more than three hundred men were in custody. The colonel stated that evidence brought out during the inquiry would be used as the basis for making recommendations to civil authorities in each case. He further stated that local draft board officials would sit in on the hearings because, as he pointed out, "the draft status of some of the persons involved may have changed recently." Those ominous words were heard with alarm by physically able young men of draft age who had secured deferment from military service because of engagement in work considered vital to the war effort. By walking off their jobs and participating in the rioting, those men had jeopardized their exempt status. The thought frightened them, but it was too late. The four military courts went into session at 9:00 A.M.

M. W. McMaster, the director of public relations at the Pennsylvania Shipyards, stated on Thursday morning that about half of the regular crew had returned to work for the Wednesday night shift and expressed confidence that Thursday would see almost a full force on duty. He made his prediction based on the establishment of martial law and the increasingly tight control of every phase of life in the city. The American Federation of Labor got in on the act and publicly urged all the workers to get back on the job so production would not be seriously hampered. Throughout the state, public reaction to the events in the riot cast a reflection on a labor force that was so easily turned aside from the critically important work of shipbuilding. Public opinion was that the workers should have stayed on their jobs to aid the United States war effort.

Chief Dickey was quoted as saying, "Anything that takes men away from the yards for a cause such as that which slowed down production when hundreds walked off the job this week is sabotage. There have been rumors of fifth column activities here and we have been checking up on them." City officials chimed in to express their thoughts that fifth columnists had fomented the riots. They noted that they did not believe the disturbance was based on racial friction. That view was not generally supported.

Dickey admitted that his department had not been successful in pinpointing saboteurs as the moving force in the event, but he stated, "There is somebody behind it and if I could get my hands on him I would wring his neck." Referring to the appearance of the mob at the city jail, Chief Dickey further commented, "I scanned the crowd and did not see a Beaumont man whom I could recognize," an opinion similar to that expressed in Sherman after the roasting alive of George Hughes in the courthouse fire there in 1930. Then, the community was staggered by a statement attributed to City Attorney Albert Tatum that "a physician's examination of the young woman who said she was attacked by a Negro Tuesday, the incident that provoked the violence, has opened the case to question!"

There could be no congregation of people of either race, so Mayor Gary ordered the cancellation of all plans by black residents for celebrations in the city in observance of Emancipation Day on June 19. To enforce the order, it was made a part of the martial law decree by Colonel Mason. However, on that Thursday night the curfew was eased a bit. It was set to begin at 9:30 P.M.

Stating that martial law was expected to be lifted on Sunday, a prospect that heartened the law-abiding people of the city, Colonel Mason announced that the military court had completed the inquiry at 5:10 A.M. on Saturday, June 19, after forty hours of continuous deliberation. The court had placed twenty-eight men in the custody of local law enforcement officers. Several faced serious charges as instigators and ringleaders of the rioting. Others were to be charged with arson and assault with intent to murder. Beaumont was returning to normal by Saturday. White employees and most of the blacks had returned to their jobs at Pennsylvania Shipyards, where there would be a full shift schedule on Sunday to make up for the time lost. The shipyards at Orange also announced full shifts for Sunday, taking up the slack caused by the walkouts there and subsequent barring of black workers from their jobs.

On Friday night, the Beaumont curfew had been moved to begin at 11:00 P.M. Soon it would be a thing of the past, but the aftermath bitterness of the rioting would haunt the people of the city for years to come. The unsung heroes in the situation there were the young National Guardsmen, who were pulled away from homes and jobs for an unpleasant and potentially dangerous task. The "Lone Wolf" had the highest regard for Texas National Guardsmen. He had seen them operate efficiently and coolly as they handled difficult situations in such places as Mexia, Borger, Sherman and the East Texas oil fields. Now they had given another shining example of their sense of duty and responsibility.

XV

The Phantom Killer

The scene for one of the most sensational cases in the history of American law enforcement was laid in Texarkana, the Northeastern Texas city that straddles the Texas-Arkansas state line. That case was also one of the most vexing in Gonzaullas' career. In mid-April 1946, the "Lone Wolf" became deeply involved in what were being referred to as the "Phantom Murders." The mysterious assailant was generally spoken of and written about as the "Phantom Killer" or the "Phantom Slayer." Before the carnage ended, five men and women had been brutally murdered, two severely beaten and abused and one critically wounded by gunfire.

That series of tragedies was made into a motion picture *The Town That Dreaded Sundown*, which was built around the work of Captain Gonzaullas in the original case. Gonzaullas' counterpart in the film was named J. D. Morales and was played by Ben Johnson. As is often true of such productions, liberties were taken with the facts. That hardly seems to have been necessary, as the truth of the series of incidents was even more gruesome than the fictionalized version.

There was a total of four attacks, the first three having occurred within a short distance of one another in and near Texarkana's Spring Lake Park. That recreational spot was just off heavily traveled Highway 67, which ran through St. Louis, Little Rock and Texarkana on southwest across Texas through Naples, Greenville, Dallas and San Angelo to Alpine and Marfa, ending at

Presidio on the Texas-Mexican border. The fourth attack took place ten miles northeast of Texarkana at a rural residence in Miller County, Arkansas. Except for the method (shots aimed at the head), the Arkansas death and attempted murder were not easy to reconcile with the sites chosen for the first three incidents. Had it become too risky in Texarkana for the Phantom Killer and was he obliged to go elsewhere to satisfy an uncontrollable urge?

The first attack came on the night of February 22, 1946, on a "lovers' lane," a popular resort for dating couples adjacent to Spring Lake Park. Twenty-three-year-old Jimmy Hollis, accompanied by nineteen-year-old Mrs. Mary Jeanne Larey, had driven to the lane. He stopped the car, turned off the ignition and lights, after which they sat there and talked quietly. Within a few minutes, there was the crunch of a footstep and a gruff-voiced man stood at the side of the car. With only starlight and the reflected glow from the nearby city to illuminate the scene, the couple perceived that the man wore over his face what appeared to be a white handkerchief with holes cut out for his eyes. He turned on a flashlight and partially blinded them with its beam. Brandishing a pistol, he ordered them to get out of the car. Then he commanded Hollis to loosen his belt and drop his trousers, which he did. At that instant, the man struck him on the back of his head with the pistol, using such force that Hollis' skull and several neck vertebrae were fractured. The victim fell to the ground as if dead.

The assailant kicked Hollis and then turned his attention to the terrified Mrs. Larey. He ordered her to run up the road, which she did, thinking that she might thereby be able to escape. His command and her flight were believed to satisfy a sexual urge for mastery, as he then ran after and quickly overtook her. He threw her onto the ground, struck her on the head with the pistol and commenced to attack her in a vicious and bestial manner. Mrs. Larey reported later that she thought he was frightened away by the lights of a car that turned into the lane, but she was not sure. The car did not come up to where she lay. Whatever caused him to run away obviously saved her life. The instant he was gone, she got to her feet to hide in the brush and trees, her heart pounding so loudly she knew he could hear it if he came back. She waited until she felt sure he was nowhere near, then stumbled to a house whose lights she saw in the distance. There she sobbed out her story and was taken to the sheriff's office where the attack was reported.

Hollis was picked up and both he and she were hospitalized. When he regained consciousness and was questioned, his description of the man was at variance with hers. He thought the man was white. She thought he was black. They could give no physical details. Mrs. Larey declared his voice sounded like that of a Negro, but she could not be sure. Was he wearing gloves? Neither knew. How tall was he? Neither could say.

Different reasons have been offered for the fact that the attack was kept as quiet as possible. It was reported that the victims asked for and received suppression of news of the incident. Another theory advanced was that the law enforcement officers believed that there would be a better opportunity to apprehend the attacker if there were no widespread sensational publicity. Hollis and Mrs. Larey were the only victims who saw the Phantom and lived to tell about it.

Terror seized the residents of Texarkana after the second assault. Later, when the national press came in on the cases, it was reported that each attack occurred at intervals of precisely three weeks, to the day, following the previous one. That was not accurate, but it made lurid copy. It was four weeks and two days after the experience of Hollis and Mrs. Larey that the next attack shocked the community. On the night of March 24, Richard Griffin, twenty-nine, and Polly Ann Moore, seventeen, drove to the Spring Lake Park lovers' lane area. Griffin pulled his car to the side of the gravel road not more than 250 feet from Highway 67, up and down which cars and trucks were traveling. The victims of the attack that night could not describe their ordeal as Hollis and Mrs. Larey had done. The next morning, the bodies of Griffin and Miss Moore were discovered. Both had died from gunshot wounds in the head. Two .38 caliber bullets had killed each of them.

In the first attack, Hollis had not been robbed, but in the second, Griffin's pockets were rifled. Trying to find a pattern, the question was raised as to whether the attacker had intended to slay Mrs. Larey, after which he would have returned to Hollis to kill and rob him. One thing was clear. In both instances, the man had been put out of the way first and then attention was focused on his female companion. A short distance from Griffin's car, a bloodstained place was noted on the grass. Officers surmised that Miss Moore had been slain there, after which she was taken to the car and placed on the back seat. Her body was removed and embalmed before tests were run to determine if she had been sexually assaulted.

The news spread through Texarkana like a racing prairie fire. It was then that the general public became fully aware of the first

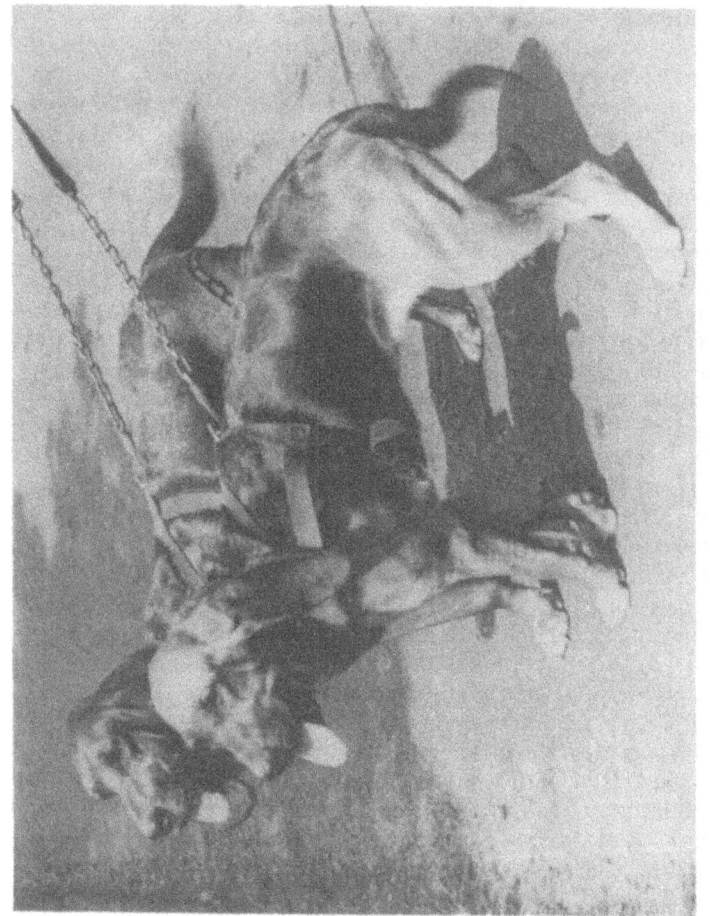

"Tex" and "Pal," Company "B" bloodhounds, were regularly used by the Rangers to track down law violators who were trying to elude capture.

incident and questions were raised about its not being given wide coverage. It was asked whether Richard Griffin and Polly Ann Moore would have gone to that spot had they known what happened to Hollis and Mrs. Larey. Some citizens suggested that they would not, and that their lack of knowledge played a part in their becoming victims. Consternation reigned in the city and a reaction based on fear of the unknown set in. Residents began leaving lights on outside their homes throughout the night. Stores sold out of locks as families attempted to barricade their doors more securely. Stocks of guns were exhausted in a matter of hours, the same being true of ammunition. The fact that the two attacks occurred in a secluded part of the city did nothing to lessen anxiety. Who knew where the killer would strike next? No one was going to take a chance.

When the bodies of Griffin and Miss Moore were found, hundreds of people flocked to the lane, effectively obliterating footprints, tire tracks or any other evidence that might have been of value to the police. Latent fingerprints on the car were smeared by the hands of the throng. Texas Rangers were called in to investigate and see what evidence might be secured at the site. Thanks to the morbidly curious, the Phantom Slayer was safely protected by the loss of any telltale clue. Gonzaullas said that that was one of the frustrating facets of the case. The Rangers were not requested to stay and patrol. The local police thought they could handle that. After the initial shock, the city settled back into complacency.

The press seized upon the time spacing between attacks two and three for thrilling news stories. The third occurred in the early morning hours of April 14, three weeks to the day following the murders of Griffin and Miss Moore. A seventeen-year-old youth, Paul Martin, and his fifteen-year-old date, Betty Jo Booker, left a dance where she had played a saxophone in the school orchestra that furnished music for the affair. She was seen placing the instrument in Paul Martin's car as they left together. It was about 2:00 A.M., but the Phantom Slayer was waiting.

The fact that Martin and Miss Booker drove to Spring Lake Park tore holes in the theory previously expressed that Griffin and Miss Moore would not have gone there had they been aware of what happened to Hollis and Mrs. Larey. Paul Martin and Betty Jo Booker did know of the Hollis-Larey experience, and they did know how Richard Griffin and Polly Ann Moore were killed there. Yet, they went to the lovers' lane and parked the car. The question that agonized people was why they did so.

The following morning a passing couple, Mr. and Mrs. G. H. Weaver, were aghast to find young Martin's blood-soaked body lying beside the road. And, again, hundreds of townspeople streamed out to the area, blotting out every possible clue that might have been of value. Miss Booker's body was not to be seen. Martin lay about a mile from his car. He had been shot first in the face and then, as he apparently ran from the killer, was again shot, that time in the back of the head. It appeared possible that Martin and Miss Booker had been forced to get in the Phantom Slayer's own car. Martin was murdered on the road after he had gotten out of a vehicle. Miss Booker was then taken up a dirt road and into a field, where she was slain. She, too, was shot in the head. The killer took no chances of these victims living to bear tales on him. A search party found her ravished body several hours after Martin was discovered. Like Hollis, Martin was not robbed, but Betty Jo Booker's saxophone was missing.

This time, the Rangers were called in to stay and the "Lone Wolf" was placed in charge of the investigative process. It was hampered by the lack of clues, those telltale bits of evidence that were swept away by the crowds of visitors to the murder sites. There was precious little on which to proceed. Nevertheless, the Rangers worked doggedly at the task to pick up a point here, a hint there. No more young couples were frequenting the Spring Lake Park lovers' lanes. Night activity in Texarkana ground to a virtual halt. After a Western Union telegraph messenger was fired at by a nervous householder who said he thought the boy might be the killer, no more telegrams were delivered after nightfall. Special delivery of mail was also suspended when the sun went down. Strangers in town were cautioned not to go onto the streets after dark. That simply was not safe in view of the number of trigger-happy people in the city.

In an effort to trap the Phantom Killer, elaborate systems were designed by the officers, complete with radio communication and a blinking of flashlights for signal. The Rangers and local police set up decoys on the lanes where the atrocities had been committed. Those decoy teams consisted of one officer in civilian clothes and a companion dressed as a woman. It had become recognized that they were up against a psychopathic killer who was sexually aroused by the sight of a couple in a secluded spot. It could not be determined whether the letting of blood was a concomitant part of his gratification, or whether the murders were committed solely to remove any possible witness of his deeds. It was also obvious to the investigators that they were dealing with a man of above average intelligence. The theory was advanced that he could be a person who stood high in the community in a business or social way and, until his uncontrollable desire took hold, was perfectly normal in behavior. More than one thousand persons, including some two hundred known sexual perverts, were checked out and cleared of suspicion. The officers waited while the decoys went out night after night. The Phantom Killer did not walk into their trap.

Because of the nationwide press coverage and the emphasis on the false "three weeks to the day" expectation of reappearance, as that time neared following the murder of Paul Martin and Betty Jo Booker, news reporters flocked to Texarkana to be on hand when "it" happened. They were disappointed. Two days before the expiration of that three-week period, the Phantom struck again, but not in Texarkana as anticipated.

Two weeks and five days after Paul Martin and Betty Jo Booker were slain, Mr. and Mrs. Virgil Starks were in their rural home in Miller County, Arkansas, about ten miles northeast of Texarkana. They were fully aware of the spate of murderous attacks in Texarkana, indeed who was not, and had discussed them with family and friends, all of whom looked upon these events with a feeling of utter abhorrence.

At their distance from the location of the two beatings and four killings, no one in that farm neighborhood even considered drawing shades at night or barricading windows and doors, as was being done in the city. But, the Phantom Slayer had selected the Starks as his next victims. Beyond question, he knew of the intensive coverage officers were providing in Texarkana. He was obliged to go elsewhere for his gratification. In the aftermath, it was wondered how he happened to choose the Starks. He must have known them personally. Judging from the tracks that he left in the soft ground following recent rains, he knew the layout of the residence and outbuildings. His car was surely parked down the road, as he walked from and then back to a pinpointed spot.

On the night of May 3, 1946, Mr. Starks was sitting in an easy chair in the living room listening to the radio, which was on a table beside him. The chair was situated by a window, the sash of which had been closed. However, the window shade was raised all the way to the top of the frame. Mrs. Starks had gone into the adjacent bedroom and undressed, putting on her nightgown, after which she lay on the bed. The bedroom window shades were raised and the light was on. Unknown to them, the Phantom Slayer was standing outside watching every move. He was armed with a .22 caliber rifle, a departure from his usual .38 caliber pistol. That fact clearly showed the investigating officers that he knew the distance from which he would fire and that he needed a rifle for accuracy.

Soon after Mrs. Starks reclined on the bed, she heard the crash of breaking glass over the sound of the radio. She did not detect the crack of rifle fire outside. She jumped up and ran to the door between the two rooms, from which she saw her husband standing in a reflex action, blood streaming from his head. Then he sank back into the chair. Rushing to his side, Mrs. Starks lifted his head in absolute horror, then turned and ran to the wall telephone to call for aid. It was the old type instrument. She cranked it twice to signal the operator and was simultaneously staggered by a shot that shattered her jaw. Instantly another shot struck her in the face.

Mrs. Starks groped her way back into the bedroom and then reeled into the darkened kitchen, frantic with fear and pain. She realized then that the unknown attacker was tearing at the screen of the kitchen window that opened onto the back porch. The door was fastened. In wild flight, she ran back through the living room and out the front door into the dark, not knowing what she might encounter there. She made her way to a house that was not far distant, but no one was at home. Mrs. Starks continued running and got to the next residence down the road where she fell into the arms of friends stunned by what they saw.

The alarm was called in to the Miller County sheriff's office, but by the time the officers, accompanied by Gonzaullas, reached the Starks' home, the killer had vanished. They found that he had entered the house through the kitchen window and tracked his footprints through a pool of blood from Mr. Starks' fatal wounds. It appeared that he even stopped to smear his hands in the blood.

No one could have foretold it at the time, but that was the last attack made by the Phantom Slayer. What brought the murders to an end, and why, was the basis for speculation in the years that followed. During the seventy-one days between February 22 and May 3, 1946, five innocent persons had been slain and three cruelly injured. Had the Phantom Killer's lust been satisfied? Had he gone to another part of the nation? Was he still alive? The body of a man was found on a railroad track close to Texarkana on May 7. He was never identified. Was he the killer and, if so, was his death an accident or did he take his own life?

The "Lone Wolf" had his opinion in the matter. Years after the series of events, he commented that the officers had a good idea

Commemorative bronze statue of Gonzaullas by Robert Summers is on display at the Ranger Museum in Waco. Thirty-one statues were cast and sold in honor of the "Lone Wolf," with proceeds going to the Moody Texas Ranger Memorial Library. (Courtesy Texas Ranger Hall of Fame and Museum.)

who the perpetrator was, but could not move in because of lack of conclusive evidence. At any rate, the activities of the Phantom Slayer ended as suddenly as they began, but it was a long time before the people of Texarkana could relax and leave their porch lights off at night. The dread they felt at the setting of the sun lingered for months. Eventually telegrams and special delivery letters were again delivered after dark and people ventured onto the streets past sundown. Haunted by the memory of the ghastly events that had occurred there, lovers' lane at Spring Lake Park never regained its old popularity as a retreat for young couples.

Gonzaullas' personal license plate, on display at the Ranger Museum in Waco, clearly shows his association with the Rangers. (Courtesy Texas Ranger Hall of Fame and Museum.)

XVI

Manhunt in East Texas

What developed into the greatest manhunt in recent years in Northeast Texas began with a singular highway incident on Tuesday morning, February 11, 1947. Soon after that, the "Lone Wolf" was sent in, accompanied by other Rangers, to work with county and municipal officers, as well as the Highway Patrol, in setting up a dragnet. Before he was trapped, the object of the search repeatedly slipped through the mesh of that net as it was being slowly tightened.

During the night of Monday, February 10, two stores were burglarized at Mount Pleasant, the Titus County seat. In the very early morning hours, two more were entered at Talco, also in Titus County. At about the time the thefts were being discovered, the man who broke into the stores brought the spotlight of law enforcement attention upon himself. He could not have done a better job had his move been deliberately planned. It turned out that he was Walter Ransom, twenty-three, who later admitted to "Lone Wolf" Gonzaullas that he was out on parole from the Minnesota state prison system.

Right after 7:00 A.M. on the eleventh, a convoy from the General Motors plant at Detroit, Michigan, passed through Mount Pleasant on Highway 67. Its destination was the dealership of Elmer P. Phillips at Henderson and Second Streets in Fort Worth. In the convoy were three Cadillacs, one Chevrolet and one Oldsmobile. West of Mount Pleasant, Joe Wood, the driver of the last car, noticed in his rearview mirror that an automobile was following him and gradually coming closer. It kept right on coming and rammed the rear of Wood's car. The offending automobile did not stop. Instead, it swerved and then passed the convoy. Wood and his companions gave chase, at the conclusion of which Ransom's vehicle was overtaken and forced to the side of the road.

When Wood and the other four drivers (two men and two women) got out, there was a shouting match between them and Ransom. The quarrel was abruptly terminated when Ransom whipped out a pistol and ordered the three men to throw their wallets at his feet. Next he forced them to turn over to him the Oldsmobile that was being transported to Fort Worth. That done, he got into the car and roared off down Highway 67, headed west. The next day the Oldsmobile was found abandoned north of Mount Vernon. It had run out of gas.

The convoy, minus the Oldsmobile, turned back to Mount Pleasant to report the encounter and theft at Sheriff Guy Coker's office. Upon inspection of the automobile that Ransom had left beside Highway 67, officers found in it burglary tools that tied him to the break-ins at Mount Pleasant and Talco. The sedan itself was traced back to Henrietta, where Ransom had stolen it. With the realization that a potentially dangerous man was on the loose, Sheriff Coker called for help from the Rangers and Highway Patrol. At the same time, neighboring county and city police were alerted to be on the lookout.

When the Oldsmobile sputtered to a stop between Mount Vernon and Bogota, Ransom got out and surveyed the situation. Wary of staying on the road, he made his way on foot through woodlands until he was at a safe distance from the abandoned car. There he waited until dark before venturing forth again. He had to have transportation. By midnight he slipped up to a farmhouse where he found a car with the keys in it. That vehicle was standing in a shed between the house and barn. Before he could appropriate it, the farm hounds stirred up such a racket that the farmer got out of bed and switched on the outside lights. Seeing the intruder, he grabbed a shotgun and began firing at him. In his haste to get away, Ransom dropped several rolls of coins. Their wrappers bore the word "Waco," which connected him with the recent robbery of about a thousand dollars at Clark's Grocery Company in the city of Waco.

By early Wednesday morning, Ransom had trudged to the edge of Bogota. His need for transportation was urgent. He went up to a service station that was just opening for the day's business. The man on duty was Edgar S. Stewart, twenty-four, who operated the station along with his brother. At that moment, W. S. Stewart, twenty-two, drove up in a spanking new Chevrolet which the brothers had purchased the day before. That was just what Ransom needed, so he pulled a gun and propelled Edgar to the car. With the two brothers held at gunpoint, the trio took off, heading for Paris. The drive to Paris was not entirely disagreeable. There was conversation, during which Ransom bragged that he was the object of a search "all over" by officers, but that he would manage to stay out of their reach. On the way, he asked the Stewarts if they had any bills. Between them they produced thirteen dollars in bills. Instead of simply taking the money from them, he swapped an equal amount in wrapped coins. Those wrappers also bore the word "Waco."

When they reached Paris, Ransom forced the Stewarts to drive beyond the city into the country. At a remote spot where there were no houses in sight, he ordered them out of the car, took the wheel himself and, as they watched in anguish, roared off down the road in their new Chevrolet just as he had done in the car stolen from the convoy. In the meantime, based on reports of the location of the abandoned Oldsmobile, officers in the command post believed Ransom was heading for the Red River and a crossing into Oklahoma. As a consequence, orders went out to set up roadblocks at all bridge crossings along that part of the stream. But he fooled them and headed southwest!

The Stewarts caught a ride into Paris and reported the theft of their car. The word went to all counties in the area. Greenville police had just received the bulletin when Chief of Police Virgil Miller and Captain L. P. Petty, in a patrol car, saw the stolen Chevrolet pass them on the street headed toward Dallas. With siren screaming and red light flashing, the officers gave chase, firing at the car, which then speeded up. There was a perilous dash through the streets of Greenville, but it came to an end for Miller when the patrol car collided with a taxicab. Chief Miller suffered eight broken ribs in the crash and was taken to the hospital. Leaving Miller in the care of others, Captain Petty commandeered a private passenger car and resumed the chase, but it was too late. Ransom had disappeared from sight.

For his part, in the hurry to get away from his pursuers, Ransom lost control of the Chevrolet when he turned a corner at a high rate of speed. The car careened through two yards and smashed headlong into a telephone pole, an encounter that demolished the front end. Shaken but unhurt, Ransom looked about frantically for other transportation. In his excitement, he dropped two pistols. He took possession of the first thing he could find with the key in the ignition switch. It was a Yellow Cab. That was hardly an ideal getaway car but at least it had wheels, a nearly full tank of gasoline, and it would get him out of Greenville. Knowing that he would be expected on down the highway to Dallas, Ransom turned to the west on Highway 380.

With word coming to the command post from Captain Petty after he returned to headquarters, the alert area was widened. "Lone Wolf" Gonzaullas, Captain George Busby of the Highway Patrol and Fannin County Sheriff Dick Wait were at the post charting strategy. They were joined by Dallas Police Captain Will Fritz and Highland Park Chief of Police Millard Gardner. The need for aerial reconnaissance was felt, so a plane was dispatched from Dallas.

After some time, the command post received a report that Ransom had been spotted in the Yellow Cab at Farmersville, apparently headed toward McKinney. It did appear that he was trying to get to the metropolitan area where he could be lost in the crowd. But, again he fooled them. Ransom turned north on the western outskirts of Farmersville, made his way to Highway 78 and took a wide circle through Leonard, then to Wolfe City and on to Commerce. He had passed through that town only a couple of hours earlier on his route from Paris to Greenville.

He knew he had to get out of the Yellow Cab. That is what the officers were sure to be looking for, and it was easy to spot. He did what came naturally to him. He abandoned the cab and stole another car. His choice this time was a 1941 black Ford sedan with red wire wheels, which he took from Homer Clifton. Now that he was less conspicuous on the highway, he sped out of Commerce, retracing his trail back to Wolfe City. From there, he headed toward Bonham, though the officers did not know it at the time. The Yellow Cab would be discovered a bit later after Clifton reported the theft of his automobile. Ransom was again nearing the Red River, which he could not cross. At the same time, he was boxing himself into an ever smaller area.

His erratic path made the "Lone Wolf" and his fellow officers at the command post swear. What in the world was the fellow going to do next, they wondered. In response to calls for more help in running down Ransom, scores of officers joined in the search and roadblocks. Now he was known to be in the black Ford sedan, license number ES*7610. Before the manhunt was terminated, almost two hundred law enforcement officers were actively engaged in trying to spot him.

Before it was learned that Ransom had gone back to Commerce, and while an intensive search was going on along the highways leading into Dallas, the reconnaissance plane crashed in a field near Cockrell Hill and the pilot was killed. It was while attention was focused on approaches to Dallas that word was flashed to the command post that the black Ford had been seen near Bonham. It was Wednesday afternoon. Additional roadblocks were quickly set up to keep him from driving out of Fannin County. Ransom's next appearance was at a bridge over the Red River north of Bonham. He tried to cross it but was turned back by gunfire from Oklahoma officers manning a roadblock at the north end.

Ransom's situation was becoming desperate. From the bridge, he headed southeast. Late in the afternoon he drove into a service station-grocery at Monkstown where he bought gasoline, a roll of bologna and a loaf of bread. Again he disappeared. By this time, his pattern of doubling back on his tracks was recognized and when he reappeared in Monkstown at the supper hour, two Highway Patrolmen, Ross Kemp and W. A. Beaty of Paris, were waiting. When he saw them, Ransom took off in a cloud of dust. In the chase, he wrecked Homer Clifton's black Ford and fled into the thicket on foot, the patrolmen firing at him. One bullet grazed his chin, but he kept going. The untouched bologna and bread were found in the wrecked car, but no guns were abandoned that time. It was not known whether he was armed. Although armed throughout the two-day chase, he had not fired at an officer. Gonzaullas realized that Ransom's primary aim was to elude his pursuers, not fight it out with them, but no one took any chances.

On his abandonment of the Ford, the net was drawing tighter. Gonzaullas, Wait and Busby moved into the field to direct the search in its narrowed confines, but darkness hindered efforts. There was little that could be done in the night, so the time was spent deploying forces. Word was out in the northeastern part of Fannin County and northwestern portion of Lamar County. Residents reacted by turning on all outside lights, locking cars from which ignition keys had been removed and placing guns within easy reach of their beds. Despite the precautions, it was a night of nervousness on the part of householders. Ransom now knew that bridges were blocked, therefore he could not try to make his way across any of them. Additional officers were sent to stations at river fords so the fugitive would be forced to swim the stream in order to get into Oklahoma. No one knew whether he could swim.

At dawn on Thursday, two planes were called in to circle the woodlands, fields and pastures. One took off from Bonham and the other from Paris. Admittedly, the only chance of spotting him from the air would be if he endeavored to cross an open area when a plane was near enough to catch him in the act. Men on horseback and on foot surrounded the land in the fork of the Red River and Bois d'Arc Creek, slowly compressing the circle as they walked and rode, ever alert, weapons at the ready. It was rough country of brush-choked thickets, some swamplands, farms and abandoned houses. Dogs had been brought in at dawn and they picked up his trail but lost it near one of the abandoned farmhouses.

A Negro resident came up to give the information that he had seen a young blond man cutting across a field during the morning. It was startling news because that field was outside the closing circle. It meant that Ransom had slipped through a hole in the human dragnet. This tip provided a fresh starting point and called for a regrouping of the searchers. The hunt was narrowed to an area approximately two miles by three miles in extent.

At about 2:00 in the afternoon, Walter Ransom surrendered on the Gil Goss farm. He staggered out of the brush on the banks of Bois d'Arc Creek with his hands held high and said, "Don't shoot me. I give up!" He was bareheaded. His clothes were torn and caked with mud and he had a three-day growth of beard. Tears streamed from his bloodshot eyes. All the fight was gone from him. On being searched, he was found to be unarmed.

Thus ended what the "Lone Wolf" called "the greatest manhunt in Northeastern Texas since the days of the Clyde Barrow gang." That day of February 11 started out with what Ransom evidently thought would be just another routine robbery, but then things got completely out of hand for him. In the Fannin County jail at Bonham, he answered questions put to him by officers, saying that on Highway 67 west of Mount Pleasant he was headed for Dallas when he accidentally rammed the car in the convoy. "When the guy argued about paying for the damage, I just got mad and pulled my gun. That was a mistake," he said. Questioned about what he would have done if he had been armed when the posse closed in on him, he replied, "I would've killed myself. I was just trying to get away. I had no special plans." One thing he conceded was that the whole affair "wasn't worth it."

Ransom admitted to Gonzaullas that he had started stealing when he was thirteen and that by the time he reached fifteen he was sent to the Texas State School for Boys at Gatesville on a burglary conviction. After that time he said that he never considered going straight. "I just tried not to get caught." One thing had been proved about him and it was that he was not a killer. He had numerous opportunities to shoot at officers or victims, but he never did fire a shot. But, he was still thinking about getting away.

He was taken from county to county to face charges filed in connection with his recent spree. While he was in the McLennan County jail at Waco, he endeavored to involve another prisoner there in his plans for escape. Ransom offered him "several hundred dollars" if the other man's wife would bring into the jail a pistol and some hacksaw blades. The offer indicated that part of the loot from the Clark Grocery Company holdup was hidden in or near Waco. The escape plot fell apart when jail personnel got wind of what was going on. The prisoner whom Ransom approached acknowledged that he had asked his wife to bring the wanted items because "I was scared of him. Everybody up there was."

From Waco, he was moved to the Red River County jail at Clarksville by Deputy Sheriff O. H. Greenwood and Deputy Marshal Jack Crader. For the trip, Ransom was double handcuffed and a chain was fastened to the cuffs, then wrapped around his waist and locked. His legs were also shackled. "You must think I'll try to escape," he chided the officers. "We are just looking out for your health. We don't want you to get any ideas," McLennan County Sheriff C. G. Alexander replied.

During the years that Gonzaullas was captain of Company "B," the unit was housed in this frontier-style building on Ranger Circle, Fair Park, Dallas. (Courtesy Texas Ranger Hall of Fame and Museum.)

XVII

A Fitting Climax

As "Lone Wolf" Gonzaullas approached the end of the sixth decade of his life, his Ranger activities were increasingly directed into the field of administration. There was a lessening on his part of on-the-ground participation in the pursuit of criminals. He was the master strategist for the Rangers of Company "B," headquartered in Dallas. The men under his command were ranked at the top of the list in capability, and he gave them more of a free hand out in the field than did many officers. His "sixth sense" fitted hand in glove with his understanding of the intricacies of law enforcement and crime control. That understanding was based not only on his extensive training but also on practical experience through the years. It had played an important role in the remarkable record that Gonzaullas achieved during his career with the force. In his position as captain, he was able to accurately plot a successful course of action to be followed on specific cases. His expertise was frequently utilized by Department of Public Safety headquarters.

Nevertheless, now and then he was to be found out on the firing line leading and directing investigation and pursuit. The spirit of the chase remained strong in his blood. One place that grated on his nerves was Top O' The Hill, a notorious gambling casino on the outskirts of Arlington, between Fort Worth and Dallas. As the name implies, it was situated on the top of a hill, and it was known not only for its exclusiveness but also for the luxury of its appointments. The floors were covered with costly rugs and lighting was provided by elegant chandeliers. Top O' The Hill owner, Fred Browning, saw to it that dinner guests were provided with sterling silver flatware, that they ate off priceless china and drank from imported crystal. The property is utilized today by Arlington Baptist College, a far cry from its heyday role as a den of iniquity. The original casino has now been replaced by a modern college building, but the grounds are much as they were.

Top O' The Hill was well protected by armed guards and an elaborate electrical system designed to provide adequate warning to those inside that unwanted guests had arrived at the gate. Those unwanted guests who set off the alarm were invariably officers of the law. When the alarm sounded, the gaming tables and all connected pieces of equipment were instantly hidden in secret compartments in the walls. On the very few occasions that officers did get in, they would find some people playing lawful card games or shooting pool, while others sipped soft drinks and chatted. In addition to the warning system, there was a tunnel through which guests could escape if need be. They could enter it by means of a hidden door in the house. The mouth of the tunnel was well camouflaged in a dense growth of brush on the side of the hill.

Because patrons were carefully selected by the management and were there only by invitation, law officers could not disguise themselves and just walk in as customers. It was more than merely frustrating. It was maddening. Top O' The Hill was considered to be impregnable, but the "Lone Wolf" was committed to finding its Achilles heel. He made up his mind that he and his men would crack the place before he retired from Ranger service.

Gonzaullas and his associates of Company "B" plotted long and hard. The first thing that had to be done was to plant an informant on the staff of the casino, which was not the simplest matter in the world. However, it was eventually done when a Ranger, of all people, succeeded in going to work after an elaborate concoction of false background records was devised for him. His was an exceedingly dangerous assignment. Had he been found out, he would have been eliminated without mercy. After he had been on the job long enough to learn all details of the operation of the casino and its system of protection—the complete layout of the building and grounds, how many guards were outside on duty, what their pattern of patrol was—minutely detailed plans were developed. The time had arrived for the Rangers to move.

They selected Sunday night, August 10, 1947. Silently making their way through the wooded grounds on the back side of the estate, they surprised and soundlessly captured the guard for that area. One Ranger was stationed at the mouth of the tunnel. Gonzaullas and the other two crawled through the bushes up to the door where they remained hidden and waiting. When the door was opened to let in a patron who had been admitted at the front gate, they rushed the doorkeeper and captured him. Then they moved quickly into the casino. Their aim was to get there before the gambling equipment could be stashed away. They had to see it in operation.

The suddenness of their movement into the house caught everyone off guard. Their entrance into the gambling hall was greeted by screams from patrons, a handful of whom decided to make a run for the secret tunnel and freedom from arrest. It was wasted effort on their part. They were met at the mouth of the tunnel by the polite Ranger, who escorted them back inside where they were arrested along with all other patrons, the owner and his employees.

When the arrests had been completed, the Rangers turned their attention to the destruction of all of the gambling tables and devices. They did not use their axes on the furnishings of the building, because the furniture of Top O' The Hill was far too magnificent and costly to destroy wantonly. That was a distinct relief to the owner, Fred Browning, who paid the fines of all guests and employees, as well as those assessed against the house.

Four months after the successful raid on Top O' The Hill, Gonzaullas became involved as an investigative officer in the robbery of the First State Bank of Bremond, which occurred on December 23, 1947. In that incident, two men entered the bank at noon and held up the employees on duty, locking them and two customers in a vault.

Back in the days when Bonnie and Clyde and their kind were roving the state on their crime sprees, many small banks had adopted the policy of simply closing their doors during the noon hour. That was a prudent practice. A reduced staff between twelve noon and one o'clock, and the further fact that most law officers would be off duty while eating lunch, provided a tempting target for bandits. How many small-town banks were thus saved from robbery can never be known.

At Bremond, the pair turned away clutching more than twelve thousand dollars. When they went out the front door, they stepped right into the arms of Robertson County Sheriff Bob Reeves of Franklin. It was a development they did not expect. Sheriff Reeves had come to Bremond to pick up a new car from G. W. Holland, whose garage was located across the street from the bank. It was one of those chance circumstances where location and timing dovetailed perfectly. When the sheriff arrived at the garage to get his car, Stash Hoblinsky, a mechanic employed there, remarked to him that something might be wrong at the bank. He had looked up to see two men get out of an automobile, which had been parked at the curb in front of the bank, and go into the institution. There was nothing extraordinary about that. However, Hoblinsky observed that they had left the motor running. That was unusual, and suspicious. In addition, the bank's blinds had been lowered. That was not customary at midday.

Accompanied by Holland, Sheriff Reeves walked across the street and peered through the front window, trying to see inside. He was not noticed by the two busy men. When they came out, they were loaded with currency and sacks of coins, but one man held a gun in his hand. On seeing Reeves and Holland standing there, and not knowing one was a law enforcement officer, the bandit ordered them to stand against the outside wall of the bank. The heisters proceeded to the car. Sheriff Reeves' hand moved toward his holster, whereupon the robber called to him, "Don't draw," but the sheriff did so speedily and shot his challenger in the forehead, "right between the eyes." He fell partly into the car and dropped his pistol in the gutter. The driver attempted to pull his dying accomplice onto the front seat, but could not do it quickly, so he sped away, allowing the body to fall to the curb. When the alarm was broadcast, Falls County Sheriff Brady Pamplin headed southeast out of Marlin to set up a roadblock. He was alone. About five miles from town on the road to Bremond, he saw the wanted car approaching rapidly. Sheriff Pamplin stepped into the road with his submachine gun ready to fire. The oncoming bandit took his hands off the steering wheel and held them up, but did not stop. Instead, he zipped past the sheriff who wheeled and fired at the car. "I think every shot struck it," the sheriff reported.

When the news of the bank holdup, shooting and flight of the remaining bandit reached the general public, the usual flood of sightings started coming in, hampering the officers in their work. Each lead had to be checked. One such report originated in Dallas and gave "positive" word of having seen the car on a street in Oak Cliff. Two men were said to have been seated in it dividing a large sum of money. And, the car was steaming, indicating an overheated engine. That was at 3:00 P.M.

Gonzaullas and other officers did not become involved in a search for the automobile reputed to be in Oak Cliff. Just fifteen minutes earlier, the actual getaway car, complete with bullet holes, bloody passenger seat and about eighteen pounds of wrapped silver coins in a burlap bag (more than five hundred dollars worth) was found sitting in front of a business establishment in the River Oaks section of Fort Worth. River Oaks Chief of Police John Boyd spotted the vehicle, whose license number had been noted by Sheriff Reeves as it sped from the bank in Bremond.

"Lone Wolf" Gonzaullas, Highway Patrol Captain Jack Sutherland and two FBI agents inspected the car for clues. The bandit slain at Bremond was identified as J. B. Hooper, twenty-one. Joe S. Fletcher of the Department of Public Safety in Austin reported that the Chevrolet had been stolen in Dallas back on August 3. Fingerprints found in the car were those of Francis M. (Bobby) Hooper, twenty-six, brother of the dead man. Later, it was disclosed that the car had been seen at Clifton soon after the noon hour. It was obvious that Hooper had threaded his way through and around the hastily assembled roadblocks at Waco and that he had traveled from Clifton through Meridian and Glen Rose, approaching Fort Worth from the southwest. A dragnet was spread over North Central Texas, with emphasis on the Fort Worth region. Nearly a month passed before Hooper turned up.

He had slipped out of Texas and flown west. After stops en route, he ended up in Los Angeles. From the airport there, he telephoned a World War II buddy with whom he had served on Okinawa. Unknown to Hooper was the fact that his friend was now a rookie patrolman. Hooper wanted to come by the house for a visit with him and his wife, so the men could talk over "old times." He was invited for dinner. Hooper's buddy had read about the Bremond bank robbery and the search for the escaped bandit, but he did not indicate that. At the conclusion of the telephone conversation, the patrolman notified the FBI and his superiors in the Los Angeles Police Department. The two agencies coordinated their plans.

While the trio sat at dinner, officers quietly surrounded the house. Hooper surrendered without resistance. He was found to have $5,750 of the bank loot in his possession. After being placed in jail, Hooper remarked that he felt no resentment against his friend for what he had done. He commented, "We killed Japs together on Tinian and Okinawa, but I'm not sore. I would've done just what he did if I had been in his place." Hooper admitted that during the conversation at the dinner table when his friend let it be known that he knew of the robbery and flight, "He advised me to turn myself in. I was considering it when I was caught."

After Hooper was returned to Texas and placed in jail at San Antonio, he told where he had hidden about fourteen hundred dollars of the bank loot. On his journey to Fort Worth, he had turned aside at Meridian, gone into the country and buried a Federal Reserve Bank sack beside a dirt road about seven miles west of the town. The money was in the form of silver dollars, half dollars, quarters and dimes. "He told us the exact location," Sheriff Reeves said, "and it was no trouble to find."

Following soon was another bank robbery, but it was one in which no one was killed. It took place at Buffalo in Leon County on Friday, February 27, 1948, just over two months after that at nearby Bremond. At Buffalo, a lone gunman went into the Citizens State Bank in the early afternoon. With that Bremond robbery fresh in his mind, Sam Boroughs, president of Citizens State, became uneasy when he looked out and saw a Buick sedan, which had no license plates, stop in front of the bank. When the driver left the car running and started walking toward the entrance, Boroughs stepped into his office at the back where he would be able to telephone police if any untoward event transpired. That is what he thought he would do, but he did not remain out of sight. The stranger walked up to the window manned by A. A. Raines, pulled a pistol from his pocket and aimed it at Raines, saying "Tell that man to come out of the back room, or I'll shoot you!"

Hearing the threat, Boroughs voluntarily came from his office. He had no opportunity to notify police. The thirty-two-year-old bandit was short and stocky, and extremely nervous. The bank personnel feared that in his trembling excitement, he might inadvertently fire the gun. The outlaw ordered Boroughs to fill a sack with cash. When the president started stacking one-dollar bills on the counter, he was brought to heel by the curt order to "give me some of that big stuff," so stacks of five- and ten-dollar bills were laid out. The man grabbed and stuffed them into his jacket.

Just as he was turning to leave, Mrs. Connie Fulks, publisher of the *Buffalo Press*, and Leon Lynch, a farmer, entered. To their astonishment, they were looking into the barrel of a pistol. The bandit ordered them to join the others and then ran outside to jump into the Buick sedan and flee. Mrs. Fulks unexpectedly was in on the ground floor of a news story she could write for her paper.

The bandit was almost caught in the act. Harry Boroughs, brother of the bank president and owner of a dry goods store next door, started into the building and saw the gunman, whose back was toward the front door. Boroughs was unseen, so he ran back to his store and telephoned the alarm to Leon County Sheriff Ben Lee, who happened to be in Buffalo on business. Lee rushed to the bank just in time to see the robber turning a corner in the Buick several blocks up the street.

A posse consisting of four area county sheriffs, namely Paul Stanford of Anderson, Jim Sessions of Freestone, Charlie Shreve of Limestone and Ben Lee of Leon County, highway patrolmen and FBI agents joined in the search. Captain M. T. Gonzaullas and members of Company "B" sped to Buffalo from Dallas. Gonzaullas directed the spreading of the dragnet. By nightfall the search had been enlarged to a statewide basis. The abandoned Buick was found by the pilot of a reconnoitering plane. It was in a grove of trees near Highway 75. Footprints leading from the car to the road indicated to officers that the robber had an accomplice who picked him up at that predetermined spot.

"Lone Wolf" Gonzaullas and his fellow officers discovered from prints on the Buick that the Buffalo bandit was B. L. Franklin. They worked closely in tracking him. It was not easy because the man remained constantly on the move, but find him they did in less than three weeks. He was picked up at 1:00 A.M. in a Texarkana, Arkansas, dance hall in company with a blond. It was said at the time that "he danced right into the arms of the law." Franklin had just requested the orchestra leader to play "Sentimental Reasons" when Deputy Sheriff Frank Riley cut in on the dance and placed Franklin under arrest. Franklin said friends warned him to stay away from Texarkana because officers had been raiding night clubs and rooming houses in a crime control drive. "They said this was a hot spot. Here I am and I'm caught." He had on his person $867 of the $2,350 he had taken from the Citizens State Bank in Buffalo.

Gonzaullas was brought into the case of a missing Dallas man in September 1948. G. S. (Jack) Rose and J. M. (Jim) Corbett decided to go coon hunting in Bosque County near the residence of Mrs. Rose's mother, Mrs. Frank Bradstreet of Clifton. Corbett was living at the Rose's Dallas residence in Oak Cliff, having rented a room there. On July 28, Rose and his wife, accompanied by Jim Corbett, drove to Bosque County, taking Mrs. Rose to visit at Mrs.

Bradstreet's home. When the two men drove away in Rose's car, that was the last time his wife saw him alive. By the following day, when the hunters had not returned, Mrs. Rose became alarmed. She finally reported her husband's disappearance. An alert was put out in Texas on Rose's automobile and was later extended nationwide.

Dallas police handled the initial phase of the investigation but were confronted by a brick wall on every angle they checked out. After it became recognized that the missing man was possibly dead, the Dallas Police Department turned the matter over to the state. The action was based on the belief that if he had been slain, it was unlikely that his death occurred in Dallas County. Captain Gonzaullas took charge of the case, since Rose resided in his Ranger district. There was nothing to go on. The two men and the car had vanished. But a month later there was a break. It happened in Jacksonville, Florida, where Patrolmen B. W. Hagen and W. C. Townsend of that city's police department arrested Jim Corbett and Fred Miller of Syracuse, New York, when they spotted the license plate number of Jack Rose's car. With Corbett and Miller was Arthur Tousant of Watertown, New York, who told police later that he knew of Rose's murder but had been picked up by his companions long after it was committed.

Miller and Corbett accused one another of murdering Rose and stealing his car. Miller said the killing took place in Bosque County where Corbett and Rose had gone on their coon hunting expedition. For his part, Corbett asserted that Miller had killed Rose near Gladewater, Texas. The only thing they did agree on was that the body was buried "on the bank of a river close to Nashville, Tennessee." Directions to the grave were vague. Tennessee, Florida and Texas officers spent more than a week probing in the area, but without success. The grave was located when the "Lone Wolf" took Corbett from Jacksonville to Camden, Tennessee. Corbett led him and the other officers to the shallow grave about seven miles from Camden. It was near the shore of Kentucky Lake on the Tennessee River. There they found a body in an advanced state of deterioration. Soon after his arrest in Jacksonville, Miller failed in an attempt at suicide.

Mrs. Rose was flown to Camden where she sobbingly identified articles of clothing as having belonged to her husband. Dental records confirmed that Jack Rose had been found. She was accompanied to Tennessee by Glenn H. McLaughlin, chief of the Bureau of Identification and Records, Department of Public Safety at

Austin. Gonzaullas said the cause of death, determined by an autopsy, was a gunshot wound in the head. "The bullet entered the left side of the head under the ear," Gonzaullas reported, "and emerged above the right temple, knocking out a part of the skull."

Corbett later voluntarily confessed that the murder was committed about two miles from Clifton on Highway 6. In his confession, Corbett said he was driving the car because Rose had been drinking excessively. According to Corbett, Rose became belligerent and removed a pistol from the glove compartment with the avowed intention of shooting him (Corbett). When Rose started trying to insert a cartridge into the chamber, Corbett said he pulled his own pistol and fired at him in self-defense. He moved Rose's body to the back seat of the car and covered it, after which he went to Dallas and picked up Miller. They drove for two days with Rose's body in the vehicle, Corbett said. When they reached Western Tennessee, they had to dispose of it so Miller stole a shovel from a construction job. The pair dug a hole and put Rose's body in it. When Corbett led the officers to that grave, the body was found to be covered by only six inches of soil. After being brought to Texas from Tennessee, Corbett, Miller and Tousant were placed in the Bosque County jail at Meridian. They were soon transferred to the Johnson County jail at Cleburne for safekeeping.

Corbett was indicted by the Bosque County grand jury and tried in the Fifty-second District Court at Meridian in November 1948. Gonzaullas and Mrs. Rose were among those giving testimony. The trial and deliberation by the jury did not last long. Corbett was sentenced to twenty-five years in the penitentiary. Miller and Tousant waived a jury trial and were immediately sentenced by Judge R. B. Cross to two years each for their part in concealing the murder. Within two hours after the sentences were pronounced on the three men, they were taken from Meridian to the Huntsville unit by Bosque County Sheriff George Grimes and his deputy, Doyle Spurlin.

Gambling casinos in Texas had been decimated in numbers due to the dedicated efforts of Rangers such as M. T. Gonzaullas. He and his associates on the force all over the state had worked tirelessly to put them out of business. But, there were still a few successfully clinging to a thread of life. That thread was cut for one when the "Lone Wolf," accompanied by Rangers R. L. (Bob) Badgett, Ernest Daniel, Jay Banks and L. C. Rigler, closed in on Sherman's Hi-Lite Club on Highway 75 during the evening of Monday,

August 1, 1949. Captain Gonzaullas stated that the Ranger force undertook that raid because so many complaints had been made by Sherman citizens who objected to the open gambling going on in their city. He did not seek the help of Grayson County or Sherman officers in investigating the complaints or in carrying out the raid itself. "I just acted on my own," he commented. Five months earlier, a "token" raid had been made by Sherman officers. It had no appreciable effect on the continued operation of the casino.

Although it was plush, the Hi-Lite Club was not as elaborate a setup as was Top O' The Hill at Arlington, but the patrons were just as astonished in one place as in the other when the Rangers entered. For certain, the Hi-Lite was easier to get into. Dressed in a gray business suit and looking every inch a successful executive who was out for an evening of fun, Gonzaullas had stood in the club watching the proceedings for more than a quarter of an hour when his associates arrived. His nonparticipation in the game did not attract notice because the place was so crowded with chance-takers it was not possible for all who were there to take part at the same time. He said he had sat downstairs for an hour and watched men and women passing up and down the stairs leading to the casino. When asked how he was able to get in, he smiled and replied, "Oh, that was easy. I was vouched for." He would not reveal whose recommendation it was that gave him entree to the place. The "Lone Wolf" was quoted as saying, "Everyone was very nice when we announced the raid." Then he added, "Of course, there were a lot of nice people there."

The patrons had no tunnel into which they could dart, so they remained calm, though embarrassed at the notoriety they feared would follow the raid and attendant publicity. Some of Sherman's leading citizens were participating in the games when the raid was announced. The raid on the casino and the charges that were filed resulted from a detailed investigation that had been conducted for over a month. Undercover Rangers had visited the Hi-Lite Club as patrons and were armed with facts to support the charges made against the owner, his employees and the customers of the place. All of the equipment in the club was confiscated, as was the large sum of money spread on the tables.

In the summer of 1950, the "Lone Wolf" told Mickey Cohen to "git." The notorious racketeer followed instructions and departed, all the while complaining about the lack of traditional Texas hospitality. As a matter of fact, Cohen had no choice but to comply since his presence in Texas was not wanted by state authorities. When word reached Austin that Cohen and two associates had turned up at Odessa, instructions went out from Colonel Homer Garrison, Director, Department of Public Safety, to Captain M. T. Gonzaullas of Company "B" and Captain R. A. "Bob" Crowder of Company "C" to eject them from the state. Garrison said he had received reliable information that Cohen intended to extend his gambling empire into Texas. It was the firm resolve of the law enforcement authorities to nip that plan in the bud.

Joined by two other Rangers, Gonzaullas and Crowder started on Cohen's trail. They missed him at Odessa but tracked him to Wichita Falls. In that city he was placed under technical arrest by the sheriff, awaiting the arrival of the Rangers, but was allowed freedom. When the "Lone Wolf," Crowder and their two companions reached Wichita Falls, they went straight to the hotel where Cohen, Harry Brooks and Dennis Morrison were staying in a suite. In the early morning hours of Thursday, August 31, Cohen, Brooks and Morrison were roused from their sleep. They were taken to the Wichita County jail, then whisked to Fort Worth, where they were questioned further. Brooks was permitted to take a flight to Cleveland, Ohio, where he was residing at the time. Cohen and Morrison were summarily placed on a Los Angeles-bound plane by Gonzaullas and the other Rangers, who maintained watch until it was in the air.

The plane was due to touch down at El Paso, so the county sheriff there, Joe Campbell, was notified to be on the lookout in order to ensure that Cohen and his companion kept going. The two men did get off at El Paso, where they were picked up by Sheriff Campbell, taken to the El Paso County jail and fingerprinted. After that, they were turned over to the El Paso city police. Those officers escorted Cohen and Morrison back to the airport and put them on another Los Angeles-bound plane, keeping them under observation until the aircraft took off.

A short time later, a large box of extra-fancy California fruit was delivered to the Gonzaullas' residence in Dallas. It was a gift from Mickey Cohen. Gonzaullas promptly returned the box, unopened, freight charges collect.

The last public official duty "Lone Wolf" Gonzaullas carried out, before his approaching retirement was announced, came when General of the Army Douglas MacArthur visited Dallas on Friday,

June 15, 1951. There was a tumultuous reception for MacArthur. A crowd estimated at more than four hundred thousand jammed the streets of the city to cheer the general who had been fired by President Truman. That evening, the Cotton Bowl was overflowing with enthusiastic Texans who came to hear him speak. Ordinarily, Captain Gonzaullas would have been involved in the security arrangements for the general, his wife and young son Arthur, but not that day. The famous "Lone Wolf" had been chosen to make a presentation to the boy on behalf of the city of Dallas.

When the chartered Constellation landed at Love Field at 3:50 P.M., the first man to greet MacArthur was the reception committee chairman, L. H. True, who introduced Mayor J. B. Adoue and Chamber of Commerce President John W. Carpenter, followed by other members of the committee. Then Captain Gonzaullas stepped forward, holding a pearl-handled .45 caliber, single-action Colt revolver, which was inscribed, "To Arthur MacArthur, from friends of his father." The revolver was in a handsomely hand-tooled leather holster. To the wide-eyed delight of the youth, the holstered gun was placed in his hands, and Gonzaullas told him that such Colt revolvers had helped make Texas history. The youth pulled the gun from the holster and first held it by the barrel. General MacArthur was openly pleased at the attention Dallasites had paid to the thirteen-year-old, and when Arthur stammered a thrilled, "Say. Thanks a lot," MacArthur laughed. The airport crowd of twenty thousand cheered.

Arthur fondled the gun, turning it over and around in his hands until the party moved forward and he was obliged to go also. A fitting climax to Gonzaullas' illustrious career was the boy's parting grin of appreciation to the veteran Ranger, an expression that conveyed a joy that could never have been expressed in words. Captain Gonzaullas felt a pang of sadness that he had no son or daughter and he controlled the urge to reach out and grasp this clean-cut youngster in a hug of warm affection. And then it was over!

XVIII

The Last Years

Five days after Captain Gonzaullas presented the Colt revolver to young Arthur MacArthur, he announced his plans to retire. The decision had been made at a much earlier date and his intentions were revealed in a letter to Colonel Homer Garrison, Jr., Director, Department of Public Safety in Austin. The fact that he would soon be leaving was known in the Ranger force after the letter was written, but one of the things Rangers were skilled in doing was keeping a secret. Word was withheld from the public until he personally made the news known in his statement to the press on June 20, 1951.

The letter to Colonel Garrison was dated May 3, 1951. It said in part:

> You will recall on various occasions in the past few years I have expressed to you my desire to retire from active duty in the Texas Rangers upon reaching the age of sixty, whereby I could enter another field which would enable me to spend more time with my family.
> After much thought and careful consideration, I have come to the definite decision to retire from active duty as a Captain of the Texas Rangers, this Department, effective at the close of business July 31, 1951, for the purpose of entering the radio, television and moving picture field . . . .
> When I first joined the Texas Rangers and took the oath at Austin, Texas on October 1, 1920, it was the fulfillment of

all my boyish hopes and dreams. At times, the road was rough and rugged and the life dangerous, but regardless of the nature of my assignments, I have always endeavored to the best of my ability to meticulously obey and carry out orders in the true traditional Ranger form. Now as I am about to come to the close of my long Ranger career, it is indeed gratifying to know that I have contributed in some small way to the success and progress of one of the finest world renowned law enforcement organizations. I shall always cherish the fond memories of the many years that I have served . . . and been associated with the wonderful personnel that makes up this magnificent body . . . .

Although he declined to reveal details at the time of the announcement, it did become known that he would go to Hollywood as a consultant. Touching on that in an editorial on June 22, the *Dallas Morning News* commented,

> So Texas Ranger M.T. (Lone Wolf) Gonzaullas is retiring—of all places—to Hollywood! Best of wishes of a thousand police reporters go with him. Ten times that many police characters are glad to see him change scenery. The man was poison! In that perilous time between crime and capture, he was great. In that split second when, pistol in hand, a shot meant death or apprehension, he was coolly accurate. That is the test of a good officer. Courage is not enough. It must be courage with composure.
> Lone Wolf will be a "technical adviser" to the boys that make Hollywood westerns. That is good news. For goodness sakes, will he please tell them how to wear western hats! Will he put his spurs on future efforts to make a cowboy star out of Victor Mature; let the latter star in *Brooklyn Bridge is Falling Down*. Gary Cooper is better, but needs the authenticity in detail that Gonzaullas can supply.

By July 8, his full Hollywood secret had slipped out. In an interview with the "Lone Wolf," Mike Dickinson of the *Dallas Times-Herald* wrote, "Although he will lay away his uniform, mild-mannered Ranger Gonzaullas will stay close to his first love. He will become technical consultant for a national radio and television series 'Tales of the Texas Rangers' in the near future. He will divide his time between Hollywood and Dallas, but will retain his home here. 'Tales of the Texas Rangers' will have authentic stories of Ranger life. Many of the scenes for television will be photo-

Company "B" Rangers at Gonzaullas' retirement party in 1951. *Front row, left to right*: John T. Cope, S. H. Denson, M. T. Gonzaullas, Robert A. Crowder, Bob Badgett and L. C. Rigler. *Back row, left to right*: G. M. Roach, Jay Banks, Jim Geer, Dick Oldham, Stewart Stanley, and Ernest Daniel. (Courtesy Texas Ranger Hall of Fame and Museum.)

graphed in Texas." As a matter of fact, the California landscape was clearly in evidence in the finished product. Although it was not made known at the time, Captain Gonzaullas had occupied his spare time for two years before retirement in assembling material to be used first in the radio program, and then on television.

For both series, all completed scripts were submitted by the studio to Gonzaullas for review by him and by Colonel Garrison. The "Lone Wolf" looked upon his connection with Hollywood as an opportunity to give the American public an overall view and understanding of the Texas Ranger force. The direct role that he and Garrison played assured that there would be no glamorizing or exaggeration of exploits and events. "Let's keep the record straight at all times," said Gonzaullas.

The *Fort Worth Star-Telegram*'s staff writer Mack Williams, reporting from Athens, where Gonzaullas' retirement party was under way at Koon Kreek Klub on July 10, quoted the captain as saying that the officers of today work harder than the old-timers. "They have to know more law," said the "Lone Wolf." He added, "They work scientifically." He told Williams that in earlier years the best way to break the spirit of an outlaw was to put him on the old iron chain. "When I handcuffed my prisoners to a chain wrapped around a tree, people would come and laugh at them. Many prisoners told me they'd get out of town and never return if only I'd turn them loose from the chain," he reminisced. That had been his experience in Wichita County, at Borger and at Kilgore. "Tear gas does the trick now," he observed. "A man can't be tough when he's crying and vomiting."

At the Athens party, Gonzaullas told his friends he would be technical adviser to the celebrated Stacy Keach, who would produce the series "Tales of the Texas Rangers." His own ambition, he told them, was to make the Rangers famous all over the world, just as they were in Texas. Questioned by reporters on one of their favorite topics, the number of men he was reputed to have killed in the line of duty, the "Lone Wolf" replied, "Let's just say there were several. I don't like to dwell on it. I did it only to protect my own life, or property, and only to enforce the law!"

Henderson County Sheriff Jess Sweeten, a longtime friend, was host at the retirement barbecue honoring Gonzaullas at Koon Kreek Klub. Gathered there were 200 top law enforcement officers of the state, plus 150 Texas business leaders. All had come to demonstrate their friendship and admiration for a man whose adult life had been spent in work aimed at making Texas a safer place in

Gonzaullas and Colonel Homer Garrison, Jr., then Director of the Department of Public Safety, at Gonzaullas' retirement party. (Courtesy Texas Ranger Hall of Fame and Museum.)

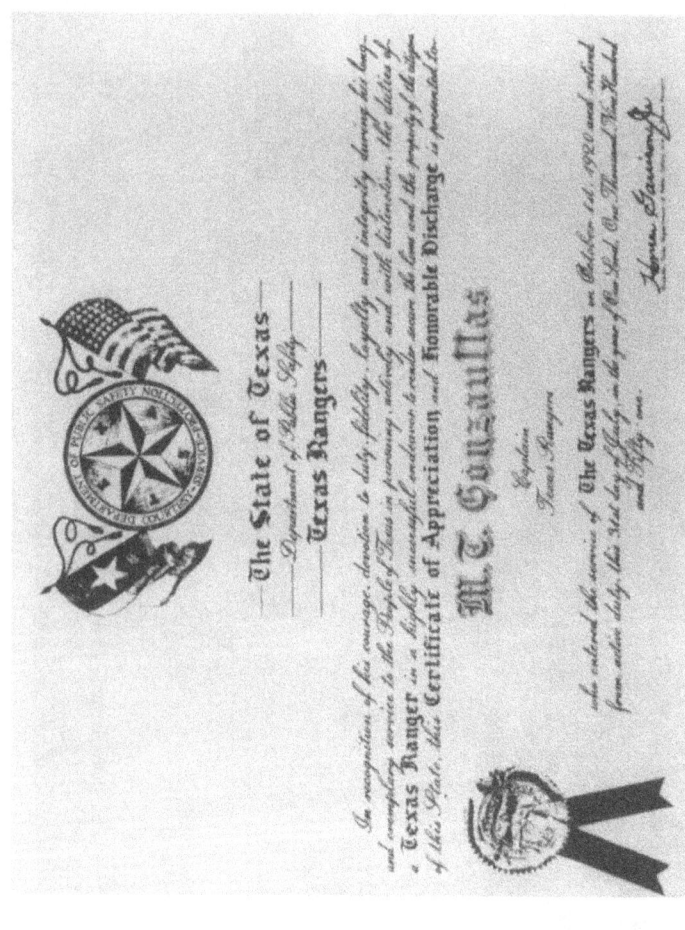

Certificate of Appreciation and Honorable Discharge presented to Gonzaullas when he retired from the Texas Rangers. (Courtesy Texas Ranger Hall of Fame and Museum.)

which her citizens could live. Tributes were paid to Gonzaullas in addresses by several of the guests. Included among those was his successor as captain of Company "B," Bob Crowder, who said of him that if a dangerous mission came up, he wouldn't send one of his men out on it. He would go himself. "That is the kind of man he is," Crowder noted. Colonel Garrison commented that Gonzaullas never questioned an order but went ahead and carried it out, "even at risk to his own life."

For his part, the "Lone Wolf" spoke of law enforcement officers with whom he had been associated during the past thirty-one years and paid special tribute to those in small towns. He said, "I have learned much about crime control by listening to small-town officers discuss their experiences and share their knowledge. They are a fine bunch of men."

News of Gonzaullas' retirement and his forthcoming role in Hollywood caught the fancy of the news media. By the dozens, newspapers from El Paso to Texarkana, from Brownsville to Amarillo carried stories of his exploits. Gonzaullas' adventures made exciting material for their subscribers, always eager to hear and read tales of the age-old, never ceasing battle between the law and outlaws. A full-page article in the *Houston Chronicle* was typical of those which lavished attention on this man, who was admired as one of the most colorful Rangers in the long history of the force.

In that *Chronicle* article, Don Hinga wrote in part, "There's one member of his family, his wife of over 30 years, who'll have no regrets when he hangs up his holsters. They bore no children. 'A Ranger's life is like that of a baby doctor,' Gonzaullas says. 'You seldom get a hurry call unless it's at night, and the weather is never good. You never know when you pull out whether you're going to be gone for a day, a week or maybe a month. My wife was always sitting up for me when I came back . . . . ' "

In commenting to Hinga on the dangers of facing the very young and the old outlaw, Gonzaullas managed to get in a blast at criminals of today. He observed, "There are two classes you have to watch out for. One is a young kid. He hasn't got sense enough to know much about danger. The other is an old man. He hasn't got much more time to live, and usually doesn't give a damn." Hinga concluded the long article, "He flatly refuses to talk about any gun fights, but he grins and tells you his philosophy. 'I'd rather be tried for killing a dozen _____s in enforcing the law than have one of them tried for killing me!' "

The excitement contained in the news stories about Gonzaullas' career and retirement spread from Texas over the United States. Articles were published in metropolitan papers from coast to coast. He was written up in *Newsweek*, which carried a photograph showing him astride Charcoal, his favorite horse. Charcoal is now buried in the pet cemetery at Marshall.

Then it was off to Hollywood where he and Mrs. Gonzaullas were to rub shoulders with the stars. They became friends of many of filmdom's leading men and women. Those people, who were accustomed to encountering autograph hounds wherever they went, became fascinated with this Ranger character fresh from Texas, a man who, in real life, personified the triumph of good over evil in what might be called the never-ending Western morality play. The stars turned autograph hounds and sought Gonzaullas' signature for their own collections.

Captain and Mrs. Gonzaullas enjoyed their life in the tinsel world that was so different from that back at home in Texas. For his part, the "Lone Wolf" was preoccupied with his responsibilities as technical adviser to Keach. Mrs. Gonzaullas laughed and said, "The Ranger force is his first love. From the beginning of his service, I knew that I would be his second love!" For episode plots in the radio and television series, he furnished authentic material gleaned from his own experiences and those of other Rangers, contemporary and earlier. The Hollywood scriptwriters were not obliged to draw on their fertile imagination. Facts furnished by Gonzaullas were as exciting as any plots the writers could have dreamed up.

Joel McCrea starred in the radio version of "Tales of the Texas Rangers," which had a nationwide following. When the televised series went on the air for its long and successful run, Craig Stevens, Willard Parker and Harry Lauter had leading roles at different times during production. The series was also taken up by Dell Comics in the publication of books bearing the same name, "Tales of the Texas Rangers." The comic book plots were the product of the author's fancy. They were not based primarily on Gonzaullas' personal experiences. In all of them, radio, television and books, the principal Ranger character was named Jace Pearson. The "Lone Wolf" owned half of the radio and television series.

By December 1952, he was touring the country promoting the new motion picture *The Lawless Breed* starring Rock Hudson in the role of John Wesley Hardin. Gonzaullas had served as technical adviser on the film, which was produced by Universal-Inter-

At Company "F" Texas Rangers headquarters in Waco, 1972. *Left to right:* retired Ranger Ernest Daniel, Mrs. Daniel, Laura Isabel Gonzaullas, and the "Lone Wolf."

national. On his promotional visit to Houston, he was interviewed and questioned regarding his attitude toward the perennial question of gun control. He told the reporter for the *Houston Post*, George Jackson, "Guns make all men equal. If the law says nobody can have a gun, the good citizens are going to obey the law, but the criminals aren't." He further said he believed the solution to crime lay in cooperation by the citizenry. "In other words," he commented, "the people who serve on juries have got to levy such stiff sentences that murder becomes unpopular . . . ." He had said much the same thing on prior occasions, and he would say it again.

When his work in Hollywood ended after five years of commuting between Dallas and the West Coast, the "Lone Wolf" finally settled down to a quiet life of retirement. It was not easy, because his had been a full and busy existence. He and Mrs. Gonzaullas had outside interests that helped him. Into these they directed their energy. Both were active in serving Gaston Episcopal Hospital in Dallas as members of the board of directors. She became secretary of the board and he was elected vice-chairman, finally stepping into the chairmanship, which post he held at the time of his death.

They were members of the West Shore Presbyterian Church, where he served on the board of deacons. Gonzaullas had been a member of Pentagon Lodge #1080, AF&AM, Dallas, since December 23, 1924. On April 24, 1925, he had attained the Thirty-second Degree of Scottish Rite, and the following day had been constituted a Noble of the Mystic Shrine in Hella Temple, Dallas. Captain and Mrs. Gonzaullas were charter members of Lakewood Country Club. Affiliation with these organizations kept them occupied. And he worked with his flowers. But there was always time out to attend any gathering of ex-Rangers anywhere in the state.

Paradoxically, the "Lone Wolf" and Mrs. Gonzaullas enjoyed legal gambling. After his retirement in 1951, during their sojourn in California they were frequent patrons of the racetracks in that state, where they played the horses. Following their return to Texas, they regularly traveled to Louisiana, Kentucky and the northeastern United States to attend horseracing events. In states where racing and accompanying betting were within the law, his attitude was "enjoy it." In others, where they were outside the law, he would say "forget it!"

Throughout his lifetime, the captain never touched alcohol. During his active years in law enforcement out in the field, he was a cigar smoker but when he retired he dropped that habit. Perhaps

Laura Gonzaullas' influence can be seen there. Her home was filled with luxurious furnishings in period pieces. Chairs and sofas were upholstered with rich fabrics, the cushions down filled. How many women would approve of having draperies and upholstery permeated by cigar smoke? The most powerful and individualistic men are frequently tamed by a gentle woman's persuasive words.

Because of the encounters he had with the criminal element and the prominent role he played in sending several to the electric chair, the "Lone Wolf" and his wife were ever conscious of the danger of retaliation. For the sake of their safety, they had ornamental iron grilles installed over window openings in their house. Doors were similarly protected. His enormous gun collection, which many people knew about, could be tempting to thieves. Captain Gonzaullas always carried a holstered pistol. Mrs. Gonzaullas kept a small gun in her purse. As long as he drove a car, the "Lone Wolf" carried within easy reach his "hand machine gun," the automatic pistol capable of firing sixty-four rounds.

He took great interest in the creation by Waldine Tauch of the Ranger statue, which was placed in the lobby of the terminal building at Dallas' Love Field. Captain Jay Banks of Dallas had been the model for the artistic work. At the dedication on April 30, 1961, Captain Gonzaullas looked over the throng gathered for the ceremony. He was soberly aware of the absence of three of his close friends, men with whom he had served on the Ranger force. In 1958, both Gully Cowsert and Johnny Klevenhagen had died. Captain Jerry Gray had left the thinning ranks of retired Rangers in 1959. In that year of 1961, the "Lone Wolf" reached his seventieth birthday, but he was still vigorous and strong, the picture of robust health. He looked ten years younger than the calendar showed. Captain Tom Hickman, under whom he had served, was destined to go in 1962, Joe S. Fletcher in 1966, Colonel Homer Garrison in 1968 and Marvin "Red" Burton in 1970. In the old Texas frontier tradition, it was said of those men that "they had heard the owl hoot." Many of the old-timers were firm in their conviction that just before death, warning of the impending event is given by the hoot of an owl sent for that special purpose.

Late in the year before Colonel Garrison died, Gonzaullas served on the committee which developed plans for an event in Waco that had double significance. There was a luncheon on December 12, 1967, honoring Garrison, whose health was rapidly failing. A second part of the program was the breaking of ground for the Fort Fisher Museum in Lake Brazos Park. It was to be a building in which Texas Ranger memorabilia would be housed, and it would also contain the headquarters of Company "F." After Garrison died on May 7, 1968, the name was changed to the Homer Garrison Memorial Museum. The building was dedicated on October 25, 1968.

Gonzaullas himself was honored on December 15 of that year when a portrait of him by Holmes Ed Jones of Beaumont was presented to the museum and dedicated. Colonel Wilson E. Speir, Garrison's successor as Director of the Texas Department of Public Safety, addressed the group and gave a resume of Gonzaullas' distinguished career in the service. The "Lone Wolf" expressed his deep gratitude for the honor paid him and said, "The place on the museum wall you have selected to hang this portrait is significant to me, and also appreciated. My idol in the Rangers was Captain John R. Hughes. His illustrious career inspired my early career. He was an example of the honest, fearless and courageous officer after whom I patterned my life. Then too, this spot on the side of the portrait of my dearest friend and former chief, Colonel Garrison, adds much to this honor to me." Garrison's large portrait hung centered on the wall above the fireplace. To the left was the portrait of Hughes. That of Gonzaullas was placed on the right. Then he praised the city of Waco for providing "this fantastically appropriate fort, this outstanding museum. We have wanted a museum, a repository for our treasures and memorabilia for many years and we are deeply grateful to you people of Waco for this honor to the Rangers, and to the honor and memory of Homer Garrison . . . ."

Among others who held Captain John R. Hughes in high regard was the famous western writer Zane Grey, whose book *Lone Star Ranger*, published in 1914 by Frank A. Munsey Company, was dedicated to him. The memory of Hughes was still fresh in the minds of the older Texas Rangers. He had died in Austin in 1947 at the age of ninety-two and was buried in the State Cemetery.

Zane Grey's dedication read,

To CAPTAIN JOHN HUGHES and his Texas Rangers.

It may seem strange to you that out of all the stories I heard on the Rio Grande I should choose as first that of Buck Duane—outlaw and gunman.

But, indeed, Ranger Coffee's story of the last of the Duanes has haunted me, and I have given full rein to imagination and have retold it in my own way. It deals with the old law—the old border days—therefore it is better first. Soon, perchance, I shall have the pleasure of writing of the border of today, which in Joe Sitter's laconic speech, "Shore is 'most as bad an' wild as ever!"

In the North and East there is a popular idea that the frontier of the West is a thing long past, and remembered now only in stories. As I think of this I remember Ranger Sitter when he made that remark, while he grimly stroked an unhealed bullet wound. And I remember the giant Vaughn, that typical son of stalwart Texas, sitting there quietly with bandaged head, his thoughtful eye boding ill to the outlaw who had ambushed him. Only a few months have passed since then—when I had my memorable sojourn with you—and yet, in that short time, Russell and Moore have crossed the Divide, like Rangers.

Gentlemen,—I have the honor to dedicate this book to you, and the hope that it shall fall to my lot to tell the world the truth about a strange, unique and misunderstood body of men—The Texas Rangers—who made the great Lone Star State habitable, who never know peaceful rest and sleep, who are passing, who surely will not be forgotten and will some day come into their own.

The "Lone Wolf" passed through Denton in January 1970 on his way to a Company "B" reunion at Rex Cauble's ranch, and visited with Bill Rives. Writing in his column, "Views," in the *Denton Record-Chronicle*, Rives caught the spirit of the old-time Ranger, much as Zane Grey did, when he wrote,

> It isn't very often that I am privileged to have a few minutes with M. T. "Lone Wolf" Gonzaullas, the retired Texas Ranger captain who has become a legend in his own lifetime. But, after those few minutes, I relish their memory because this is a man of whom stories are told, radio sketches are unfolded, historical essays are written, television documentaries are produced, and columns, such as this one, are printed in newspapers all over the land.
>
> Gonzaullas represents an era, and there aren't many representatives of that era left. He was a Texas Ranger when the name meant much more than it does now. In his day, the Ranger stood tall. His eyes were clear, his draw was swift, his aim was straight, his courage knew no bounds, and his sense of justice was precise and correct. There were few men more envied than he. And, there were few men who could meet his qualifications. The Texas Ranger probably came closer to being the complete man than anybody in history . . . .

Gonzaullas is saddened by the fact that the Rangers of today don't command the universal respect and admiration they used to. "These men of today," he said, "are just as good as—maybe better than—any Rangers we ever had." He said the Rangers are caught in the apathy that extends to law enforcement everywhere. It is becoming increasingly difficult for a man to do his duty as a law enforcement officer, he said, and therefore it becomes more difficult to recruit them.

"Officers," he said, "are tired of being abused. Nowadays it is the officer who is handcuffed instead of the criminal. Why, an officer practically has to get shot before he can even defend himself." In such circumstances, with the courts coddling the criminals, how can an officer throw his whole heart into his job? Gonzaullas asks. And then he answers the question himself. "He can't. He simply can't."

In the interview, the "Lone Wolf" pointed out that a part of the solution to America's alarming rise in crime is for the people to get behind their peace officers. "Give them support and they'll get the job done . . . ." he told Rives.

During the last decade of his life, he spoke out firmly on the subject of restrictions placed on the work of officers. He blamed those restrictions on legislators catering to special interest groups for votes, and on rulings by courts that are gentle on the lawbreaker. He exploded that he never thought he would live to see the day when crime was so rampant in Texas, and in the nation as a whole. It was Gonzaullas' belief that the law enforcement officer has the hardest job in the United States. "I'm sick and tired of those bleeding hearts who cry when an officer has to shoot a murderer to keep him from killing more innocent people," he said. "Why, you'd think the officer is the wrongdoer, not the criminal. And another thing that irks me," he continued, "is to see vicious killers, outlaws like Billy the Kid for instance, played up as heroes. It's the law enforcement officers who are the heroes, not the murdering punks we see all around us."

Drawing his finger across his throat, he said, "I'm fed up to here by all this talk about police brutality. Who ever hears those bleeding hearts talk about the brutality of muggers and rapists and killers toward their victims? Another thing that will help in reducing crime is to make the punishment so severe and so swift that the violator will draw back from breaking the law!" That was sage counsel. The fact that he knew how to handle tough situations had never been more clearly demonstrated than in the aftermath of

With Gonzaullas at the Homer Garrison Memorial Museum on October 30, 1975 is Jarvis P. Garrett, son of former Texas Ranger Pat Garrett. On July 14, 1881, when he was sheriff in Lincoln County, New Mexico, Pat Garrett shot and killed William H. Bonney, Jr., alias "Billy the Kid." (Photo by Bob McNellis.)

the Texas City disaster in April 1947. Sent to the scene to help maintain order, one of the first things the "Lone Wolf" did was announce that all looters caught in the act would be shot on sight. He was taken at his word. There was no further looting.

Early in March 1970, his curiosity took him to the Southwestern Historical Wax Museum to see a lifesize figure of himself as a young Ranger. Pleased with what he saw, the "Lone Wolf" commented, "It kind of shakes you up to see yourself standing there!" At that time, the museum was in Fair Park, but two years later it was moved to Grand Prairie, where Gonzaullas' figure was again placed on display, along with 113 other representations of notable persons. Just weeks later, he was honored by the presentation to the Homer Garrison Memorial Museum of a lifesize bust of himself. It was the work of Waco sculptor Arlin Horne.

After they sold their home in Dallas, Captain and Mrs. Gonzaullas lived at Homestead Manor, a luxury apartment complex located on East University Boulevard in Dallas. As an ex-Ranger skilled in investigative work, he assumed the responsibility of overseeing the safety of the apartments and their residents. The *Dallas Morning News*, in commenting on Gonzaullas' duties there, quoted one tenant as saying, "I think he knows every noise and footstep for the entire complex. Any time there's anything unusual going on outside, you can look out and see the captain going along to investigate it." The paper attributed the "spotless record—not a single break in or theft," to the ex-Ranger.

He took an interest in the Former Texas Rangers Association and, in 1972, was appointed to the Texas Ranger Commemorative Commission by Senior Ranger Captain Clint Peoples. Plans were in the making for a fine structure at Waco to complement Fort Fisher and the Homer Garrison Memorial Museum. The new project was to be the Texas Ranger Hall of Fame. The program was launched and carried through to completion by a group of eminent Texans who had long admired the Rangers and wished to see erected a fine building with an art gallery, gift shop, library, dioramas and various audiovisual displays that would tell the story of the Ranger force. Those admirers formed the Texas Ranger Commemorative Foundation and set about raising funds for the ambitious project.

Ground was broken on August 4, 1973, one day short of the 150th anniversary of the date on which Stephen F. Austin hired ten frontiersmen, paying them fifteen dollars per month out of his own funds, and directed them to "range" Texas to protect the settlers against Indians and outlaws. The building, completed at a cost in

Certificate of Captain Gonzaullas' election to the Texas Ranger Hall of Fame, issued February 7, 1976, when the building housing the Hall of Fame was dedicated. (Courtesy Texas Ranger Hall of Fame and Museum.)

excess of $750,000, was dedicated on February 7, 1976. It was turned over to the city of Waco and, along with the Fort Fisher replica, museum, camping and picnic areas, is maintained by the municipal parks and recreation department. The Moody Texas Ranger Library in the Hall of Fame is rapidly being developed into a primary research center on the Texas Rangers and closely related subjects. United States Marshal Clint Peoples, who as Senior Ranger Captain was the first chairman of the Foundation, stated that the Texas Ranger Hall of Fame was the first memorial dedicated to a law enforcement agency.

On an inspection tour the day of dedication, the "Lone Wolf" was highly pleased with what he saw. As the May 1976 issue of *Texas Highways* observed, ". . . And the result is 'magnificent' in 'Lone Wolf' Gonzaullas' words. If this 84 year old Ranger, who has lived through some of the wildest and bloodiest times of Texas' 20th Century history is impressed by the Hall of Fame, . . . the City of Waco should have no trouble entertaining the general public." When he was touring the Hall, the comment was made by one of his friends that he, meaning Gonzaullas, would be enshrined there, to which he replied, "I would consider it a great honor, but even so, I would rather visit the Hall of Fame than be enshrined in it. I enjoy life!"

But, he was not well. It was apparent that the robust health he had enjoyed for eighty-five years was failing. The problem was not simply the normal aging process. There was a deeper underlying cause. Friends noticed and commented out of his hearing that he was obviously declining in vigor. He had lost weight and his color was not good. Never one to discuss personal problems, he kept his counsel. Yet, there was evidence that he knew what lay in the near future. He accelerated the process of selectively disposing of his collection of 580 guns, of knives, daggers and clubs he had removed from criminals during his career. He gave to this friend and to that, with never a word about the real reason why. "I just want you to have it," he would remark in his quiet manner.

More of his cherished Ranger friends had departed this life, among them Tom White and Charles Miller, who died in 1971, Robert A. "Bob" Crowder and Zeno Miller in 1972 and Martin N. Koonsman in 1974. The "Lone Wolf" realized that he would be numbered among their ranks before long. But, he retained his sense of humor. He enjoyed retelling one of Charlie Miller's feats. The two men were kindred souls in temperament. Miller was on border duty when he and a companion went into a restaurant for coffee. It

The popular Ranger postcard held by Company "F" Captain Robert K. Mitchell was made from the photograph of "Lone Wolf" Gonzaullas on Charcoal in the 1940s. Gonzaullas and Mitchell were in the Fort Fisher replica at Waco on October 30, 1975.

had already become evident that their presence was bitterly resented by the residents of the area.

The little cafe was a busy place, Gonzaullas noted: "All of the seats were occupied, so they ordered two cups of coffee which they said they would drink while standing." It seems that the proprietor was as noncooperative as everyone else in town. He refused the order, telling Miller that he did not serve patrons who were standing. "So, they swallowed their pride and waited a bit for a couple of empty seats, but no one left. Everybody just kept on sitting and ordering more coffee," he chuckled. "It didn't take long for the boys to figure out what was going on. They also realized that they couldn't simply walk out. That would have been a serious loss of face." Gonzaullas laughed heartedly when he told of the solution. "Charlie just pulled a pistol and fired two shots into the great big coffee pot. It was one of those tall things, an urn, that's what it's called. Then he picked up two cups and held them under each stream of coffee spurting out from the holes. They took their time and enjoyed their coffee standing. Oh, they could have sat down then because all the customers suddenly decided they ought to be somewhere else as soon as the shooting started." What happened after that? "Charlie Miller was suspended from the force for a little while, but he didn't care one bit," Gonzaullas said. "He had proved his point. After that, whenever he went into a cafe anywhere along the border and ordered a cup of coffee, he got it, 'pronto.'"

As a part of his process of relinquishing possessions, Captain Gonzaullas turned over to the Homer Garrison Memorial Museum a number of personal items, including his bulletproof vest, his chaps, a personalized license plate, etc. In one of the cases at the museum, there is a .38 caliber Colt revolver that had been stolen from his car in the East Texas oil field many years before. When Clyde Barrow was killed in a 1934 ambush near Gibsland, Louisiana, the gun was found in Barrow's possession. It was then confiscated by Rufus Pevehouse, sheriff of Navarro County. Pevehouse did not know at the time that the pistol had originally belonged to "Lone Wolf" Gonzaullas.

At the beginning of February 1977, Gonzaullas received some visitors who wanted to fill in some gaps in their knowledge of Ranger history. His drastic enfeeblement was readily apparent, but he was his usual hospitable, courteous self. Despite weakness, in the conversation he got in a last blast at privilege. He was speaking of Special Rangers and their commissions in the 1920s. Gonzaullas remarked, "There were an awful lot of Special Ranger commissions out, and I doubt whether they even have records on any of them [in Austin]. And you know, whenever the average Special Ranger goes any place if he is working for a corporation or something, he doesn't say, 'I am a Special Ranger.' He says, 'I am a Ranger,' so we used to get a lot of grief from some people that got out of line. There were too damned many Special Ranger commissions out. Too many politicians had them. And, some of them had red lights on the front of their cars, and sirens . . . ."

He had his say and the interview soon came to an end, as his strength waned. When his guests departed, they knew when they would see him next, and they were right. "Lone Wolf" Gonzaullas had heard the owl hoot! With his beloved Laura holding his hand, he died quietly at the age of eighty-five on Sunday, February 13, 1977. Death was not a stranger to him. He had brushed it countless times during his career. At the end, he met death from cancer with the same gallant courage for which he had long been famous.

Gonzaullas' gold badge of captain, Texas Rangers.

BIBLIOGRAPHICAL NOTE

The core of the public record of Texas Ranger exploits from the early 1920s to the mid-1970s is in Captain M. T. "Lone Wolf" Gonzaullas' scrapbooks. The material concerning his own eventful career reaches out to bring in a great number of his associates in the field of law enforcement during a turbulent era in the history of Texas. That period covered oil booms and prohibition, the depression and war, efforts to control gamblers, gangsters and narcotics smugglers, and related activities.

His five carefully prepared scrapbooks, containing nearly five hundred 11½- by 16-inch sheets, provide scholars and students with fingertip insight. It would be not only burdensome to the reader but also impractical to list in a formal bibliography all of their more than thirteen hundred references. Those readers who are interested in obtaining more details on any subject covered in this volume can review Gonzaullas' scrapbooks, which have been placed in the Moody Texas Ranger Library at the Texas Ranger Hall of Fame in Waco by Mr. and Mrs. Henry Rosser, he being executor of Mrs. Gonzaullas' estate. The scrapbooks contain much more material than it was possible to include in this published work on Gonzaullas and the Texas Ranger force.

The scrapbooks are not a compilation of what Gonzaullas wrote or thought about himself and his career. Instead, they comprise a collection of what others saw and recorded. In those books are to be found eyewitness reports by participants in sensational events in Texas' unending battle against crime—accounts of detection, pursuit and apprehension; of court proceedings, convictions and sentencing; even of executions.

His work in compiling the mass of original news articles is of great value to a scholar. Everything is in chronological order, with all sources named. True, one could go to the archives of newspapers that are still being published and, by laborious searching, ferret out needed material on him and his fellow Rangers. But, that is not necessary because of his having put it all together in one place!

In addition, much of the material now is available nowhere else. Many noted crime-ridden oil boom-towns flourished briefly, then declined into mere shadows of their former selves, or disappeared. When those boom-towns crumbled after production in their once boisterous oil fields dwindled and when the populace moved on to greener pastures, the newspapers collapsed, and with them went their files. Today, few copies of those papers can be found in the several great archives of the state. Without the articles that the "Lone Wolf" preserved in his scrapbooks, there would be gaps in the Ranger story and in that of his own career.

It cannot be denied that "Lone Wolf" Gonzaullas had a book in mind sixty years ago. He never got around to writing it himself, but because of his nose for news he set about, at the inception of his Ranger service, to gather the newspaper and magazine articles that would become the basis of a biographical sketch.

The story of Captain Gonzaullas, as well as that of many of his contemporaries and predecessors, comes alive in the more than five hundred 8- by 10-inch photographs in his fifteen-volume collection. In those large albums, many men of the stalwart Ranger breed can be seen, from the days of the beginning of frontier photography right on down to the present. With few exceptions, all of the individuals and scenes are carefully identified. The photograph albums have also been placed in the Moody Texas Ranger Library in memory of Captain Gonzaullas, whose expressed wish was that all of his collections go to that depository.

Scholars and students of Texas Ranger history are referred to Captain Gonzaullas' scrapbooks, photograph albums and tapes of reminiscences for one of the most complete and detailed accounts to be found anywhere.

The following brief bibliography contains other sources of information about Captain Gonzaullas and the Texas Ranger force:

UNPUBLISHED SOURCES:
    General Personnel Files of the Texas Rangers. Texas State Archives, Austin, Texas.
    Personnel File of Captain M. T. Gonzaullas. Texas Department of Public Safety Headquarters, Austin, Texas.
    Rosser, Henry. Personal correspondence with the author in the possession of the author.

PUBLISHED SOURCES:
    Handbook of Texas, The. Vols. I and II. Austin: Texas State His-

torical Association, 1952.
Handbook of Texas, The. Vol. III. Austin: Texas State Historical Association, 1976.
McGiffin, Lee. *Ten Tall Texans.* New York: Lothrop, Lee and Shepard Company, Inc., 1956.
Sterling, William Warren. *Trails and Trials of a Texas Ranger.* Norman, Okla.: University of Oklahoma Press, 1959.
Texas Almanac. Dallas: A. H. Belo Corporation, n.d.
Wolters, Jacob F., compiler. *Martial Law and Its Administration.* n.c.: Gammel's Book Store, Inc., Printers, 1930.

INDEX

Abernathy, Sheriff Gib: 72
Abilene, Tex.: 43-44, 85
Acker, C. M. (Buddy): 142-143
Adamson, Mrs. C. V.:101
Adjutant General's office: 7, 14, 20, 68, 71, 93, 125
Adoue, Mayor J. B.: 188
aerial reconnaisance: 73, 172-174, 183
Aikin, Jr., Acting Governor A. M.: 154
Alcorn, Bob: 62
Aldrich, Captain R. W.: 7, 19, 29, 57-58
Alexander, Sheriff C. G.: 175
Allred, Governor James V.: 120, 122, 127, 135-136
Alpine, Tex.: 159
Alspaugh, Dr. H. B.: 69
Amarillo, Tex.: 64, 84, 92, 195
American Federation of Labor: 157
American Legion Post: Gladewater, 116-117; Shamrock, 90, 92
Ames, J. B.: 13, 17
Anderson, Sheriff Gordon: 146-147
Anderson County: 183
Anderson Furniture Co. (Dallas): 60
Andrews, Cleo: 145-147
Arcadia Oil Co.: 16
Archer County: 25-26
Arizona: 145
Arkansas: 62, 136, 143, 160, 165-166, 183
Arlington, Tex.: 145, 177, 186
Arlington Baptist College: 178
Arlington Downs: 92
Asher, Johnnie H.: 27
Associated Press: 41
Athens, Tex.: 192
Atlas Pipe Line Co.: 120
Atwell, Judge William H.: 51, 53
Austin, Stephen F.: 136, 204

Austin, Tex.: 13, 20, 29, 36-37, 40, 68, 71, 77, 90, 99, 116, 135, 138, 181, 185, 187, 189, 200, 209
Avant, G. B.: 24

Badgett, R.L. (Bob): 146, 185
Baer, U.S. Marshal Phil: 43
Bahama Islands: 42, 54
Baker, D. D.: 135
ballistics tests: 125, 130-131
Banks, Captain Jay: 185, 199
banks (robberies): Citizens State, Buffalo, 182-183; First National, Cisco, 69-73; First State, Bremond, 179-182; Krum, Sanger, Tioga and Valley View, 61
Baptist Church: Desdemona, 13; Gladewater, 116; Kilgore, 105-106
Barrow, Clyde: 32, 120, 146, 174, 179, 208
Bartlesville, Okla.: 24
Beaty, W. A.: 173
Beaumont, Tex.: 37, 42, 53-56, 122, 151-158, 200; mob action, 151-158; streets: Eleventh, 152; Forsyth, 152; Gladys, 152; Main, 151
Becke, Charles: 64
Beecherl, Lieutenant Louis A: 96
Belgian refugees: 79
Berkley, Mayor G. C.: 90-91
Billy the Kid: 202
Blackwell, Captain C. J.: 14
Blasengame, Mrs. B. T.: 70
bloodhounds: 143, 145, 149
blue books: 45, 49, 63-64
blue laws: 90-91, 113
Boggs, Brady: 70
Bogota, Tex.: 170
Bois d'Arc Creek: 174

213

Bonham, Tex.: 172-174
Booker, Betty Jo: 163-165
bootlegging: 12, 13, 20-29, 31, 34-40, 42-56, 62-63, 78, 113, 122
border: (with) Arkansas, 159; Louisiana, 19; Mexico, 7, 31, 35, 160; Oklahoma, 85, 111, 171, 174
border raids on ranches: 31
Borger, Tex.: 64-65, 75-80, 100, 110, 158, 192; flight of criminals, 79; official corruption, 75-80; "the line," 75-80
Boroughs, Harry: 183
Boroughs, Sam: 182
Bosque County: 126, 183-185
Boulder, Colo.: 145
Boyd, Chief John: 181
Boy Scouts of America: 26, 121
Brabham, Rev. T.W.: 84
Bradford, Chief G. E.: 70
Bradford, No. 3 Daisy: 103
Bradley's Corner, Tex.: 9, 10, 20-27 passim
Bradstreet, Mrs. Frank: 183
Brady, H. P.: 13, 17
Brazoria County: 148
Brazos River: 73
Breckenridge, Tex.: 12, 14, 18-19
Bremond, Tex.: 179-183
Bridgetown, Tex.: 8-10
Brite, L. C.: 132
Broadway shows: 7
Brooklyn, N. Y.: 7
Brooks, Harry: 187
Brown, Ellie Cleveland: 153
Browning, Fred: 178-179
Brownsville, Tex.: 195
brutality, police: 202
Buffalo, Tex.: 182-183
Bullington, Orville: 119
Bunger, Tex.: 73
Burkburnett, Tex.: 7, 9, 22
Burton, M. (Red): 113, 199
Busby, Captain George: 172-173

Cadiz, Spain: 1
Calaveras: 42

Caldwell, Deputy Sheriff H. G.: 49
Calhoun, Clem: 78
California: 192, 198
Camden, Tenn.: 184
camouflage; 17, 25, 38, 39
Campbell, Sheriff Joe: 187
Camp Wolters: 145
Canada: 7, 35, 137
Canton, Tex.: 82
Carmichael, George: 70
Carmichael, Colonel H. H.: 113, 136-- 138
Carpenter, John W.: 188
Carpenter's service station: 141
Carrasco, Antonio: 131-135
Carter, Judge R. M.: 93-95, 98, 101-- 102
Carter, Mrs. R. M.: 102
Cash, Robert Lacy (see Lacy, Robert): 145
cattle: border raids on ranches, 31; fever ticks, 31-32; smuggling of, 31-32
Cauble, Rex (ranch): 201
Cedar Springs: 50
Central Texas: 41, 60
Chalk, J. W.: 64
Charcoal: 196
Charon: 46
Childress, Tex.: 67-68
Childress County: 68
Chisos Mountains: 130
Chitwood, Roy: 134
"Choc" beer: 23, 28
Choctaw Indians: 23
Choctaw Settlement: 93-94
Christian Courier, The: 58
Chrysler dealership: 114-116
circus performance: 89-92, 113
Cisco, Tex.: 69-74
Clark Grocery Co.: 170, 175
Clarksville, Tex.: 175
Claude, Tex.: 64
Clay County: 63
Cleburne, Tex.: 185
Cleveland, Ohio: 187
Cliett, Oscar: 70
Clifton, Homer: 172-173

Clifton, Tex.: 126, 181, 183, 185
Cockrell Hill: 173
Coffman, David: 53
Cohen, Mickey: 186-187
Coker, Sheriff Guy: 170
Collingsworth County: 86
Colt revolver: 188-189, 208
Comanche Indians: 136
Comer, Laverne: 70-71
Commerce, Tex.: 172-173
Compton, Sheriff John B.: 67-68
Comstock, Tex.: 1
Constellation plane: 188
Cooper, Gary: 190
Cope, John T.: 126
Corbett, J. M. (Jim): 183-185
Cotton Bowl: 188
courts: Fifty-second District, 185; Fifty-fourth District, 131; Thirty-first District, 88
Cowsert, Gully: 199
Crader, Jack: 175
Crawford, Pete: 130
Crim, Mrs. Lou Della: 103, 112
Crim, Mayor J. Malcolm: 103, 112
Crim, No. 1 Lou Della: 103
crime, accessory to: 12
crime syndicates: 37
Cross, Judge R. B.: 185
Cross Plains, Tex.: 145
Crowder, R. A. (Bob): 141, 149, 187, 195, 206
Crowdus, Major Earl: 100
Culberson County: 131, 133-134
curfew at Beaumont: 154, 158
Curry Field: 149

Dallas, Tex.: 34, 43-46, 49, 53-54, 60, 63-64, 82, 85, 96-99, 135, 146, 148, 153-154, 159, 171-174, 177, 180-190 passim, 198-199, 204; Police Department, 184; streets: Alaska, 148; Alton, 43; Burnside, 149; Commerce, 46; Elm, 61; Gould, 49; Grand, 45; Harwood, 60; Lancaster, 148; Ledbetter, 148; Marburg, 68; Michigan, 148; Olive, 60; Pacific, 60; University, 204; Wood, 44
Dallas County; 62, 69, 145, 184
Daniel, Ernest: 141, 145, 185
Davenport, John: 21
Davidson, Colonel Louis S.: 97-98, 100
Davidson, U. S. Commissioner R. V.: 50
Davis, Frank: 145
Davis, L. E.: 71
Davis Mountains: 129
Dawson, Harry: 146
Day, R. L.: 70
Dean Law: 107, 122
death penalty: 89, 131, 135, 138-139, 199
Decker, Bill: 149
Dell Comics: 196
Del Rio, Tex.: 1, 31-32, 34
Democratic Party: 119
denatured alcohol: 36
Denison, Tex.: 46, 93, 96, 111, 145
Denton, Tex.: 201
Denton County: 61
DeQueen, Ark.: 62
Desdemona, Tex.: 12-13
Detroit, Mich.: 169
Dial, Chief W. A.: 110
Dibrel, U. S. Commissioner Charles G.: 35
Dickey, Chief Ross: 151-152, 157
Dickinson, Mike: 190
disguises: 64, 86
Dix, Dorothy: 45
Dixon, N. K.: 149
Dixon Creek: 76
Donovan, Major General Richard: 154
Duane, Buck: 200
Duncan, Judge Ivy: 83
Duncan, Levi: 130

East Texas oil boom: 103-117
Eastland County: 13, 43-44, 71-72
Eighteenth Amendment: 36, 52, 122
Eighth Service Command: 154
Einstein, Izzy: 55
Eliasville, Tex.: 25
Elk City, Okla.: 85

215

El Lobo Solo: 1
El Paso, Tex.: 1-2, 27, 134-135, 187, 195
El Paso County: 134, 187
El Rio Bravo del Norte: 34
Emancipation Day, 1943: 158
Emergency Hospital (Dallas): 69
Empire Oil Co.: 24
Erick, Okla.: 85
Estes, Judge William Lee: 43
Eubank, Mayor J. S.: 100
Evans, Dr. A. N.: 101
Ewing, Judge W. R.: 88, 92
execution: 62, 89
extortion: 82

Fair Park (Dallas): 204
Falls County: 180
Fannin County: 172-174
Farmersville, Tex.: 172
Federal Building: 45, 51
Federal Bureau of Investigation: 138, 181, 183
Federal control of oil production: 113, 116
Federal Reserve Bank: 182
Ferguson, Governor Miriam A.: 62, 120, 122; inauguration (1933), 119
Fletcher, Joe S.: 140, 181, 199
Florida: 184
Floury, Jess: 110
Floyd, G. M.: 35
Former Texas Rangers Association: 204
Fort Davis, Tex.: 130
Fort Fisher replica (Waco): 199, 204, 206
Fort Worth, Tex.: 64, 71, 97-98, 116, 149, 153, 169-170, 177, 181-182, 187; Bureau of Identification, 71; streets: Henderson and Second, 169; Main, 116; Seventh and Commerce, 116
Foster, Sheriff Jim: 73
Fowler, T. R.: 142-143
Franklin, B. L.: 183
Franklin, Tex.: 179
Freestone County: 183

Frisco Hotel (Sherman): 97
Fritz, Will: 62, 148, 172
Fry, Sheriff Bill: 61
Fulks, Mrs. Connie: 182

Galveston, Tex: 35, 37-38, 42, 100; bathing girl revue, 37
gambling: 10-13, 22, 25, 27, 65, 78, 122, 145, 177-179, 185-187, 198
Gant, Charlie: 110
Gardner, Chief Millard: 172
Gargoyle (magazine): 107
Garren ranch: 132
Garrison, Jr., Colonel Homer: 122, 138, 140, 187, 189, 192, 195, 199-200
Garrison Memorial Museum, Homer (Waco): 200, 204, 208
gasoline rationing coupons: 147, 149
Gaston Episcopal Hospital (Dallas): 198
Gatesville, Texas State School for Boys: 71, 175
General Motors Corp.: 169
Georgetown, Tex.: 2
German Army: 79
Geron, H. C.: 55
Gibsland, La.: 32, 120, 208
Gillon, John A.: 32
Gilmer, Tex.: 145-146
Gladewater, Tex.: 110-111, 116, 145-146, 184; Bozman Corner Road, 146
Glen Rose, Tex.: 181
Gonzaullas, Helen von Droff (mother): 7
Gonzaullas, Laura Isabel Scherer (wife): 7, 139, 198-199, 209
Gonzaullas, Manuel (father): 7
Gonzaullas, Captain M. T. "Lone Wolf": birth, 1; Borger duty, 64-65, 75-80; brothers murdered, 2; bust, 204; candidate for sheriff, 121; captain of Company "B" (appointment), 140; chief special agent, 120-121; crime (theories on control), 27-28, 192, 195, 198, 201-202; Chrysler coupe, 114-116; death, 2, 209; disguises, 43, 52-53,

216

64; enlistments, 1, 7, 58, 65; Hollywood consultant, 190, 192, 196; indictment for murder, 42; jailed, 13, 42-43; Kilgore duty, 103-118; "Lone Wolf" (first reference), 20; marriage, 7; men killed, 6, 192; Mexican Army service, 9; murder trial, 56; parents 1-2, 7; physical description, 5-6, 107; portrait, 200; possessions (disposition of), 206, 208; prohibition agent, 34-60, 62-65, 75; race at Arlington Downs, 92; religious attitude, 2, 5; retirement, 188-196; special agent with Treasury Department, 9, 125; on staff of district attorney, 121-122; style of operation, 5, 6, 9, 12; tour with Carmichael, 138; weapons, 6, 86-87, 107, 116, 199, 206; weapons engraved with code, 6, 107; (weapons) swivel mounted machine gun, 116

Goose Neck Bend of Brazos River: 73
Goss, R. G. (Bob): 85, 88, 92, 98, 106-108, 110, 113
Goss farm, Gil: 174
Graham, Tex.: 17, 25, 73
Grand Prairie, Tex.: 204
Granite, Okla.: 86
Gray, Captain Jerry: 199
Gray County: 86, 88
Grayson County: 56, 93, 95, 98, 186; courthouse (see Sherman)
Grayson Hotel (Sherman): 99
Greenville, Tex.: 159, 171-172
Greenwood, O. H.: 175
Gregg County: 106, 110, 121, 146
Grey, Zane: 200
Griffin, Richard: 161, 163
Griffin, Sam D.: 36
Grigsby, Louis: 146
Grimes, Sheriff George: 185
Grisham, A. O.: 64
Groesbeck, Tex.: 38
Gross, U. S. Marshal Samuel L.: 62
Guinn, W. C.: 43

Hagen, B. W.: 184
Hamer, Captain Frank: 32, 57, 75, 93-95
Hamilton, W. B.: 82-83
Hardesty, Roy W.: 25
Hardin, John Wesley: 196
Harding, Tex.: 25
Harris, Woodrow: 70-71
Harvard University: 70
Hayes, Sheriff Will H.: 121
Hays, Sheriff Martin: 110
Hella Temple (Dallas): 198
Helms, Henry: 73
Henderson, John: 62
Henderson, Tex.: 103, 106
Henderson County: 192
Henrietta, Tex.: 170
Hercules: 38
Hickman, Captain Tom: 25, 61-62, 65, 71, 73, 75, 92, 98, 106, 113, 116, 119, 122, 135, 199
Highland Park: 172
Highway: No. 6, 185; No. 67, 159, 161, 169-170, 174; No. 75, 183, 185; No. 78, 172; No. 380, 172
Hi-Lite Club (Sherman): 185
Hill, Robert: 73
Hinga, Don: 195
Hobart, T. D.: 83-84
Hoblinsky, Stash: 180
Hoguet, Sheriff Si: 143
Holland, G. W.: 180
Hollis, Jimmy: 160-161, 163
Hollywood, Calif.: 148, 190, 192, 195-196, 198
Holmes, District Attorney John: investigative work, 77, 80; murder, 77-78
Homestead Manor (Dallas): 204
Honey Grove, Tex.: 85
Hood, Hal: 62
Hooper, Francis M. (Bobby): 181-182
Hooper, J. B.: 181
Horne, Arlin: 204
hot oil thefts: 24, 116
Houghton, Major S. J.: 96, 100
Houston, Tex.: 35, 52, 55, 142-143,

217

146, 153, 198
Houston Bar Association: 51
Huddleston, J. P.: 83, 85, 88, 105-106
Hudson, Rock: 196
Hudspeth County: 134
Hughes, George: 93, 95-97, 157
Hughes, Captain John R.: 2, 27, 200
Hugo, Okla.: 143
Huntsman, U. S.: 108, 113-114
Huntsville, Tex.: 62, 143, 145
Hutchinson County: 78-80, 84
Hydra: 38

Independence, Mo.: 62
indictments: 42, 51
Interocean Oil & Refining Co.: 24
interurban: 96-98
Iowa Park, Tex.: 8
Isbell, C. M. (and Mrs.): 62
Ivan, Texas: 25

Jackson, George: 198
Jackson, Penn: 126
Jacksonville, Fla.: 184
Jefferson County: 42, 56, 152
Johnson, A. S.: 122, 136-137
Johnson, Ben: 159
Johnson, John: 153
Johnson County: 185
Johnston, W. R.: 24
Joiner, C. M. (Dad): 103
Jones, Fletcher: 43
Jones, Captain Frank: 2
Jones, Holmes Ed: 200
Jones, Mayor Will P.: 67-68
Jordan, Frank: 88

Kamey, Tex.: 28
Keach, Stacy: 192
Kemp, Ross: 173
Kemp, Tex.: 28
Kemp City, Tex.: 120
Kentucky: 198
Kentucky Lake: 184
Kermit, Tex.: 129
Kidd, J. A.: 13
Kilgore, Tex.: 103-118, 192; drilling activity, 112-113; streets, 112-113
Kinney County: 32
Kirby, W. H.: 84-85, 88, 92, 98
Klevenhagen, Johnny: 199
Knight, Walter J.: 63-64
Koon Kreek Klub (Athens): 192
Koonsman, Martin N.: 13, 17, 206
Krum, Tex.: 61
Ku Klux Klan: 67

Lacy, Robert (also Robert Lacy Cash): 145-147
Laird Hill: 108
Lake Brazos Park (Waco): 199
Lake City, Tex.: 25
Lakewood Country Club (Dallas): 198
Lamar County: 141-143, 173
Langley, Bill: 92
Laredo, Tex.: 60
Larey, Mrs. Mary Jeanne: 160-161, 163
Lathrop, No. 1: 103
Lauter, Harry: 196
Law and Order League: 13
law enforcement, problems of: 27-28, 58-59, 192, 195, 198, 202
Lawless Breed, The: 196
Leach, F. P.: 146
Leach, J. H.: 146
Lee, Sheriff Ben: 183
LeMay, Walter: 148-149
Leon County: 182-183
Leonard, Tex.: 172
LeSeur, W. L.: 18
Limestone County: 38-41, 183
Little, Rube: 62
Littlefield Building (Austin): 40
"Little Mexico" (Dallas): 63
Little Rock, Ark.: 159
Little Wichita River: 26
Lone Star Ranger (Zane Grey): 200
longshoremen's strike (Galveston): 100
Longview, Tex.: 103, 106, 110, 121-122; streets: Fredonia, 110, Ware, 110
looting (looters): 204
Loper, Sheriff W. S.: 38
Los Angeles, Calif.: 181, 187

Louisiana: 114, 143, 198; Bureau of Identification, 114; Highway Police (Patrol), 114
Louisiana Purchase: 111
Love Field (Dallas): 188
lovers' lane: 160-168
Lowery, Pat: 62
Lufkin, Tex.: 135
Luther, J. T.: 148-149
Lynch, Leon: 182
lynching: 74, 85, 151

MacArthur, Arthur: 188-189
MacArthur, General Douglas: 187-188
McCleskey, Tex.: 25
McClure, E. B.: 32
McCormick, J. W.: 20, 28-30, 63, 135
McCrea, Joel: 196
McDuffie, Dan L.: 110
McElroy, Curtis: 129
McFall, Emmett: 108
McGee, Jasmine: 101-102
McGee, Colonel L. E.: 96, 99
McGraw, C.G.: 122, 127
McIntosh, Chief P.K.: 106, 108, 113
McKinney, Tex.: 149, 172
McLaughlin, Glenn H.: 184
McLemore, Sheriff W. K.: 85-86, 88, 90-91
McLennan County: 175
McMaster, M. W.: 157
McMurray, Sheriff Bill: 108

Mace, Albert: 80
machine gun, swivel mounted: 116
Madisonville, Tex.: 35
Manchen, Louis: 149
Manss, Louis B.: 37
Marfa, Tex.: 132, 159
Marine Corps, U. S.: 90
Marlin, Tex.: 180
Marshall, Sheriff Schuyler: 60-62
Marshall, Tex.: 110, 196
martial law: 78, 99-101, 113, 153-154
Martin, Paul: 163-165
Mash, Leon: 148
Mason, Prohibition Agent James: 49

Mason, Lt. Colonel Sidney C.: 154, 156, 158
Mature, Victor: 190
Memphis, Tenn.: 143
Meridian, Tex.: 126, 181-182, 185
Mershon, C. M.: 148
Methodist Church: Travis Street (Sherman), 101
Mexia, Tex.: 38, 40, 158
Mexico: 31, 35, 130-134, 136, 143
Miami, Tex.: 88-89
Miles, Bassett: 36
Miller, A. H.: 63
Miller, Charles: 206
Miller, Fred: 184-185
Miller, Chief Virgil: 171
Miller, Zeno: 206
Miller County (Arkansas): 160, 165-166
Minnesota State Prison System: 169
Mitchell, Sheriff C. L.: 143
mob action: 8, 9, 84-89, 93-102, 152-153, 156-157
Mobile, Ala.: 42, 54-56, 60
Moffett, Will: 62
Monkstown, Tex.: 173
Moody, Governor Dan: 67, 77-78, 82-85, 90-92, 94, 97-100
Moody Texas Ranger Library: 206
moonshiners (see bootlegging)
Moore, C. O.: 67-68, 80
Moore, Floyd: 145
Moore, M. A.: 43
Moore, Polly Ann: 161, 163
Morales, J. D.: 159
Morris, David H.: 34, 43
Morrison, Dennis: 187
Mount Pleasant, Tex.: 169-170, 174
Mount Vernon, Tex: 170
Munsey Company, Frank A.: 200
murder in Wheeler County: 84-85
Murphy, Jack: 54-55
Murray, Governor William H. (Alfalfa Bill): 111-112
Myers, W. H.: 34-35

Naples, Tex.: 159

narcotics: 20, 27, 31, 41, 54, 64, 68-69, 148
Nashville, Tenn.: 184
Navarro County: 208
Naylor, Major John W.: 100
Neches River: 54
Neff, Governor Pat: 51-52
Neill, J. D.: 134
New Boston, Tex.: 110, 145
New Orleans, La.: 41-42, 46, 54-55
New York, N.Y.: 7; draft riots, 93
New Waverly, Tex.: 143
Newcastle, Tex.: 25
Newspapers: *Buffalo Press*, 182; *Dallas Dispatch*, 45; *Dallas Morning News*, 44, 120, 136, 147, 190, 204; *Dallas Times-Herald*, 107, 190; *Denton Record-Chronicle*, 201; *Fort Worth Star-Telegram*, 192; *Houston Chronicle*, 195; *Houston Post*, 198; *Pioneer Oil Herald*, 44; *San Antonio Express*, 125; *Shamrock Texan*, 91; *Sherman Democrat*, 101; *Shreveport Times*, 114; *Van Free State Press*, 81; *Wichita Falls Daily Times*, 20, 29
Newsweek (magazine): 196
Newton, Tex. (Newton County): 9
Newtown, Tex. (Wichita County): 9-10, 22
Nitschke, R. E.: 36
Nitzer, W. A.: 42-43, 56
Nixon, Sheriff W. P.: 82
Northern and Northeastern Texas: 7, 41, 45, 60, 101, 142, 146, 148, 169
Nudleman, Mr. and Mrs. Nathan: 61

Oak Cliff (Dallas): 49, 180-181, 183
Oakhurst, Tex.: 143
Odessa, Tex.: 187
oil fields: East Texas, 19, 81, 103-117, 120, 158, 208; Eastland County, 13-14, 16, 43, 64; Hutchinson County, 75; Limestone County, 64; North Texas, 12, 29, 81; Panhandle: 75, 81; proration: 113, 116; Stephens County, 13, 19, 64; unitized development: 81; Van Zandt County, 81; Wichita County, 10, 12, 14, 20, 22-23, 27, 64
Okinawa: 181
Oklahoma: 9, 19, 23, 85, 100-101, 112, 136, 142; Highway Department, 111; Highway patrol, 143, 173; National Guard, 112
Oldham, Dick: 145-146
Olga (steamship): 41
Olson, Marion: 70
Orange, Tex.: 153-154, 158
Orange County: 154
outlaws: 1-2, 5, 130, 192, 200

Palace Royal Dance Hall: 110
Palmer, Homer: 15
Palo Pinto County: 72
Pampa, Tex.: 83-89 passim
Pamplin, Sheriff Brady: 180
Panhandle, Tex. (city): 79
Panhandle, The Texas (region): 76, 84-86
paraffin test: 138
Paris, Tex.: 141, 143, 145, 171-174; streets: Lamar, 141, Twenty Third, 141-143
Parker, Bonnie: 32, 120, 179
Parker, Willard: 196
Parkland Hospital (Dallas): 60
Parsons, H. B.: 61
Pearson, Jace: 196
penitentiary (at Huntsville): 62, 89, 145, 185
Penn, John W.: 134
Pennsylvania Shipyards (Beaumont): 151-158 passim
Pentagon Lodge #1080, A.F.&A.M.: 198
Peoples, Senior Ranger Captain Clint: 204, 206
Perkins, W. E.: 60
Perry, Kent C.: 108
Petty, Captain L. P.: 171
Pevehouse, Sheriff Rufus: 208
Phantom Killer (Slayer): 159-168 passim

220

Phantom murders: 159-168 passim
Phares, L. G.: 122, 125, 135-136
Phillips, Elmer P.: 169
Phillips, Captain Royal: 140
Phoenix, Ariz.: 143
Pinkerton detective agency: 24
Pinto Switch: 32, 34
Pioneer, Tex.: 43-44
police brutality: 202
Port Arthur, Tex.: 37; streets: Eighth, Houston and Procter, 37
Port Lavaca, Tex.: 41
Powderly, Tex.: 142
Presbyterian Church: 2; West Shore (Dallas), 198
Presidio, Tex.: 160
prohibition (law and agents): 20, 34, 58, 64, 84; opposition to, 52; repeal, 122
proration efforts: 113, 116
prostitution: 10, 13, 27, 65, 76
Purvis, H. B.: 135

racial problems: at Beaumont, 151-158 passim; at Childress, 67-68; at Sherman, 93-102 passim; discrimination alleged, 132; Panhandle, 84-89 passim
raids: 20-29 passim, 37, 43-50 passim; 55, 61-63, 65, 82, 106-108, 110, 113, 116, 121-122, 177-179
railroads: Atchison, Topeka and Santa Fe, 79; Galveston, Harrisburg and San Antonio (Southern Pacific), 32; Gulf, Colorado and Santa Fe, 126; Louisville & Nashville, 54-55; Panhandle and Santa Fe, 79
Raines, A. A.: 182
Ranger, Tex.: 12-14, 17, 83
Ranger statue (Love Field, Dallas): 199
Ransom, Walter: 169-175
Ratliff, Sheriff J. H.: 141
Ratliff, Marshall: 71, 73
Red River: 9, 23, 27-28, 111, 142-143, 171-172, 174
Red River Bridge Co.: 111
Red River County: 175
Reeves, Sheriff Bob: 179-182

Republican Party: 119
Retrieve Prison Farm: 145-146, 148
Rheudasil, Scott: 88
Rice Hotel (Houston): 51
Richardson, Sheriff Bill: 152
Richardson, W. H.: 135
Rigler, L. C.: 185
Riley, Frank: 183
Ringling Brothers, Barnum & Bailey Circus: 90-92
Rio Grande River: 1, 7, 31, 34, 60, 130, 134, 200
Rising Star, Tex.: 70
Ritchey, E. F.: 88
River Oaks (Fort Worth): 181
Riverside, Calif.: 7
Rives, Bill: 201
roadblocks: 153, 171
robbery: 10, 14-15, 61, 69-74, 110, 113-114, 179-183
Roberts, Steve: 148
Roberts County: 88
Robertson, George: 141-145 passim
Robertson, General Robert L.: 65, 68
Robertson County: 179
Robinson, Emma May: 70-71
Rocky Point, Tex.: 38
Roosevelt, President Franklin D.: 136
Rose, G. S. (Jack): 183-185
Rose, Mrs. Jack: 183-185
Rush, C. G.: 145
Rusk County: 108
Rutherford, Pete: 70

St. Louis, Mo.: 159
Salem witch hunt: 93
San Angelo, Tex.: 159
San Antonio, Tex.: 41-42, 137, 182
San Antonio Public Service Co.: 137
Sanger, Tex.: 61
San Jacinto County: 143
San Jacinto Day: 42
Santa Claus bank robbery: 69-74
Savannah, Ga.: 42, 55
Sayre, Okla.: 85
Scherer, Abraham and Caroline Greenbaum: 7

Schmid, Sheriff Smoot: 145
Scotland, Tex: 25
Scottish Rite: 198
Seale, Allen: 62
Seay, Tully: 149
Secret Service: 136
Sessions, Sheriff Jim: 183
Shamrock, Tex.: 85-92 passim, 113
Shannon, K. C.: 134
Shannon, T. W.: 24
Shelton detective agency: 24
Sheppard, U. S. Senator Morris: 136-- 137
Sherman, Tex.: 46, 56-57, 93-102, 157-158, 185-186; burning of courthouse, 95-102; hanging of dead prisoner, 97-98
shoe ration stamps: 149
Shreve, Sheriff Charlie: 183
Shreveport, La.: 46, 114
Sierra Blanca, Tex.: 135
Sitter, Joe: 201
Skeen, Bryant: 62
slot machines: 65, 78, 145
Smith, Dave: 62
Smith, Evans (letter): 120, 147
Smith, Sheriff Lonnie: 146
Smith, Mr. and Mrs. Riley: 131-135
Smith County: 81
Smith and Wesson: 131
smugglers, smuggling: 2, 31-32, 35, 41-42, 54, 60, 130
snortin' pole: 78
South Bend, Tex.: 25, 73
Southern Texas: 41
Southwestern Historical Wax Museum: 204
Spain: 7
Spartan Refining Co.: 120
speakeasies: 37-38
Spear, Alex: 69-70
speed limit: 8
Speir, Colonel Wilson E.; 200
Spring Lake Park (Texarkana) 159-168 passim
Spurlin, Doyle: 185
Stafford, Captain Tilton D.: 96

Stanford, Sheriff Paul: 183
Stanley, Stewart: 61, 113, 116, 145
Starks, Mr. and Mrs. Virgil: 165-166
Stephens County: 13-20 passim, 72
Sterling, Governor Ross: 111, 113, 117, 119
Sterling, Adjutant General W. W.: 116
Stevens, Craig: 196
Stevenson, Governor Coke: 154
Stewart, Edgar S.: 171
Stewart, W. S.: 171
Stinnett, Tex.: 78, 84
Stone, C. L.: 14
Stone, Major Fred: 152
Styx, River: 46
submarine whiskey cache: 46
Sutherland, Captain Jack: 181
Sweeten, Sheriff Jess: 192
Syracuse, N. Y.: 184

Talco, Tex.: 169-170
Tales of the Texas Rangers: 190, 192, 196
Tatum, Albert: 157
Tauch, Waldine: 199
Taylor, G. M.: 94
Tennessee: 184-185
Tennessee River: 184
tequila: 32, 34
Texan Theater (Kilgore): 114
Texarkana, Tex. (Ark.): 136, 159, 183, 195; Spring Lake Park, 159-168 passim
Texas, State of:
— centennial celebration: 136
— Department of Public Safety: 120, 122, 126, 135, 138, 140, 177, 181, 184, 187, 189, 200; Bureau of Identification, 122, 125, 127, 140, 184; Bureau of Intelligence, 122, 125-127, 129, 131, 137-140; Bureau of Training and Education, 122; Crime Detection Laboratory, 127, 138, 140; Drivers License Bureau, 136; Highway Patrol, 122, 125-126, 136, 139, 143, 153-154, 169-170, 172, 181, 183

— Highway Commission: 111
— Highway and Public Transportation Department: 111, 139
— Legislature: 120, 122
— Public Safety Commission: 122, 125, 135
— Railroad Commission: 113, 116
— State Cemetery: 200
— State School for Boys (Gatesville): 71, 175
Texas City disaster: 204
Texas Highways (magazine): 206
Texas National Guard: 90, 95-96, 99-101, 113, 142, 152-154, 158; A, B, E, and Headquarters Companies, 96; Fifty-sixth Cavalry, 78; 112th Cavalry, 96; 124th Cavalry, 97-98; 114th Infantry, 98; 144th Infantry, Company F, 61; 144th Machine Gun Corps, Company H, 97
Texas Rangers: 14, 52, 67-68, 78, 83, 93, 122, 125-139 passim, 145, 154, 163-164, 170, 192, 201; airborne, 130; Companies: Headquarters, 75; A, 135, 153; B, 29, 65, 75, 113, 140-141, 153, 177-178, 183, 187, 195, 201; C, 31, 64, 187; D, 2; F, 200; conflict with Governor Ferguson, 119; discord, 135-136; exodus in 1933, 119; political activity, 119, 137; Special Ranger commissions, 208-209
Texas Ranger Commemorative Commission: 204
Texas Ranger Commemorative Foundation: 204
Texas Ranger Hall of Fame: 204, 206
Thompson, J. N.: 126
Thompson, William M.: 42
Thornberry, Tex.: 63
Thrift, Tex.: 9
Tinian: 181
Tioga, Tex.: 61
Titus County: 46, 52-53, 169
Top O' The Hill: 177-179, 186
Tousant, Arthur: 184-185
Town That Dreaded Sundown, The: 159
Townsend, W. C.: 184
Travis Street Methodist Church (Sherman): 101
Trice, Carl: 146
Trinity Heights (Dallas): 148
Trinity River: 46
trotline: 105
True, L. H.: 188
Truman, President Harry: 188
Twenty-first Amendment: 122
Tyler, Tex.: 117
Tyson, L. H.: 63

Uniform Oil & Gas Co.: 24
unitized plan of oil field development: 81
United Press: 91
United States: 34-35, 42, 137, 196, 198, 202; Army, 99; Border Patrol, 130; Coast Guard, 130; Customs agents, 130; indictments for conspiracy against, 51; Treasury Department, 9, 125
Universal-International: 196, 198
Upshur County: 146

Valley View, Tex.: 61
Val Verde County: 32
Van, Tex.: 81-82
Vandiver, R. C.: 8
Van Horn, Tex.: 131-134
Van Zandt, R. C.: 64
Van Zandt County: 81-82
Vaughan, Sheriff Richard: 93-96
Victoria County: 41
Volstead Act: 31, 34-35

Wachtendorf, Herman: 88
Waco, Tex.: 67, 131, 170, 175, 181, 199-206 passim
Waggoner, E. P.: 92
Waggoner, G. L.: 92
Wait, Sheriff Dick: 172-173
Walker County: 143
"War of the Bridges": 111
Warnken, C. A.: 43

223

Washington, Jesse Lee: 85–86, 88
Washington, D. C.: 36, 154
Watertown, N. Y.: 184
Weaver, Mr. and Mrs. G. H.: 164
Weaver, Deputy Sheriff: 21, 25
Webb, George: 49
West, Mae: 6
West Shore Presbyterian Church (Dallas): 198
Western Texas: 130, 132
Western Union: 164
Wheatley, J. B.: 93
Wheeler, Tex.: 88
Wheeler County: 85, 88; murder in, 84–85
whiskey making (see bootlegging)
White, Tom: 206
Wichita County: 7–13 passim, 19, 24, 30, 63, 110, 187, 192
Wichita Falls, Tex.: 8, 9, 14, 16, 20, 23–24, 27, 63, 65, 68, 82, 119, 153, 187; Brook Street, 14–15, 82; robbery of poker game, 14–16; Welfare Board, 63
Williams, Claude A.: 121
Williams, Mack: 192
Williams, Ray: 129
Williams Hotel (Sherman): 99
Willis, Mrs. Fred: 101
Willow Springs, Tex.: 143
Wilson, Fred: 35
Wolfe City, Tex.: 172
Wolters, Brigadier General Jacob F: 78
Wolters, Camp: 145
Wood, Mayor A. J.: 117
Wood, Joe: 169–170
Wooton, Howard: 108
Wooton, Marvin: 108, 113–114
World War I: 79, 125
Worsham Buick Co.: 60
Worthington, Hugh: 62
Wray, Inc., George D.: 114
Wright Hotel (Pioneer): 44
Wylie, Carl: 72
Wylie, R. C.: 72
Wynne, Letters to Mrs.: 45
Wynne Prison Unit: 143

Yellow Cab: 172
Young, W. E.: 113
Young County: 25, 72–73
youths, involvement of: 23, 27–28
Ysleta, Tex.: 134

Zent, W. L.: 64
Zutler, Edith: 43